D1572090

DAILY LIFE BEHIND THE

IRON CURTAIN

Recent Titles in
The Greenwood Press Daily Life Through History Series

The New Inuit
Pamela R. Stern

The Indian Wars
Clarissa W. Confer

The Reformation
James M. Anderson

The Aztecs, Second Edition
David Carrasco and Scott Sessions

The Progressive Era
Steven L. Piott

Women during the Civil Rights Era
Danelle Moon

Colonial Latin America
Ann Jefferson and Paul Lokken

The Ottoman Empire
Mehrdad Kia

Pirates
David F. Marley

Arab Americans in the 21st Century
Anan Ameri and Holly Arida, Editors

African American Migrations
Kimberley L. Phillips

The Salem Witch Trials
K. David Goss

DAILY LIFE
BEHIND
THE

IRON
CURTAIN

JIM WILLIS

The Greenwood Press Daily Life Through History Series

AN IMPRINT OF ABC-CLIO, LLC
Santa Barbara, California • Denver, Colorado • Oxford, England

Library of Congress Cataloging-in-Publication Data

Willis, Jim, 1946 Mar. 19–
  Daily life behind the Iron Curtain / Jim Willis.
    pages cm. — (The Greenwood Press daily life through history series)
    Includes bibliographical references and index.
    ISBN 978–0–313–39762–2 (cloth : acid-free paper) — ISBN 978–0–313–39763–9 (ebook) 1. Europe, Eastern—Social life and customs—20th century. 2. Europe, Eastern—Social conditions—20th century. 3. Communism—Social aspects—Europe, Eastern—History—20th century. 4. Communist countries—Social life and customs. 5. Communist countries—Social conditions. 6. Berlin Wall, Berlin, Germany, 1961–1989. I. Title.
DJK50.W55   2013
947.0009′045—dc23   2012036348

ISBN: 978–0–313–39762–2
EISBN: 978–0–313–39763–9

17 16 15 14 13   1 2 3 4 5

This book is also available on the World Wide Web as an eBook.
Visit www.abc-clio.com for details.

Greenwood
An Imprint of ABC-CLIO, LLC

ABC-CLIO, LLC
130 Cremona Drive, P.O. Box 1911
Santa Barbara, California 93116-1911

This book is printed on acid-free paper ∞

Manufactured in the United States of America

This book is dedicated to the collective source of my wisdom:
Mom, Dad, C. J., and Annie

CONTENTS

Preface: From War to Oppression . . . Then Hope   ix

1. Eastern Europe under Communism   1

2. The Rise of Communism, Fascism, and Nazism   17

3. The Berlin Wall Goes Up   31

4. The Rules of the Iron Curtain   47

5. Many Resist and Pay the Price   81

6. *"We're Getting Out of Here!"*: Escape Attempts from the East   109

7. Depictions of European Communism in Movies   129

8. The News Media's Role under Communism   151

9. The Final Years of European Communism   169

10. November 9, 1989: The Night of the *Mauerfall*   183

11. Russia and Germany after the Wall   203

Selected Bibliography   227

Index   231

PREFACE: FROM WAR TO OPPRESSION . . . THEN HOPE

Imagine you are a young Berliner, 16 years old, when World War II finally comes to an end in 1945 Europe. If you are a boy, you have managed to escape conscription into the war by an army that was drafting some teenagers even younger than you. But, for as long as you can remember, you have lived in a country consumed by angry rhetoric, violence, and now the devastation wrought by the Allied victory that has crushed the German army and the cities and towns of Germany along with it. You are a bundle of mixed emotions because, although your country has just lost this war and you have lost loved ones in it, the war is—in fact— finally over. You may be standing in streets filled with rubble from what used to be beautiful buildings, but at least you are standing. You are alive, and the fighting is over. No more bombing raids at night or during the day. Tomorrow may bring many questions about what comes next, but at least the fighting and the bombing are over.

As the days, weeks, months, and years progress, you pitch in and help find ways to feed your family and to start rebuilding your home and neighborhood. The end of the war has brought people from different lands to that neighborhood: American, French, British, and Russian soldiers are regular sights in the streets and evening places. You have been tossed a few candy bars yourself by passing American GIs, and they have been luxuries you've treasured. News of the Berlin airdrops has reached your neighborhood, and it looks like help has come in the form of food from your country's former enemies. The days start to look brighter; indeed the entire future does.

Before long, however, you see that your country of Germany and your city of Berlin are going to have to pay the price for the imperialism that brought on the onslaught of the Allied armies. Your country is being divided into East and West Germany, and your Berlin is in the East. But only part of the city is becoming a part of East Germany; the rest is being divided into three other sectors to be controlled by France, Great Britain, and the United States.

Unfortunately, as you will soon come to see, East Berlin will fall under a new totalitarian regime, and the political party controlling it and all of East Germany is known as the Communist Party. You quickly come to learn the new rules of life for living in East Germany, and they don't seem to offer too much in the way of personal freedoms, despite the name given to your new country: the German Democratic Republic, or GDR.

At the age of 20, when most that age are thinking they have their whole lives ahead of them to plan out as they wish, you wonder seriously about that. Travel restrictions have already been imposed, and there are many stories of East Germans who are already finding ways of getting out of what appears to be some oppressive years ahead. There is still some freedom of movement, however, so you decide to stick it out and start your career, perhaps in a construction trade, working for the new collectivist system known to you as Communism.

You marry, start a family, and often give thought to joining others who are escaping to West Berlin. About the time you develop the resolve to do that, however, it is the summer of 1961. As you fine-tune your plan to get your family out to the West, it is already August. Then one morning during that month, you wake up and discover that the path to the West is blocked. Overnight, construction has begun on a new set of barriers to keep you, your family, and all your countrymen and -women locked into East Germany. The new barrier is coming to be known as the Berlin Wall. It starts with barbed wire, but it will end with a 10-foot concrete-and-steel wall surrounding the city of West Berlin that will be fortified by an inner wall on the eastern side of a region. The land in between will be covered with mines and guard dogs and will become known simply as the death strip.

Will you ever achieve the hope and dreams you had when you realized the last Allied bombs had fallen on your city in 1945? It doesn't look good. In reality, you will be 60 years old before that Wall comes down and the oppression of Communist rule has vanished from East Germany and all of Eastern Europe.

What was it like to live behind the barrier, known alternatively as the Berlin Wall, the Monster, or the Iron Curtain? That is the question that this book will seek to answer. Much of the focus will be on the countries and people of Germany and Russia, because:

1. Russia was the epicenter of power for Communist East Europe, and the policies and daily regulations of the Soviet-bloc countries were often enforced with Soviet tanks.

2. Germany was the country straddling the East–West, or Communist–Free Europe divide. Following World War II, this country was split in half, with the West becoming the Federal Republic of Germany (FRG) and the East becoming the German Democratic Republic (GDR). As was noted earlier, despite the name given East Germany, it was anything but democratic and was controlled entirely by the oppressive Communist Party. The city of Berlin was the flashpoint for East–West confrontations because—like the country of Germany—it was divided into Communist East Berlin and democratic West Berlin. However, since the city was entirely in East Germany, it came to be totally surrounded by the 10-foot Monster of the Berlin Wall, which the GDR euphemistically called the anti-fascist protective rampart. It was at the base of this Wall that the life-and-death issues of living in free versus Communist Germany were played out with regularity.

Much of this book will be told anecdotally, through the eyes of those who lived behind the Iron Curtain, and some will be told in narrative stories that focus on those individuals who tried to resist and even escape the East to find freedom in the West. Again, most of those refugees first found freedom in West Germany. Many of these stories are told in italic type, which is used when the narrative turns to focus on individuals and how they coped with the Communist system or how they resisted and often paid the price for that resistance.

However, a few parts of this book—most notably the first two chapters—will take more of a broader historical overview of Eastern Europe and how it came under the influence of communism. This backdrop is necessary to put the stories of these people and these places into context. It is not the intent of the author to make this a definitive historical look at the rise of the Communist era or the Cold War era that followed it. The plan is to try and stay focused, as much as possible, on how the overall system of communism affected everyday citizens.

Any book is a result of much labor that has gone before by others, and this is one is no exception. I have tried to credit the many sources from which much of this material has come. I stand in awe of the body of work that has been produced by people who lived to tell these stories, and by others—journalists and researchers—who discovered many of these stories hidden behind the Iron Curtain. I have personally had the privilege of working in Germany off and on for the past 17 years, ever since the U.S. State Department (then in Bonn, now in Berlin) asked me to come to Central and Eastern Europe to conduct lecture tours and develop lasting friendships with people there. I have also been privileged to cover, as a working journalist for the *Oklahoman* newspaper, both the tenth and twentieth anniversaries of the fall of the Berlin Wall. I have never in my life been so moved than on the nights of November 9, 1999, and November 9, 2009. The fall of the Berlin Wall stands as hope to the world that no wall of oppression will endure forever.

I would personally like to thank my wife Annie, for giving part of me up to write another book, and for her always-helpful comments as I've told her parts of these stories. Usually that insight has led me to poke around in places I had never thought of doing, often with good results. I would also like to thank my colleagues at Azusa Pacific University, in Southern California, where I teach and write in the serene surroundings of our Rose Garden Quad.

In the stories that follow, I hope you find the inspiration I did in hearing about the courageous people of Eastern Europe during some of the darkest days in their history.

—Jim Willis, PhD

1

EASTERN EUROPE
UNDER COMMUNISM

I miss the communist era sometimes (at least when I'm not hungry).

The main difference between Poland then and now is that during the miserable real-socialism era people had money, but couldn't buy anything because shop shelves were empty. Now they can buy whatever they want, but many can't afford it.

To cut the whole story short—I wouldn't import any features of a socialist country into modern, capitalistic society.

These three comments come from anonymous Polish citizens who have lived both under Communist and non-Communist regimes.[1] They are reacting to a question on a blog about what it was like for everyday people to live under two different economic systems: one Communist and the other capitalist. We start with these observations because most Eastern Europeans have lived their lives under two—and sometimes three—different economic and political systems. For the Poles, there has been Communism, National Socialism, and capitalism. Two of those systems also brought them autocratic rulers.

But Communism was certainly not the first economic system Eastern Europeans knew. In fact, it surfaced fairly late in the development of these very old countries.

Nevertheless, for most Americans living in the twentieth century, the thought of Eastern Europe conjured up the overarching specter of Communism because it seemed the countries making up that region had always been under a Communist regime and always part of the former Soviet Union or what President Ronald Reagan referred to as "the evil empire." Evil or not, The Union of Soviet Socialist Republics (or, more commonly, the USSR or Soviet Union) was not created until 1922. It would die officially in 1991, although Communism in Eastern Europe had been rendered fairly impotent after the Berlin Wall came down in 1989. However, equating of the USSR and Communism is correct because the Soviet Union was unified under one, and only one, political power and economic system: Communism.

THE COUNTRIES OF EASTERN EUROPE

Before proceeding further, we should define what we are talking about geographically when we talk about Eastern Europe, and what countries constitute that geopolitical region of the world. The countries that officially comprise Eastern Europe are as follows:

- Russia
- Czech Republic
- Poland
- Hungary
- Romania
- Moldova
- Croatia
- Lithuania
- Latvia
- Estonia
- Slovenia
- Slovakia
- Bulgaria
- Ukraine
- Belarus
- Serbia

- Montenegro
- Bosnia
- Herzegovina
- Albania
- Kosovo
- Macedonia

To this list should be added one of the most important of the former Communist states: the German Democratic Republic, or East Germany. Although geographically in Central Europe, East Germany was partitioned following World War II to Soviet control. Up until Germany was reunified following the fall of the Berlin Wall in 1989, East Germany was its own country under a Communist regime. It has now ceased to exist as a separate country, although Germans often still refer to themselves or their heritage as Wessis (West German) or Ossis (East German). If St. Petersburg was the city where modern-day Communist rule began in Eastern Europe in 1917, East Berlin was the city where it dramatically and symbolically came to an end in 1989.

The preceding list of countries shows at least three things:

1. It contains several countries that most Americans have heard of only tangentially and have no idea where they are on a world map. Take, for example, Albania. In the 1997 movie *Wag the Dog*, a crisis communication specialist decided to fake a war with Albania to distract voters' attention from a presidential scandal shortly before the election. When asked if people would not get wise to the ruse, the specialist replied, "Why should they? Whoever heard of Albania?"[2]

2. Not all of the countries of Eastern Europe were part of the USSR and its state-controlled Communist system. In fact, only seven of the 22 countries that today comprise Eastern Europe were part of the Soviet Union. They are Russia, Moldova, Lithuania, Latvia, Estonia, Ukraine, and Belarus. The USSR contained 15 different countries, however, so the remaining eight came from the North Asian countries of Armenia, Azerbaijan, Georgia, Kazakhstan, Kyrgyzstan, Tajikistan, Turkmenistan, and Uzbekistan. So another popular misconception is exposed, and that is that the former Soviet Union consisted only of Eastern European nations.

3. Although only seven of the countries that currently comprise Eastern Europe were officially a part of the USSR, Communism was entrenched in all of them, to a greater or lesser degree.

COMMUNISM TAKES ROOT

With the concept of Eastern Europe defined by countries, let us turn to the focus of this chapter: What was this region like before and under Communism, and how did that economic and political system take root and transform more than a third of the nations into Soviet states? We will do this by focusing on a sample of the most influential countries of Eastern Europe because their stories follow patterns similar to all the countries of the region. First, though, here is an overall thought about the Communist era in Eastern Europe[3]:

> *If an intelligent layman were asked which was the most significant event of the 20th century, strong chances are that he would say the collapse of communism. If the same question had been asked of such a man in the 1970s, the answer, in all probability, would have been the Bolshevik Revolution of 1917. The victory of communism in Russia, the regimes it unleashed in Eastern Europe and the collapse of those regimes mark the beginning and the end of an epoch. This epoch saw the establishment of one of the most oppressive political and social systems in human history. The irony was that this system identified itself with communism, which at one time was seen as the ideology of liberation and emancipation of all human kind.*
> —Rudrangshu Mukherjee, the *Telegraph*, Calcutta, India

Russia

We will start with Russia because it would prove to be the most powerful and influential of all the Communist countries in Eastern Europe. Up until 1917, Russia had a vast empire that ranged from Eastern Europe all the way west to the Pacific Ocean. It was a poor country and much more of a developing nation than an advanced one when it came to literacy, education, standard of living, and any kind of real progress. Agriculture was the main source of income for most Russians, and four out of five people were peasants. The methods farmers used were primitive, and the harvests were often small as production lagged. Horses and plows were everywhere in the countryside; tractors almost non-existent. With a huge increase in population, Russia found it impossible to feed everyone under its near-feudal system of farming, and great famines ensued in 1601 and 1891. Millions died as a result.

Overarching all this was a dictatorship of autocratic elites, ruled by a tsar that emanated from a royal family. In the early twentieth century, this was Tsar Nicholas II, a descendant of the Romanov family. As much as is possible to do over a territory of several million square miles, the tsar ruled with an iron fist, using a secret police force, the Department for Protecting the Public Security and Order, called the *Okhrana (an acronym for the Russian words)*, to enforce his orders and to put down any opposition among rebels. The Okhrana would prove to be an early forerunner of later secret police units like the KGB in Russia and the Stasi in East Germany. They were always needed as enforcers when government policy was to deny citizens basic freedoms and severely restrict their emigration—or even travel—to more democratic countries.

In Russia's vast rural areas, farm labor was provided by peasants who worked for the landowners. It would be more correct to say that the peasants were actually *owned* by the landowners, as a system of serfdom reigned in many areas. Officially, serfdom had been abolished in 1861 following earlier revolutionary activity in the Russian Empire. But the terms of that arrangement proved even more unfavorable to the peasants, who never reaped economic benefit from it. So, by the twentieth century, the peasants were still badly paid and their resentment against the landowners—most of whom were aristocrats—grew with each passing year. In the cities, people were in a similar economic bind. Like their counterparts in the fields, urban workers usually shared living quarters, suffered through poor working conditions for 11-hour days, and were poorly paid.

The tsars did little or nothing to improve the conditions faced by so many everyday Russian citizens. The situation became volatile during the first two decades of the twentieth century under Tsar Nicholas II, and it was exacerbated by the added hardships imposed by Russia's entry into World War I.

It would have taken very strong leaders, in the best of conditions, to rule 125 million people who were scattered across some 2,000 miles of countryside. That was the Russian Empire at the start of World War I. And, with Tsar Nicholas II demanding that he read every proposed regulation himself, the process of governing slowed even more, and months might pass before decisions were reached. Historian John D. Clare offers the following description of events leading up to the collapse of the tsarist regime in Russia[4]:

The (Russian) army had recently been defeated in a war with Japan (1904) and the secret police were chaotic [occasionally they arrested each other by accident]. The economy was backward [mainly peasant farmers] and could barely produce enough food to feed people; where industry was developing, in towns such as St Petersburg, living and working conditions were so awful that the workers were angry and rebellious.

There were many opposition parties. The Cadets were middle class people who wanted Russia to have a parliament like England. The Social Revolutionaries wanted a peasant revolution. And the Communists [split into moderate Mensheviks and fanatical Bolsheviks] wanted a working class revolution. There was continual unrest. In 1905 there had been a revolution, and the Tsar had been forced to allow a parliament [called the Duma], but by 1914 he was ignoring it. In 1911 the Prime Minister, Stolypin, was assassinated. Workers organized themselves and elected committees called "soviets,"

Nevertheless, in 1914 the Romanov dynasty had ruled Russia for 300 years, so it cannot be described as all that weak. It was supported by the army, by the Church, by the secret police, and by the natural conservatism of the peasants, who worshipped the Tsar as appointed by God. . . . All the things that threatened his (the Tsar's) power were the modern things that were growing stronger (industrialization and communism).

Perhaps the main thing which led to the collapse of the Tsarist regime was the First World War. If the Tsar's government before 1914 was weak, the war pushed it to breaking point. The war took men from the farms and food to the front, and it clogged up the railway system, so that people starved in the towns. Prices rose, and there was famine in the winter of 1916 to 1917.

In March 1917, things reached a head. Many workers went on strike. On March 8, demonstrations held in conjunction with International Women's Day turned extreme and were blown into riots At first soldiers shot into the marchers, but on March 12 many of the troops mutinied and joined people doing the protesting. That same day the Duma also deserted the Tsar and established what came to be a provisional government. It was a busy day because the new force of deserted soldiers and protesters established a Soviet of 2,500 "deputies" elected by the people.

The Tsar lingered too long before boarding a train. Deputies of the Duma intercepted him before he reached St. Petersburg, ordering him to abdicate his office. The people's revolution had won a great victory in bringing down a Tsar.

With a provisional government now in place, people hoped for some stability. However, it was short-lived when that government was replaced eight months later by the Bolsheviks in the Russian Revolution. This interim government was not made up of Communists, but of middle-age politicians who wanted to usher in a democratic form of government. They offered no immediate relief to the farmers and industrial workers, and they failed to produce the food supplies needed by the people. So in the end, the needs of the day would win out over democratic ideals.

Obviously, conditions were rife for a full-blown revolution, and the City of St. Petersburg was to be the epicenter of the revolt that came to be known as the October Revolution. The year was 1917, and Russia as it had previously been known, was about to disappear in the onslaught of a new economic and political system called Communism. Five years later, the Union of Soviet Socialist Republics, or the Soviet Union, would emerge and dominate Eastern Europe for most of the twentieth century.

German Democratic Republic

Much discussion will be devoted later to the former German Democratic Republic (GDR) or, as it was more commonly known, East Germany. It was such an important Communist country, it is important to introduce it here. Before the end of World War II, East Germany did not exist. The country was only the eastern portion of a unified larger Germany. However, the war would change that for a period of four and a half decades.

The change began at the Yalta Conference in February 1945, when leaders of the United States, Great Britain, and the Soviet Union met to agree on dividing Germany into "occupation zones." The Yalta Conference set the lines of demarcation for the different occupied areas, each to be overseen by one of the conquering Allied powers. After the surrender by Germany, representatives of the United States, Great Britain, France, and the Soviet Union assumed governmental control of the different zones. These zones were then made official at the Potsdam Conference held later that year. The Soviet occupation zone included the former German states of Thuringia, Mecklenburg-Vorpommern, Saxony, Saxony-Anhalt, and Brandenburg. The city of Berlin was also divided among the four powers, with the territory east of the Oder-Neisse Line given to Poland and the Soviet Union for annexation.

So, within the single year of 1945, Germans who lived in the new Soviet Zone saw their way of life change dramatically. For most middle-aged East Germans, it would change forever because they would not live to see the reunification of Germany, which would not occur until 1989. In a short time, millions of people went from life in a western-oriented country with parliamentary rule (albeit

British prime minister Winston Churchill (left), U.S. president Franklin D. Roosevelt (center), and Soviet leader Josef Stalin (right) at the Yalta Conference. The "Big Three" met in Yalta, Crimea (in what is now the Ukraine) on February 4 through 11, 1945 to discuss military and political strategy for ending World War II. (Library of Congress)

one that was recovering from an impotency wrought by the Third Reich) to an eastern-oriented country with Communist rule and a life that was regulated by GDR leaders who were influenced heavily by Soviet leadership.

A single example of a female East German teenager shows the terror that many of her fellow citizens faced. Her name is Erika Riemann, and she lived in East Germany, where she was arrested by the secret police, the Stasi. Her crime? She drew a bow on the moustache of a portrait of Joseph Stalin. Meant as a schoolyard prank, the East German government did not find it funny. She was tried in a military court and, hard as it is to believe, was sentenced to 10 years of hard labor in Siberia. After police arrested her, they took her to the dungeon of an East German castle, or schloss. It was there she was subjected to harsh interrogation. Her captors made her sit up straight in a chair for hours on end. If she moved at all, she was slapped. She received nothing to eat and nothing to drink. Totally exhausted, she confessed to all the charges against her, although she said she did not really understand many of them.

She was summarily convicted and transported to a Dresden area prison, and was locked in a cage. From there, she was transferred to the brutal fortress of Torgau, where guards regularly raped the inmates. Each prison to which she was transferred seemed worse than the last. After enduring several beatings, she lost her sense of taste and smell and, once, tried to hang herself. She was finally released in January 1954, at age 22.[5]

Poland

A life of limited personal freedom was nothing new to the everyday citizens of Poland. Before Communism, Poland was a nation that, from 1926 to 1939, lived under an authoritarian system. The Sanacja Movement was a ruling force in Poland, and its members gained power after the May 1926 coup by Jozef Pilsudski. The name Sanacja came from a Latin word meaning healing, and Pilsudski used it to spur his followers to achieve greater social, economic, and political reforms. Pilsudski was an authoritarian leader who set the stage for later authoritarian rulers who allowed no opposition. Government leaders nationalized the country's assets and involved themselves in the country's economy. It was difficult for Poland to develop under this system. In the 1930s, when Hitler embarked on his plan for European domination, he set his sights on Poland and invaded it on September 1, 1939. The Nazis subdued Poland and brought it under control of the Third Reich until it was liberated by Allies during World War II. The Nazis attacked from the west, the north, and the south; resistance was futile. A month later, Polish Jews and non-Jews were stripped of all rights and were subjected to special, freedom-restricting laws. Rationing of food and medicine was established, and there was not enough of either to go around. Among the laws targeting the Poles were the following:

- All Polish men of a certain age range were required to join the German army.
- All Poles were required to learn the German language, as the Polish language was banned from use.
- The Nazis closed all Polish secondary schools and universities.

- Poland's media were brought under Nazi control.
- Libraries and bookstores were closed or burned.
- Polish culture was eliminated, and Polish art was either destroyed or confiscated.
- Polish churches and synagogues were burned. Most priests went to concentration camps.
- Hundreds of Polish community leaders, mayors, local officials, priests, teachers, lawyers, judges, senators, and doctors were executed in public squares. Many others, along with members of the intelligentsia, were sent to concentration camps.

The Baltic States

The three Baltic states of Latvia, Estonia, and Lithuania have long held ties to the Soviet Union, although they have not always wanted those ties to exist. In the eighteenth century, what was then the Russian Empire took control of most of the current Baltic states. Latvia, Lithuania, and Estonia became sovereign states following World War I, and announced their independence in 1918. They were recognized as independent countries in 1920. However, it was an independence that would last only two decades, as the Soviet army entered the Baltic states under the threat of a full-blown, military invasion. The Soviet military occupied all three states and created governments friendly to the USSR after manipulating the electoral process to the point of letting only pro-Soviet candidates run for office. It was not long before the three states were annexed by the USSR.

Things went from bad to worse for the three countries when, in 1941, the Nazis invaded and stayed for three years. When the Russians ousted the Germans, the Red Army reoccupied the Baltics. This time, it was not without organized resistance. In each of the three Baltic nations, revolt arose from groups of Baltic partisans known as the Forest Brothers, Latvian National Partisans, and Lithuanian Partisans. For eight years, from 1944 to 1953, these insurgencies lasted in the form of guerilla warfare in hopes of ultimately claiming independence for Estonia, Lithuania, and Latvia. This goal was not to be reached, at least not for another four decades.

The road to independence began to be built again in the late 1980s when anti-Communist demonstrations and reforms were

Lithuanian people seen during the run "Heartbeats for the Baltics" dedicated to the 20th anniversary of the Baltic Way at the Cathedral Square in Vilnius, Lithuania, Saturday, August 22, 2009. (AP Photo/Mindaugas Kulbis)

occurring in the Soviet Union and East Germany. In the Baltic states, protests took the form of a widespread campaign known as the Singing Revolution. This was a crusade of civil rebellion against the rule of the USSR. In a highly significant and memorable event, known as Baltic Way, 2 million insurgents created a 600-kilometer human chain from Tallinn to Vilnius. This occurred on August 23, 1989, just three months before the breach and fall of the Berlin Wall in Germany. This event convinced most of the Soviet leadership, including Mikhail Gorbachev, that the Soviet Union had lost its Baltic states.

Czechoslovakia

Following World War I, Czechoslovakia was created in 1918 out of a region that had been part of the Austro-Hungarian Empire. The new country had a significant mix of nationalities as a result. For example, in addition to the 7 million Czechs, there were also about 2 million Slovaks, more than 700,000 Hungarians, and nearly 500,000 eastern Slavic/Ukrainian people, sometimes called

Ruthenians. All this was in addition to the 3.5 million German-speaking people in the newly formed country. The country made attempts to become a good neighbor to other countries by reaching out through the League of Nations. Although Czechoslovakia had never been part of Germany, many in the country felt an affinity with Germany because of their language and because they inhabited the Sudetenland, a region on the Czech border with Germany. It was not long before German-speaking Czechs began complaining about the Czech-dominated government discriminating against them. Many Germans who had been annexed into the Czech nation lost their jobs in a national depression and thought, in the mid-1930s, that they might fare better in Adolf Hitler's Germany.

Czechoslovakia became a target of invasion by Hitler, but his military advisors warned that the terrain would not favor them in battle. They added the caution that if other countries—most notably France, the United Kingdom, or the Soviet Union—allied with Czechoslovakia, it could lead to serious trouble for Germany and its expansionist plans. Hitler found a way around these obstacles in 1938 by convincing Great Britain and France—neither of whom wanted war—to allow Germany to occupy the Sudetenland in exchange for Hitler's promise that he would not invade Western Europe. So the German army marched into the Sudetenland in the fall of 1938. That was only the start of German intentions, however. Since most of Czechoslovakia's mountain fortresses were in this region, the country as a whole was unable to defend itself against further German aggression, which would come by 1939. In that year, Germany took control of Czechoslovakia.

The Czech leadership was already thinking about postwar years, however, even though they were doing their thinking in exile. In 1941, Eduard Benes was named head of a provisional Czech government in London. Benes saw allies in Joseph Stalin and the Soviet Union, who could help them regain control of Czechoslovakia from the Nazis. So in 1943, Benes signed a treaty of friendship with the Soviet Union. Two years later, he went to Moscow and agreed on a plan with Stalin to accept a number of Soviet-schooled Czechs in Benes's coalition. When the Russians helped liberate Czechoslovakia from the Nazis in 1945, Benes became president. The next year, the Communist Party won a majority of parliamentary seats, and a National Front government was created that led to a Russian-style political system under the banner of Communism that lasted until the 1990s. When Communism fell in

Eastern Europe, the country regained independence from the Soviet Union's control and was renamed the Czech Republic in 1993, installing a parliamentary democracy.

Ukraine

In terms of geographical size, Ukraine is the second largest country in Europe, encompassing more than 230,000 square miles (about 600,000 km). It is a large plain, most of which is bounded by the Carpathian Mountains in the Southwest and by the Black Sea and the Sea of Azov in the south. Formerly annexed by Poland and Lithuania in the fourteenth century, much of modern-day Ukraine became assimilated into the Russian Empire (with a small piece going to the Hapsburg Empire) around 1800. Ukraine has always been a largely agricultural region with a few cities containing industries. World War I and the Russian Revolution destroyed the Russian and Hapsburg empires, and Ukrainians declared themselves an independent state. What ensued, however, were three years of civil war in Ukraine, and the western region of the territory was annexed by Poland (later to be transferred to Soviet control when the Nazis invaded Poland in 1939), while the larger portions were annexed by the Soviet Union. In 1922, the country became The Ukrainian Soviet Socialist Republic.

As happened in other countries annexed by Stalin's Soviet Union, the USSR created a terror campaign that took apart the intellectual class in Ukraine. Again as happened in other countries, Stalin created an artificial famine that resulted from his collectivization orders, virtually shutting down many private family farms. Millions of Ukrainian peasants, who were formerly independent farmers, died as a result. Thus it was not surprising that many Ukrainians welcomed the Nazi invasion of the Soviet Union in 1941 because they saw it as liberation from the deadly Communist regime under Stalin. That hope was quickly dashed, however, as the Nazi jackboot descended in brutal fashion on Ukrainian Jews, and an estimated 1 million of them were killed by the invaders.

Following World War II, the Soviets regained control of Ukraine, despite armed resistance that flared for several years, into the 1950s. When Nikita Khrushchev came to power in the Soviet Union, several years of liberalization occurred until 1964. Conditions were easier on Ukrainians under Khrushchev, but when he was replaced in 1964 by Leonid Brezhnev, restrictions would become tighter again. Living conditions would not ease again until the period of perestroika under Soviet leader Mikhail Gorbachev.

But whatever hope remained by everyday people that the Soviet system was working was quickly dashed following the 1986 Chernobyl nuclear power plant disaster. Chernobyl is located in Ukraine, and the country's citizens saw the efforts by Soviet leaders to hide the extent of carnage to the world. With the fall of Communism across Eastern Europe, Ukraine became an independent nation in 1991. It then became a cofounder of the Commonwealth of Independent States (CIS) following the dissolution of the Soviet Union, although it has not yet officially joined this commonwealth. Today Ukraine has a presidential-parliamentary system of government.

Hungary

In the book *The Hungarians: A Thousand Years of Victory and Defeat*, Paul Lendvai notes that one cultural thread that runs through Hungarian history is a feeling of aloneness in Europe. The people of Hungary have always been aware that they are bordered by Germans and Slavs, two nationalities who speak languages that are totally unrelated to Hungarian. It is partly because of this geographical placement that Hungary has been home to so much violence and turmoil in its long history.[6]

Two examples of that violence came in the mid-nineteenth and mid-twentieth centuries. When Hungarians revolted in 1848 against Russia, the revolution was put down harshly by Russian troops in 1849. A little over a hundred years later, the same thing happened in 1956 when Soviet troops brutally crushed an ill-fated Hungarian rebellion against totalitarian rule. That armed reaction by Russia was so severe that it won Hungarians great sympathy from all freedom-loving countries in the world. But it did not change the reality of the blood that was shed or the grip the Soviets had on Hungary.

Each of these two Russian invasions burst the bubble of hope and optimism that Hungarians had allowed themselves to begin feeling. Although Hungary was experiencing the down side of Communism in the 1950s, attempts were made to liberalize the system and raise living standards. But the Soviet tanks in 1956 aborted these attempts and eliminated the possibility of significant political change.

The many tragedies of Hungarian history took their toll on the spirit of the Hungarian people, snuffing out optimism and replacing it with pessimism. The Hungarian writer Tibor Dery remarked following the 1956 Soviet crackdown: "What is Hungarianness? A joke dancing over catastrophes." A fellow countryman, writer

Arthur Koestler, wrote that "the peculiar intensity of their existence can perhaps be explained by this exceptional loneliness. To be a Hungarian is a collective neurosis."[7]

Still, Hungary has refused to remain crushed. Like the rest of Eastern Europe, the country has broken loose of Communism, joined the North Atlantic Treaty Organization (NATO) and the European Union, and has produced scientists and artists who have brought the country its measure of worldwide prominence.

Romania

Romania is located in east-central Europe in the northern region of the Balkan Peninsula. Its land is marked by the Carpathian Mountains, the Danube River, and the Black Sea. Like other countries in the region, it is hard to find a time when this land was not inhabited, and archaeologists believe human presence there dates back 40,000 years.[8] Today, Romanians are the only descendants of Eastern Roman people, and their language comes from Latin, blended with some French, Italian, and Spanish. It has been said that Romania is an oasis of Latinity in this region of Europe.

From the mid-nineteenth century to 1923, Romania was a constitutional monarchy, with the country proclaiming full state independence in 1877. When World War I began, Romania declared itself neutral. It did the same thing in World War II. As a state that was once squeezed between the Ottoman, Austro-Hungarian, and Russian Empires, Romania seemed vulnerable and looked to the West, particularly France, for models of government. But in 1940, it received an ultimatum from the Soviet Union that carried a veiled threat of invasion if it did not cede certain regions to Russian states. So Romania joined the Axis powers to receive support from Germany. Following the war, Romania was under direct military and economic control of the Soviet Union until the late 1950s. That Soviet occupation led to the formation of a Communist "People's Republic." Russian troops withdrew in 1958, and Romania came under the dictatorship of Gheorghe Gheorghiu-Dej, who ruled Romania until 1968. At that time, power passed to Nicolae Ceausescu, whose policies forced Romanians into poverty, gave new heavy-handed powers to the secret police, and terrorized the people. His reign culminated in the Romanian Revolution of 1989, which claimed more than 1,000 lives but resulted in the execution of Ceausescu and the end of the

Communist regime in Romania. Presidential and parliamentary elections were held in 1990 as the country began its transition to popular rule and a free market.

SUMMARY

The countries of Eastern Europe have had tumultuous histories and have gone through periods of great struggle, poverty, oppression, and changing political and economic systems. They all fell in the path of Soviet expansionism, and some were faced in the early twentieth century with choosing between the lesser of two evils: Communism or fascist Nazi rule. The period following the two world wars leading up to 1989 when Communism crumbled in Europe saw all of these countries either directed by Soviet policies or as integral parts of the Soviet Union. The people in each of the countries breathed a sigh of relief when the windows of freedom opened with the fall of Communism and they were allowed to determine their own policies. The problem for average citizens in each of these countries was how to make a living without the basic economic subsidies they had received under their former Communist systems. As everyone discovers at one time or another, freedom usually comes at a price.

NOTES

1. "Life in Pre and Post Communist Poland," *PolishForums.com*. Retrieved from http://www.polishforums.com/archives/2009/everyday-life-7/life-pre-post-communist-poland-6215/ on November 9, 2010.
2. Barry Levinson, director. *Wag the Dog*. New Line Cinema, 1997, movie.
3. Rudrangshu Mukherjee, "Life under Communist Rule," *Telegraph* (Calcutta, India), May 1, 2009. Retrieved from http://www.telegraphindia.com/1090501/jsp/opinion/story_10898817.jsp on May 23, 2011.
4. John D. Clare, "Russia: 1917–1941." Retrieved from http://www.johndclare.net/Basics_Russia.htm on January 3, 2012.
5. Source for this story is found at http://www.telegraph.co.uk/education/3323564/Torture-memoirs-revive-horrors-of-communism.html, a review by Tony Patterson of Miss Riemann's book Die Schleife an Stalins Bart.
6. Paul Lendvai, *The Hungarians: A Thousand Years of Victory and Defeat*. Princeton, NJ: Princeton University Press, 2003.
7. Ibid.
8. Source is Trinkaus, E.; Milota, S; Rodrigo, R; Mircea, G; Moldovan, O (2003), "Early Modern Human Cranial remains from the Peştera cu Oase" (PDF), *Journal of Human Evolution* 45 (3): 245–253.

2

THE RISE OF COMMUNISM, FASCISM, AND NAZISM

Europe in the twentieth century faced twin threats to freedom and democratic forms of government. Coming from opposite ends of the ideological spectrum, the two threats were Communism and Fascism. The latter system became focused in the Nazi movement in Germany from the 1920s until the end of World War II. It was an extreme authoritarian system with supreme control placed in the hands of one man, Adolf Hitler. The Nazi movement was also called National Socialism, where leaders of the government controlled society. Communism, although ostensibly a workers movement where the proletariat (workers) ruled, nevertheless resulted in tightly controlled societies where leaders of the Communist Party controlled entire countries and the regions of Eastern Europe and North Asia. Both systems resulted in the deaths of millions of people, either through starvation, mass executions, or forced labor, which drove many to death.

This chapter will look at the rise of these dual behemoths that engulfed much of Europe and parts of North Asia during the twentieth century.

THE RISE OF COMMUNISM

In its essence, Communism is an economic and political system that strives for a classless and stateless society that is built upon the concept of common ownership of the means of production. It also envisions free access to goods and services, and the end of wage labor and private property.[1] It is, in effect, a societal commune not that far removed—in theory anyway—from the kind of society that Native Americans used to embrace on the North American continent. Like many movements that endure past a decade or two, Communism came along at the right time in Eastern Europe. As will be discussed later, many workers were on the verge of starvation, and the policies and attitude of the ruling classes in government seemed to be working against the daily needs of the masses. The time was ripe for revolution in Europe.

AN AMERICAN DALLIANCE

Communism was also an ideology that fascinated some important nineteenth century American writers, poets, and philosophers like Ralph Waldo Emerson. Its American cousin was known as Fourierism, named for its founder Charles Fourier. This philosophy envisioned people working and living in communes and letting farm machinery work for them rather than having it replace them, as was threatening to happen with the industrial revolution.

The Brook Farm Community, or Brooks Farm Community, was one result of Fourierism in America. It began in the early 1840s as a way for people to realize the ideals of cooperative communal living and working. It was founded by George Ripley, a Harvard graduate and a Unitarian pastor. He decided to join social reform with his theology and latched onto the writing of Fourier, who envisioned a classless society of equals. So in 1840, Ripley and his wife Sophia Dana Ripley lived and worked for several weeks on the Ellis Farm in West Roxbury, Massachusetts, near the city of Boston. They would spend hours each day immersed in poetry of writers like Robert Burns. Ripley knew Ralph Waldo Emerson and wrote him about his idea for organizing a socially utopian community that he planned to call Brook Farm. The letter read, in part:

> Our objects as you know, are to insure a more natural union between intellectual and manual labor ... guarantee the highest mental freedom, by providing all with labor, adapted to their tastes and talents, and securing to them the fruits of their industry ... thus to prepare a society of liberal, intelligent, and cultivated persons, whose relations with each other would permit a more simple and wholesome life, than can be led amidst the pressures of our competitive institutions.[2]

Soon, Ripley had relinquished his church pulpit; preached a farewell sermon to his congregation on March 28, 1841; and he, along with his wife and about a dozen friends, established the cooperative they called, a Practical Institute of Agriculture and Education at the Ellis Brook Farm. The community grew and came to be a place where intellectual life thrived, helped along greatly by its membership and visitors list, which included Emerson, Nathaniel Hawthorne, Charles A. Dana (who founded one of the first large American dailies in the *New York Sun)*, and Horace Greeley (who founded the *New York Tribune)*.

Fourierism had been introduced to Americans in 1840 when New York writer Albert Brisbane published a volume of Fourier's writings called *The Social Destiny*. Brisbane was a columnist at Greeley's *New York Tribune* and also spread his gospel through those writings. Fourier believed that "the cause of conflict and suffering was the perversion of natural human goodness by faulty social organization. He advocated a solution of small planned communes, and he called then phalansteries."[3] He developed a plan for each "phalanx" or individual community, which were to become cooperatives of both producers and consumers. Eventually, these phalanxes would grow economically and provide for everyone's needs and passions. "The result was to create a situation where 'Attractive Industry' would contribute to the rise of social harmony and unimaginable bliss."[4] That was the plan, anyway. But the movement never took serious root among the general population in New England. Brook Farm ran into problems with illnesses and inadequate food production, as well as a more complex organizational structure that had never been envisioned as part of the ideal. It closed in 1846.

DIFFERENT INTERPRETATIONS

Probably no ideology has different specific interpretations and manifestations as does Communism. And, like most ideologies, there emerges an often wide gap between the theory and the practice of the philosophy. Whereas Marx envisioned Communism as a *specific stage of historical development* that is the obvious result of productive forces and that leads to an equal distribution of wealth based on need, Lenin envisioned the notion of a *vanguard party that would lead the workers' revolution and retain all political power after it.* The ideals of Ripley and Emerson were much more closely aligned with Marx than with the later ideas of Lenin.

What really differs among Communist thinkers is the *way to build* the kinds of institutions that would be substituted for the existing economic drivers of capitalism. In fact, some wonder whether there should be any legislative bodies at all and whether it wouldn't be best to have more of an anarchical system of government where there are no designated rulers.

In operational terms, Communism in Eastern Europe was characterized by states controlled by Communist Party leadership, regardless of the prevailing theory of what Communism actually entailed. In fact, it became abundantly clear over time that the ideals of Communism, and its goals of equality and prosperity for all, were far removed from the reality of classes that *did* exist in society and the *scarcity of goods and services* that frustrated average citizens living under Communism in these Eastern European states.

THE RUSSIAN REVOLUTION

No revolution happens overnight, despite popular conceptions. Initial straws in the wind, suggesting resentment with the current system, are often mistaken for the final straws leading to the first shots fired. As we will later see, many in America saw the demonstrations by East Germans in 1989 and the November breach of the Berlin Wall as comprising the full range of events leading to the fall of Communism in a divided Germany. But the resentments there were as old as the Wall itself, and rebellion was in the hearts of many East Germans shortly after the barrier went up to separate democracy from Communism.

The same was true of the Russian Revolution in 1917. Its causes ran deep and spanned many decades of hardships among the Russian population. As was noted earlier, Russia was gripped by widespread poverty in its largely rural economy. When wages did start to improve, goods became scarcer and millions went hungry as the tsarist government kept food production lower than was needed by the population. In the urban areas, conditions in factories grew worse. When people are denied basic needs over a long period of time, they become emboldened and, with little to lose, strike back against ruling governments.

Such was the case at the turn of the twentieth century when citizens began demonstrating in large numbers in the streets of St. Petersburg. Some 150,000 factory workers signed a petition stating their grievances, and many took to the streets on January 22, 1905, to deliver the petition to Tsar Nicholas II at the Winter Palace.

When they neared the gates, Cossacks and palace guards opened fire, killing more than 100 Russian citizens and injuring another 300. The event became known in Russian history as *Bloody Sunday*, and it began the 1905 revolution. The workers were led by a priest named George Gaspon who later wrote of the massacre:

> There was no time for consideration, for making plans, or giving orders. A cry of alarm arose as the Cossacks came down upon us. Our front ranks broke before them, opening to right and left, and down the lane the soldiers drove their horses, striking on both sides. I saw the swords lifted and falling, the men, women and children dropping to the earth like logs of wood, while moans, curses and shouts filled the air.
>
> Again we started forward, with solemn resolution and rising rage in our hearts. The Cossacks turned their horses and began to cut their way through the crowd from the rear. They passed through the whole column and galloped back towards the Narva Gate, where—the infantry having opened their ranks and let them through—they again formed lines.
>
> We were not more than thirty yards from the soldiers, being separated from them only by the bridge over the Tarakanovskii Canal, which here masks the border of the city, when suddenly, without any warning and without a moment's delay, was heard the dry crack of many rifle-shots. Vasiliev, with whom I was walking hand in hand, suddenly left hold of my arm and sank upon the snow. One of the workmen who carried the banners fell also. Immediately one of the two police officers shouted out "What are you doing? How dare you fire upon the portrait of the Tsar?"
>
> An old man named Lavrentiev, who was carrying the Tsar's portrait, had been one of the first victims. Another old man caught the portrait as it fell from his hands and carried it till he too was killed by the next volley. With his last gasp the old man said "I may die, but I will see the Tsar."
>
> Both the blacksmiths who had guarded me were killed, as well as all these who were carrying the icons and banners; and all these emblems now lay scattered on the snow.[5]

But from that day forward, this 1905 revolution would prove to be a peaceful one, however, despite the blood shed by the Cossacks on January 22. It resulted in a general strike the following October that wound up sweeping Russia. It was that strike that resulted in a promise by the Tsar of a new constitution and parliament (the Duma), which proved ineffective and which the Tsar dissolved in 1906, shortly after creating it. Conditions for workers failed to improve, and workers continued with their general unrest until the outbreak of World War I in 1914.

The war was not going well for Russia and, by 1917, the country was staging a losing fight with Germany largely as a result of having industry inadequate to build and maintain a war machine. Added to that was the problem of an insufficient rail system that was needed to transport supplies to the troops fighting in the battle zones. Tsar Nicholas II was still leading the Russian government but was seen as ineffective by the general population.

Meanwhile, in the country's second-largest city of St. Petersburg (which was renamed Petrograd in 1914 because St. Petersburg sounded too German), factory workers faced terrible conditions. The war effort was hurting food production, supply, and distribution to the population. In addition, unemployment was rampant, and inflation was wreaking havoc with the economy. As they did in 1905, the workers organized and protested conditions, this time joining revolutionary groups known as soviets. Tempers were at a fever pitch when nearly 400,000 Petrograd workers went on a labor strike to protest the miserable conditions. One historian noted what so many believed was a single condition that sparked the revolution when he said, "It was the lack of bread that provided the spark to light the dry tinder of revolution, in a city whose military garrison sided with the insurgents at the critical moment."[6]

The workers had totally lost confidence in Tsar Nicholas II, saw nothing to lose in fighting for their survival, and took to the streets demanding changes, including redistribution of land. This time, the tsar was outmatched, and he abdicated his throne on the last day of February in 1917. With this abdication, his Cossack guards surrendered and his ministers were thrown into jail. This successful February Revolution, as it came to be known, marked the end of tsarist regimes in Russia. The monarchy was to be replaced with a Provisional Government made up of a combination of socialists ranging from conservative to liberal. In particular, this government was composed of parties called Mensheviks and Socialist Revolutionaries. Aleksandr F. Kerensky, the justice minister, was one of the key officers of this Provisional Government.

This Provisional Government coexisted for a while with the worker soviets, creating a dual-power structure in Russia. These worker soviets intensified their power base after the provisional government took over, voting to free political prisoners and thereby causing some of the most radical leaders to return to Petrograd.[7]

The February Revolution was extremely important, and it set the stage for a second revolution, the October Revolution, when the Bolshevik Party would rise up and take over the reins of government in Russia. As welcome a change as the Provisional Government was, its leaders seemed powerless—at least in the short term—to reverse workers' miserable conditions that gave rise to the February Revolution. Radical Russian political prisoners who had been released whipped up a renewed fervor among the masses of Russian workers, demanding that more be done to produce needed changes for the people. It was a situation described by American journalist John Reed in this way: "The property owning classes were becoming more conservative, and the masses more radical."[8]

The members of the Provisional Government didn't help their cause when they started going after the radicals, many of whom had just been freed from prison, and closed down newspapers seen as supporting the radical cause. A name that would live in Communist history, Vladimir Ilyich Lenin (born Vladimir Ilyich Ulyanov), was one of these freed political prisoners who inspired workers to revolt with phrases such as, "Bread, Peace, and Land" and "Down with the Provisional Government—All Power to the Soviets!"[9]

Years before, Lenin had founded a faction of the Marxist Russian Social Democratic Labour Party (RSDLP), which split from the Menshevik faction at the Second Party Congress in 1903.[10] This faction was known as the Bolsheviks, and they would become the most important group in Russian Communist history. They ultimately became the Communist Party of the Soviet Union.

The Bolsheviks had supported the Provisional Government of Kerensky, who became something of a dictator but wound up freeing the radicals he had arrested and supplying them with arms to take down the man that he had appointed leader of the armed forces, Lavr Kornilov. The reason was that Kornilov had designs on seizing total power for himself and his government coalition. The Bolsheviks sensed the makings of a power vacuum, their voices grew louder among the people, and they won a majority of seats in the local governing soviets in Petrograd and Moscow, Russia's largest city.

With their strength and numbers increased, the Bolsheviks convinced the military to storm the Winter Palace on October 24 and 25, 1917, and the members of the Provisional Government were arrested and taken into custody. This was the "bloodless coup" that catapulted the Bolsheviks into power. On October 26, elections were held that resulted in most of the ruling government seats going to the Bolsheviks. When they lost that majority in later elections, the Bolsheviks simply dissolved the government and took control. A civil war ensued with factions loyal to Kornilov (the

White Guard Volunteer Army) that were comprised of Cossacks, former noblemen, and moderate socialists who wanted a return to the days of the monarchy.[11]

Ultimately, the Bolsheviks proved victorious with the help of Latvian troops loyal to the Bolshevik cause. The Latvians would prove just as useful in helping defend the Bolsheviks (now being called Communists) not only from the "Whites" but also from the Allies, comprised of Great Britain, France, Japan, and the United States. The civil war between the Bolsheviks and the Whites would come to an end in 1920 when the Allies withdrew their troops from the growing Soviet Union.[12]

The Bolsheviks became the Communist Party of the Soviet Union and founded the Russian Soviet Federative Socialist Republic, which would in 1922 become the chief component of the Soviet Union, or the Union of Soviet Socialist States (later "Republics."). Communism was the official ruling ideology of the Soviet Union, and it would cast its influence all across Eastern Europe and North Asia before it crumbled some six decades later. The control the Soviet Union had on this vast area was helped by its success— and the spoils of that victory—as an Allied power in the war to come: World War II.

World War II changed everything in Eastern Europe. Following the war, Communists took control of eight Eastern European nations. The new economic and political system ended the previous governments of these nations some of which were living under varying degrees of democracy. However, even before the war, conditions had eroded in these countries, thanks to a mix of ethnic populations as well as differences, political corruption, and the Great Depression. During World War II, Eastern Europe found itself squeezed between the Soviet Union and Nazi Germany. Several of the Eastern European countries, including Romania, Bulgaria, and Hungary, joined the Nazis. Some of the other nations supported resistance groups and fought the Nazis. The strongest of these were Yugoslavia and Albania, both under Communist rule. By the time the war was over, the Red Army of the Soviet Union occupied all of Eastern Europe, except for those two countries that resisted the Third Reich.

Because World War II resulted in all of Eastern Europe falling under Communism, it is important to look at how Nazi Germany rose to power and the ultimate showdown between its extreme system and the opposite but equally extreme system of Soviet Communism. Both systems were vying for control of Eastern Europe, but only one would win.

THE RISE OF FASCISM

When people think of Fascism in Europe in the first half of the twentieth century, they normally think of the German form of it that was found in the National Socialist, or Nazi, movement. However, in its purest form, Fascism came out of Italy when members of the national *syndicalist movement* started combining left- and right-wing political philosophies of totalitarianism and socialism into a morphed ideology. This is one reason some people have seen Fascism as a leftist movement, while others see it more as a rightist cause. Operationally, it drifted to the extreme right in 1919 when it became championed by a former revolutionary socialist named Benito Mussolini. The Italian people were facing uncertain times and economic hardships when Mussolini started a movement he called Fascismo. Essentially, this movement called for a state-controlled society that was run by an all-powerful dictator who would do what was best for the people. Unlike communism, which has more of a global focus, Fascism historically is concerned only with what happens to the nation/state. Communism is a socioeconomic system that stands for a classless, stateless, and egalitarian society. Fascism is an ideology that tries to bring together radical and authoritarian nationalism.[13]

Fascists wanted to expel forces and ideas that they perceived as the root cause of degeneration and decadence in society. They insisted on a popular commitment to the national community to give rise to a new Italy that would be built on a kind of organic unity. People would be unified by common ancestry, blood, and culture.[14] To ensure that this society would exist, strong leadership was required to enforce a singular, collective national identity and to build a military force adequate to defend it and ensure national security. Opposition was perceived as only getting in the way and undermining these worthy goals, so opposition was not permitted.[15]

Mussolini, using his infamous Black Shirt squads, began gaining control of Italy. In October of 1922, the Fascists marched on Rome and Italian King Victor Emmanuel III declared Mussolini prime minister of Italy. Over the next four years, Mussolini changed the role of prime minister into dictator, made it illegal for political parties other than fascism to exist, wiped out civil liberties, and installed his totalitarian regime over the Italian people, subverting the nation's constitution and enforcing his control through a sustained campaign of physical terror.

To give his regime some measure of international legitimacy, Mussolini embarked on a program of public works projects meant to show improvements in the country, incorporated an effective propaganda machine to tout his "successes" and to give an appearance of orderly administration of the government. In 1929, he signed the Lateran Treaty with the papacy that resulted in an increase in his popularity. This treaty, which stayed in effect until 1985, resulted in the papacy recognizing the State of Italy, with Rome as its capital. In return, Italy recognized papal sovereignty over the Vatican City, a 109-acre sector of Rome, and also recognized the full independence of the Pope from the Italian government.[16]

The synergy between the Nazi and Fascist movements is readily apparent, as both stress totalitarian control to achieve the goal of singular "superior" societies based on a common blood and culture. Nazism was to become a unique kind of Fascism that added biological racism and anti-Semitism to the ideological mix.[17] Like Facism, Nazism drew from both extreme right- and left-wing philosophies, but both movements hated Communism. In fact, this is one reason America tolerated the movements for a while, seeing them both as obstacles to communism in Europe. Operationally, both Nazism and Fascism came to epitomize extreme right-wing ideas, however. Nazis believed (as neo-Nazis still do) in the superiority of the Aryan race. They believed that Germany represented the purest of the Aryan nations.[18] They also saw the Jewish population as the greatest internal threat to Aryanism and perceived Jews to be a parasitic race that could subvert Aryan goals if they were not forcibly subdued. As leader of the Nazi movement, Hitler believed that the security of Germany and of the Nazi movement depended on its expansion into Europe, creating an empire so large that it could not be threatened by opposing forces or ideologies.

Given the similarities of their ideologies and goals, it was not at all surprising for Hitler and Mussolini to join forces to dominate Europe, giving rise to World War II.

THE RISE OF NAZI GERMANY

The roots of World War II and all the changes it would bring to Eastern Europe are found in the ashes of World War I when Germany felt humiliated in defeat and had trouble getting back on its feet after sanctions imposed on it by the Allied powers. Germans are a proud people, although today they don't often express it in symbols or rhetoric the way Americans do, and many were looking for a leader to make them strong once again. That leader came in the unlikely guise of an Austrian-born man with an appearance and voice that leave many wondering how he could have such great charisma with large crowds. The man was Adolf Hitler.

As a political leader, Hitler emerged in the early 1920s. His party was the NSDAP, or the Nationalsozialistiche Deutsche Arbeier-partei. More familiarly, of course, this was the Nazi Party. The Nazis first tested their influence and power by trying to take over the Bavarian state government in the Beer Hall Putsch. For his role in this attempt, Hitler was arrested by Bavarian authorities and sentenced to time in Landsberg Prison. He made good use of his time, however, writing the infamous book *Mein Kampf* (*My Struggle*, or *My Battle*). In this two-volume work, he laid out his belief system, strongly anti-Semitic, and his vision of European domination. The Nazi Party grew in power in the late 1920s and early 1930s with the help of the Strumabteilung (or Storm Troopers) that were a kind of brown-shirted cheering squad that spread enthusiasm for the Nazi movement even as it intimated other political parties or movements.

By 1933, the Nazi Party had gained sufficient strength to become the second largest party in Germany. At that time, government leaders invited Hitler to become chancellor in a coalition government. Communism had gained popularity in Germany, however, and was in opposition to the Fascist policies of the Nazis. So Hitler knew the Communists had to somehow be reduced in power, if not eliminated. The opportunity came on February 27, 1933, when a deadly fire broke out as a result of an arson attack on the Reichstag building in Berlin. This was the seat of the German parliament, and the building was completely engulfed in flames by the time firefighters arrived. There was little they could do. Chancellor Hitler pointed the finger of blame at five Communist leaders, who were arrested for arson and crimes against the government. Hitler used the incident as justification to get laws passed that stripped Communists of their political power and some of their civil liberties. Although historians still debate who actually set the fire, the result was that the Nazis were able to break the back of the Communist party as a political influence in Germany.

Using Article 48 of the German Constitution to have legislative processes suspended, Hitler ruled from 1933 forward by decree. He took over sole, supreme power by combining the offices of president and chancellor, then started calling himself Der Fuerher (the leader). All military officers were required to swear personal allegiance to him, the nation's media were brought under Nazi control, and the last free election occurred in March of that year.

In 1934, Germany launched the campaign to rearm itself and prepare for expansion of German territory. In violation of the Treaty of Versailles, which ended World War I, Hitler increased the size of the army from the imposed maximum of 100,000 to 500,000 troops. The army was, of course, required to pledge loyalty to Hitler and his policies. What followed were several internal "purges" of political opponents and of Jews, who were stripped of their civil rights, their citizenship, and—in many cases—their lives.

All the pieces were in place for Germany to start its march through Europe, gobbling up Austria, Czechoslovakia, Poland, Denmark, Norway, Belgium, and France. In 1941, Germany attacked the Soviet Union, which was a mistake. The Russian army, the Soviet people, and the Russian winter were all too much for Hitler's forces. The battle of Stalingrad would cost the Germans 600,000 soldiers, and this became a huge turning point in the European War. When America joined the war in December 1941, the combination of Americans coming from the west and south, and the Russians coming from the north and east, were to spell doom for the Nazis four years later with the Allies crushing the German army and winning the war.

With the Nazi movement eradicated, the door was opened for Communism to strengthen its hold on new parts of Eastern Europe. Many borders were redrawn following World War II as the victorious Allied nations were given control over territories that were previously under other flags. Because of this, entire populations suddenly found themselves living under alien governments and systems. Communism was one of those main systems, as the Soviet Union became the main beneficiary of these redrawn borders. The Union of Soviet Socialist Republics (USSR) now had control over East Germany, Finland, Poland, Romania, and Czechoslovakia in Eastern Europe. The Soviets were also ceded three formerly independent Baltic states—Latvia, Estonia, and Lithuania—all of whom had declared their neutrality prior to the start of World War II.

SUMMARY

This chapter, along with the preceding one, has set the stage for what is to follow in the post–World War II separation of Eastern and Western Europe; of the physical and metaphorical dividing line between democratic capitalist societies and Communist societies. Communism emerged victorious in the minds of many in Eastern Europe because Fascism was not a workable solution for a

A high wall of concrete blocks, topped with barbed wire, divides Sebastian Strasse in the Kreuzberg district of Berlin, Germany, on February 15, 1962. To the left is the American sector and beyond the wall to the right is the Russian sector. (AP Photo)

society seeking equality, while the works, words, and actions of Marx, Lenin, and Stalin were diametrically opposed to the principles of capitalism, which go hand in hand with a democratic society. What would result would be a Europe divided and, even more serious than that, families and loved ones divided by the Berlin Wall that came to be known to many as simply the Monster.

The Soviet Union, which had been an ally of the United States in the war over Nazism, would prove to be a formidable adversary in the fight for the hearts and minds of countries and people who would have to make a choice between democracy and Communism. The epicenter of that dangerous battle would often be found at the foot of the Berlin Wall and its Iron Curtain extensions up and down Europe. In the decades to come, many Eastern Europeans would pay for their decision with their lives.

NOTES

1. "Communism," *International Encyclopedia of the Social Sciences*. Retrieved from http://www.encyclopedia.com/topic/communism.aspx on May 25, 2011. *Columbia Encyclopedia*. 2008.

2. "The Brook Farm Community." Retrieved from http://www.age-of -the-sage.org/transcendentalism/brook_farm.html on July 27, 2011.

3. Ibid.

4. Ibid.

5. George Gapon, *The Story of My Life*. New York: E. P. Dutton, 1906. Available at http://www.spartacus.schoolnet.co.uk/RUSsunday.htm. Book not in copyright.

6. David Kirby, *The Baltic World 1772–1993: Europe's Northern Periphery in an Age of Change*. London: Longman, 1995.

7. Paul LeBlanc, "Russian Revolutions of 1917," *Microsoft Encarta Online Encyclopedia*. Retrieved from http://www.encarta.msn.com on June 4, 2011.

8. John Reed, *Ten Days That Shook the World*. New York: International Publishers, 1934.

9. LeBlanc.

10. Ronald Grigor Suny, *The Soviet Experiment*. London: Oxford University Press, 1998, 57.

11. Walter Kirchner, *Russian History* (7th ed.). New York: HarperCollins, 1991, 228–246.

12. Ibid.

13. "Difference between Communism and Fascism." Retrieved from http://www.differencebetween.net/miscellaneous/difference-between -communism-and-fascism/#ixzz1OIpZjRyK on June 15, 2011.

14. Cyprian Blamires. *World Fascism: A Historical Encyclopedia, Volume 1*. Santa Barbara, CA: ABC-CLIO, 2006, 670.

15. Blamires, 140–141.

16. "Lateran Treaty," *Encyclopedia Brittanica*. Retrieved from http://www.britannica.com/EBchecked/topic/331566/Lateran-Treaty on June 4, 2011.

17. Mark Neocleous, *Fascism*. Minneapolis: University of Minnesota Press, 1997, 23.

18. Blamires, 61.

3

THE BERLIN WALL GOES UP

Anna Husarska talks candidly about the Wall as a metaphor: "The Wall was not merely 106 kilometers of concrete elements and 68 kilometers of metal lattice fence with 302 watchtowers bisecting a German city. It was instead the most conspicuous part of the physical and metaphorical Iron Curtain dividing free and unfree Europe . . . But even worse was the wall inside each of us, the one that made us live a schizophrenic existence in two worlds—homes and company of family and friends where one could be oneself and a second world— false but increasingly familiar—in which we could wear a mask of obedience."[1]

One of the most significant changes in the aftermath of World War II was the dividing of Germany into East and West and the partitioning of its capital city of Berlin into four occupation zones, each controlled by one of the Allied powers: the United States, Great Britain, France, and Russia.

It might be best if we start with a little history of the Berlin Wall, when it went up and why, and the visual cue it provided the world about the massive tension that existed then between Eastern Communism and Western democracy.

THE PARTITIONING OF GERMANY AND BERLIN

Following World War II, the eastern portion of Germany was ceded to Russia for its contributions to winning the war for the Allies. As the Soviet empire grew into the post–World War II USSR, East Germany became a country within that Communist coalition. The former Germany became two Germanies: East and West, Communist and democratic.

Ironically to those living in democratic societies, Communist East Germany was known as the German Democratic Republic, or GDR, and was officially so founded and named in 1949 by the Soviet leadership that would hold sway over the country until the wall came down and eastern Communism fell apart under its own weight.

The German partitioning arose out of the rubble resulting from World War II. In Berlin itself, it is estimated there were some 500 million cubic tons of rubble in the streets resulting from sustained and long-term bombing raids from Allied powers. To their credit, the German people took much of that rubble and rebuilt entire structures, stone by stone and brick by brick. It was a long, backbreaking effort, but it also provided some needed direction and purpose in a time of chaos. Unemployment was rampant in the immediate aftermath of the war because factories and businesses had been some of the first targets bombed. There was little left. To this day, you can travel through Germany and have your German friends and guides tell you that this town was 80 percent leveled in World War II, or that city was totally destroyed.

HUNGER AND THE MARSHALL PLAN

I remember in the weeks and months following the end of the war, I was scavenging in the streets of Berlin, looking for anything of value to use to buy food for my family who were hungry. Although I was only a boy, it didn't make any difference. Each of us had to do what we could to help put some food on the table. I will never forget when an American soldier walked by and saw me, reached into his pack and pulled out a chocolate candy bar. He reached down and gave it to me. America has been a friend to me ever since that day.[2]
   —Fritz Hattig, former vice president of German Television ZDF

As a result of large-scale unemployment and the disruption to the German food production and distribution system, millions went to bed at night on the edge of starvation. For the average German citizen, life was pretty miserable as they sought simply to feed themselves and their children, and keep some kind of roof over their head. Into this situation came the Marshall Plan in April 1948. Named for its originator, Secretary of State George C. Marshall, the plan provided American assistance to Europe in helping to rebuild its infrastructure. Western Europe—including Germany—welcomed it, and historians say it helped avert widespread famine and political anarchy. Shortly after the American aid began flowing in, the Soviet Union blockaded Berlin and attempted to halt the flow of Allied supplies to the city. Undaunted, the United States turned instead to airlifting needed food and supplies into West Berlin. Many feel the United States learned a lesson after World War I, and the lesson was that it would be better for future relations to help Germany rebuild than to leave it in a state of humiliation.

As the Marshall Plan became established, opposition to Communism grew in the country. That, of course, was one of the purposes of the plan in the first place. To further stave off Communism and to help Germany's economic picture, the United States proposed a united Western European market based on the elimination of tariffs that would boost trade between Europe and the West, and help European nations rebuild and grow. This proposal was the genesis of today's European Union.

Communist reaction to this proposal was swift and predictable. The French newspaper *L'Humanité* was typical of Communist newspapers and magazines, asserting, "After disorganizing the national economies of the countries which are under the American yoke, American leaders now intend conclusively to subjugate the economy of these countries to their own interests."[3]

OCCUPATION FORCES

As a result of postwar treaty conferences in 1945 at Potsdam and Yalta, joint sovereign power over Germany was ceded to American, British, French, and Soviet powers. Each country's forces would occupy one of the four zones. Matters involving the nation would be settled by Allied Control Council composed of the commanding officers of the four occupying armies. The city of Berlin offered a special challenge at the Yalta and Potsdam conferences. It was located deep inside the Soviet zone in eastern Germany. But it was such an important city that the Allies decided it should likewise be partitioned to the four Allied powers rather than leaving it all to the Soviet Union. So, despite the fact that the city was encircled by the Soviet zone of Germany, Berlin was divided into four quadrants, each governed by one of the four occupation powers.[4] The zones occupied by the Allies lay on the west side of the city, and East Berlin was occupied by the Soviets. West Germany and West Berlin received massive injections of U.S. capital, which attracted many workers from miserable economic conditions in the East.

In the American sector of Berlin, the occupation army worked to achieve disarmament and demilitarization of the country, rooting out and dispensing with any influence Nazism had over German life. The Nuremberg Trials, wherein American officials helped prosecute and decide the fate of 22 major leaders of the Nazi movement, were an important part of that process. Twelve were handed death sentences, seven were imprisoned, and three were set free.[5]

The Office of Military Government supervised German civil affairs inside the American-occupied zone of Berlin, working together with local, state, and zonal agencies of the German government. Americans also set up a U.S. Constabulary to operate as a mobile police force in West Berlin.

The other three Allied powers set up similar structures in their appointed zones. One of the major problems that arose from administering the city and country as a whole, however, was the requirement that the Allied Control Council act only by unanimous agreement. Since the four occupying powers perceived Germany through different prisms and—especially the Soviets—through different ideologies, unanimity was hard to achieve. So many issues involving political parties, trade, currency, trade, economics, land reform policies, and labor organizations went unresolved. As a result, each occupied zone became a self-contained island operating under its own policies and rules. That system did little to assist reconstructing German life at the national level.

THE FRG AND GDR

Ultimately, in 1949, it was decided the country should be divided into two countries. These would be the Federal Republic of Germany in the American, French, and British sectors as well as West Berlin, and the German Democratic Republic in the Soviet sectors of Germany and East Berlin.

It was during this same time that the United States began to develop policies aimed at countering what were seen as Soviet plans for expansion in Germany, Korea, and other regions of the world. As early as 1946, Winston Churchill warned in a speech at William Woods College in Fulton, Missouri, that the USSR was installing an "iron curtain" across Europe. It was not idle rhetoric, as the USSR moved speedily to draw in eastern Germany (including East Berlin), Hungary, Poland, Bulgaria, Romania, Albania, and Yugoslavia behind Churchill's description of the Iron Curtain. American policy came to focus on containing Soviet power where it was, preferably through diplomatic and economic means.

The partitioning of West and East Germany went ahead and, on May 23, 1949, it became official. It was not a happy day for many in Germany who realized this would spell doom for any hope of a unified country. Among those displeased with the partitioning was Konrad Adenauer, the anti-Nazi German who was leading the country at war's end and who dreamed of unification. Instead of that, Germany got occupying troops under four different flags for each of the assigned sectors of the country and of Berlin itself. Although West Germany was occupied by Allied powers, the Allies began turning over more power to the West German government and putting German leaders into places of authority. The Allies also helped the West German government write what would become a federal constitution that would be the law for the three occupied zones in West Germany, or what became the Federal Republic of Germany.

West Germany was starting to show signs of political and economic life for the first time in a very long time.

THE BERLIN WALL

By 1961, the partitioning of Germany had been in place for 12 years, and the individual sectors were getting used to the new boundaries and conditions of life. That didn't mean that everyone liked the situation, however, and most international leaders—including President John F. Kennedy—felt it needed a resolution. Germany seemed to be the focus of so much debate about European Communism because it represented the westernmost front of Communism in Europe, and it involved a country that was divided against itself as a result of the GDR/FDR forced split. Because it was the epicenter of the fight between the two ideologies of Communism and democratic capitalism, it is no surprise that so many spy films of the 1960s and 1970s were set in Germany. It was also the place where families had been ripped apart by the newly created partitions and travel restrictions placed on East Germans who had only limited travel privileges to the west.

A meeting between President Kennedy and Soviet Premier Nikita Khrushchev in June 1961 brought no new hope to the stalemate represented by the partitioning. In fact, just a few days after this meeting, Khrushchev declared he would sign a separate peace treaty with the East German government that would end the West's right of access to Berlin. In July, he increased Soviet forces stationed in East Berlin and also increased the arms budget for defense of the region. Kennedy responded by asking for a new mobilization of NATO forces in the area. The Cold War was threatening to turn hot, and many East Germans took this opportunity to flee to West Germany, a risky move for them to attempt. Still, within the first six months of 1961, More than 103,000 East Germans fled west across the border.[6] This loss of many young and skilled East German workers was not a situation that the Soviets would tolerate for long. To stem the migration of workers to the West, the East Germans began barricading the Soviet sector of Berlin and started building what came to be known as the Berlin Wall. This would be the most visible barrier preventing freedom-loving people in the East from fleeing to the West, it would remain in place for some 28 years, and it would lead to untold hardship and loss of life for those trying to escape over, under, or through it. It was the final barrier to freedom to be put in place after the previous plan of securing all other parts of the East–West German border and then Berlin itself had failed to prevent emigration to the West. The entire border was now officially closed, and East German soldiers at the border were ordered to guard it with their lives.

BERLINERS AWAKE TO A NIGHTMARE

"Troops in East Germany have sealed the border between East and West Berlin, shutting off the escape route for thousands of refugees from the East," the British Broadcasting Corporation (BBC) reported on August 13, 1961. "Barbed wire fences up to six feet (1.83 metres) high were put up during the night, and Berliners woke this morning to find themselves living in a divided city. Train services between the two sectors of the city have been cut, and all road traffic across the border has stopped."[7] Showing the heartrending nature of this stark reality, West German Chancellor Konrad Adenauer proclaimed, "They are and remain our German brothers and sisters. The Federal Government remains firmly committed to the goal of German unity."[8]

West Berliners, at right, watch East German construction workers erect a wall across Wildenbruchstrasse and Heidelbergerstrasse in West Berlin in August 1961. (AP Photo)

BARBED WIRE SUNDAY

The day the Wall's construction began became known as Barbed Wire Sunday. As Agence France-Presse reported, "Overnight on August 12, tens of thousands of guards, soldiers and police hastily erected checkpoints and barbed-wire barriers, imprisoning their own people and cementing—literally—the Cold War division of Europe. Some awoke to find themselves suddenly trapped in the Soviet sector, separated overnight from families, friends and loved ones who happened to live on the other side of the Wall."[9]

The overnight barrier produced hundreds of different, frantic scenes like this one:

In one famous image, the Church of Reconciliation on Bernauer Strasse [just inside the Soviet Sector of East Berlin, abutting the border with West Berlin] was actually walled off and congregation members from West Berlin were not allowed entrance to worship. One of those prevented from entering was Frieda Naumann, who was a university student in West Berlin at the time. She later recalled that neither she nor anyone else had any idea what was about to happen.

"I spoke to the priest of the church the day of August 12. Like all of us, he knew nothing about it," she told a reporter with Agence France Presse.

In another instance, Karola Habedank, then a young child living in East Berlin, recalled that her father was also unaware that a barrier was going up. Luckily, she said that she and her family were rescued by friends in West Berlin who had heard rumors about the impending border closing and who gave them identity passes to flee East Berlin on the morning of August 13.

"If it wasn't for them, I would have been stuck in the East for all that time," she said. "But I had little friends living in the same house whom I never saw again." She said many people who found themselves on the wrong side of the barrier were saved by families and friends from West Berlin. "It happened fairly frequently," Habedank said. "Our story was by no means an isolated case."[10]

The overnight erection of the barbed-wire barrier—which would morph into the Berlin Wall—drew thousands of angry protestors from West Berlin who gathered on their side of the newly constructed barrier. It took East German guards with bayoneted rifles to push back some of the demonstrators who tried to beat down the barbed wire with their feet. Adenauer appealed for calm among his people, fearing violence might reach out and engulf West Berliners, leading to even more international trouble. In fact, however, outrage was the reaction from much of the international community. British authorities declared the new barrier and its restrictions to be illegal because they ran contrary to the four-power status of the partitioned Berlin. And U.S. Secretary of State Dean Rusk rhetorically framed the new barrier as a "flagrant violation" of East–West agreement. He promised strong protests would follow from the American government to Russia.

The BBC noted that the new barrier was indeed intended to stem the flow of refugees from the East to the West. "The tide of people fleeing East Germany has grown to a flood in recent days, as the Soviet Union has taken an increasingly hard line over breaking away from the three Allied powers and forming a separate peace treaty with East Germany over Berlin," the BBC said. "Nearly

West Berlin youths carrying a black cross with the slogan "We Accuse" are driven back from the sector border wall by tear gas from grenades fired by East German border guards near Wilhelmstrasse, Berlin, on August 13, 1962. The protest marks the first anniversary of the Berlin Wall. (AP Photo)

12,500 people left East Germany this week—over 2,000 more than the previous week."

THE MONSTER

When the Wall was finished many years later, the forbidding Monster, as it came to be known, would divide the two Berlins, virtually encircling West Berlin along the border created by post–World War II negotiations. The Wall included guard towers atop the concrete structure that circumscribed a swath of no man's land often called the death strip, which contained antivehicle defenses. A "baby wall" was built on the eastern edge of this death strip. Defection came to a standstill among East Germans wanting to flee. In the months and years ahead, many brave souls would try; many would fail and lose their lives in the process.

When the border was closed, a large number of Berlin families were split off from each other, and many would not see their loved ones again. West Berlin became a virtual island of freedom in a hostile land. West Berliners demonstrated daily against construction of the Wall. West German Chancellor Willy Brandt criticized the United States for not trying to stop construction of the Wall.

For its part, the East German government officially declared the Wall the anti-Fascist protective rampart. GDR leaders said defection to the West was an act of political and moral backwardness and depravity.[11]

The Wall and the extensions of its closed border that separated all of East from West Germany were often referred to in world affairs as the Iron Curtain. That curtain would remain closed until Communism began to crumble in Eastern Europe in the mid- to late 1980s.

While there were many tragic stories involving people in East and West Germany who were caught unaware by the construction of the Wall in August 1961, there were also some humorous ones about individuals who didn't have so much at stake but who still found themselves in a predicament because of the new barrier. One of those stories involved a young high school senior who lived in Turkey in 1961 with his parents while his father worked on assignment from the U.S. government. Because of his father's government status, his family could take space available on military planes going to various European cities for practically no cost.

Steve (who, out of embarrassment, prefers not to divulge his last name) goes to East Berlin for a weekend of fun, drops in at a bar for some beers, and meets a young woman who invites him over to her place. The route to her apartment, however, takes them down a dimly lit street where Steve feels something hard hit him on the back of the head. When he wakes up, it's the middle of the night and he is in the street, but he is there without any clothes. His money and passport are gone, he knows absolutely no German, and he is wearing only his birthday suit. So Steve does the only thing he can do: he gets up and flags down an East German policeman, which turns out to be a big mistake. Instead of helping Steve, the cop—who turns out to be a Stasi officer—arrests him on the spot.

Steve pleads, "Hey, just let me cross the border to West Berlin," but this was the night in August 1961 when East Germany officially closed its Berlin border to the West. Construction on the Berlin Wall itself would begin the next day. There was no way out. So Steve winds up in an East Berlin jail for two weeks while the Stasi try to figure out if he is some kind of spy, pervert, or both. American diplomats have to get involved, and ultimately he is discharged with a one-way ticket out of East Germany. And some borrowed clothes on his back.

Now all he had to do was to explain all this to his dad when he got home. Later, he said he preferred the East Berlin jail to that.

SEVEN YEARS LATER

"Berlin is the only divided city in the world," announced Bill Craig of the Canadian Broadcasting Company (CBC) in a June 9, 1968, television special called "Behind the Berlin Wall."[12] "Its division is marked by a wall, 12 miles long (as of 1968) and 10 to 18 feet high."

This was one of myriad news reports, still being done years after the Wall was constructed, worldwide on the Berlin Wall and what it was like to live in the city it divided.

Reporter Charles Wasserman noted on the same CBC broadcast about life for the East Berliners, *"The wall does make life for them somewhat special. It cuts them off from the rest of Europe, from the Western world. It limits them in their travel and in their freedom to move about; to experience the kinds of ideas and trends we know in the West. Lives must be lived under the special conditions that exist there and in the front-line atmosphere of communism that is in East Berlin and East Germany."*[13]

Wasserman headed up a reporting crew that went behind the Wall in search of young East Germans who might be willing to talk about their experiences of living there. He noted that the East German government was reluctant to let any kind of filming by Western cameramen take place in East Berlin but that it was possible to do it if you were willing to fill out mounds of paperwork and wait a long time. That is what he and his crew did. But that was only the start of their challenge. "Once inside East Berlin, we had to film so as to not attract attention of the East German police," he said. "Then, once we found young East Berliners, we found them generally reluctant to talk openly about themselves or their country. Some did, however"[14]

STUDENTS DESCRIBE THEIR LIVES

One student who did talk was a young woman who would give her name only as Edith K. A student at Berlin's Humboldt University, she tried to present a balanced view of life in the GDR. It is interesting that some of the themes she hit on, in terms of the positives of the experience, were echoed three decades later by former East Berliners looking back on the GDR as the tenth anniversary of the fall of the wall approached.[15]

"It's very cheap to study in the GDR," Edith said. "You don't have to pay any tuition at all. And about 80 percent of students get a stipend, from 90 marks to 205 marks. You can get along if you economize."

On the other hand, she noted, "Some things are most expensive. Nice, modern clothing is sometimes horribly expensive. But there are also cheaper things and, if you are talented, you can make your own dresses. Food and lodging are very cheap; mainly the basic foods of bread and milk. A two-room flat, an old one, in the center of East Berlin: 50 marks per month."

Edith also discussed the freedom to read books and see films, noting that some books and films are off-limits.

"I like very much to read a good book. Our book market in the GDR is quite alright. But again, I must confess, the latest English and American books are not to be seen on our market. Sometimes it is often a question of policy. There is no Eugene O'Neil, for example. I can see Western films— American, Canadian, and French films. 'My Fair Lady' is extremely popular among GDR audiences. Of course, some things are not shown for political reasons."

While 1968 was the height of the hippie and drug cultures among young people in America, apparently such was not the case in East Germany, according to Edith. She said young people did not do drugs in East Berlin, including LSD. She said there were no problems there like in the West. The city did have its share of hippies but, she added, "If they become too rowdy, the authorities will do something about them."

Edith said East German students were interested in politics, as well as art and music. They also wanted to travel, but therein was the rub. "We want to make tours, to see foreign countries," she said. "That's really a very big problem. There are no restrictions within the socialist countries. But it is impossible to make a trip to England. Politics attach us so much in our daily lives. It is one of the biggest problems we've got here. Politics and lack of travel."

WHAT WEST BERLINERS THOUGHT

The same CBC broadcast also included interviews with West Berlin college students about what they thought of the wall and the East Berliners living behind it. One of those students was Hans Kroener, an officer in the West German Student Federation.

He said he and his friends had been trying to establish contact with students in East Germany for two years but that the East German government and its policies kept getting in the way. Kroener said he had never had personal contact with an East German student inside East Germany. That contact had come only through international youth and student organizations. On the up side, Kroener noted that East German students had better education facilities than in West Germany, and they got more subsidies from the government than in the West. But he said their leisure time was regulated by East German state organizations and that they had to do voluntary agricultural service as well as military training.

"They have less time for music and parties and so on," he said. *"Most of the East German students are interested in politics, but the younger generation has not had contact with West Germany so they have a one-sided image. But the same can be true of the West. There is one difference, however. In West Germany we can read anything we want to, including East German newspapers."*[16]

Kroener said even students in the Communist nations of Poland and Czechoslovakia were freer than students in East Germany. He disagreed with the belief that most East German students were, themselves, Communists despite the fact that this is the ideology that they are taught in school. He predicted more liberalization for East Germany in the future.

NOTHING LASTS FOREVER

During George Bush presidency, the fall of the Berlin Wall brought the two Germanies back together in 1989. The event also marked the beginning of the demise of the Soviet Union and the beginning of the end of the Cold War.

The Wall and the extensions of its closed border that separated all of East from West Germany was often referred to in world affairs as the Iron Curtain. That curtain would remain closed until Communism began to crumble in Eastern Europe in the mid- to late 1980s. In East Germany, peaceful demonstrations occurred regularly in 1989, and all of it led up to the opening of the wall on the night of November 9, 1989. That opening, however, caught everyone—East and West Germans alike—by surprise when it happened.

U.S. President Ronald Reagan acknowledges the crowd after his speech in front of the Brandenburg Gate in West Berlin, where he said, "Mr. Gorbachev, tear down this wall!" on June 12, 1987. (AP Photo/Ira Schwartz)

NOTES

1. "Those were the days, my friend . . . " by Anna Husarska. In George Clack (Ed.), *The Berlin Wall: 20 Years Later.* Washington D.C.: U.S. Department of State. Bureau of International Information Programs. 2009. Retrieved from http://www.america.gov/publications/books/berlin_wall.htm on June 13, 2011.

2. Personal interview with Fritz Hattig, in Mainz, Germany, June 19, 2002.

3. "West Germany: Foreign Affairs." Retrieved from http://www.u-s-history.com/pages/h1886.html June 14, 2011.

4. Ibid.

5. Ibid.

6. "West Germany: Foreign Affairs."

7. "Berlin Awakes to Divided City," Retrieved from http://news.bbc.co.uk/onthisday/hi/dates/stories/august/13/newsid_3054000/3054060.stm on June 10, 2011.

8. Ibid.

9. Richard Carter, "Barbed Wire Sunday: The Day the Berlin Wall Went Up," Agence France Presse, August 13, 2009. Retrieved from http://www.expatica.com/de/news/german-news/_Barbed-Wire-Sunday__-the-day-the-Berlin-Wall-went-up_59682.html?ppager=2 on July 27, 2011.

10. "Barbed Wire Sunday: The Day the Berlin Wall Went Up," Agence France Presse on WAtoday.com.au, August 10, 2009. Retrieved from http://www.watoday.com.au/world/barbed-wire-sunday-the-day-the-berlin-wall-went-up-20090811-eglw.html#ixzz1hOGt0eHW on December 23, 2011.

11. Jim Willis, "Auf Wiedersehen, Berlin," *Berlin Wall* Blog. Retrieved from http:/blog.newsok.com/berlinwall/ on June 9, 2011.

12. "Behind the Berlin Wall" episode of "Through the Eyes of Tomorrow." June 9, 1968. Retrieved from, http://archives.cbc.ca/war_conflict/cold_war/clips/15240/ on June 17, 2011.

13. Ibid.

14. Ibid.

15. Ibid.

16. Ibid.

4

THE RULES OF THE IRON CURTAIN

On the day of August 13, 1961, when Berliners awoke to find their city carved in half, 77-year-old Frieda Schulze found herself in a dramatic tug-of-war between East and West as she dangled from her apartment window, her arms gripped by East Berlin officials inside the apartment and her legs gripped by West Berlin firefighters on the street below. This became a defining icon for the impact of this new barrier of the Berlin Wall on the day its construction began.[1]

With the building of the Berlin Wall and its extensions separating Communist East Europe from democratic West Europe, the rules for everyday life changed for people living in the Communist countries. Although many of these people had been living under Communist governments for years before the East–West barrier went up, they had still been relatively free to travel where they wanted, including Western European countries. This chapter will look at some of the changes that occurred for people living in Communist countries that, after 1961, found themselves cut off from the West.

Many of the dramatic East–West moments were played out along the Berlin Wall that separated the east and west halves of that city. It was not only the citizens of East Berlin who were worried, though. West Berlin Mayor Willy Brandt worried that his city, totally encircled by the Soviet zone, would become a strange kind of concentration camp. West Berlin was certainly free and did not belong to the Soviet sector, but the larger city of Berlin was cut in half, and West Berliners were walled in and separated from friends and family.[2] The following vignette shows how traumatic that separation was for families.

Anna Kaminsky was a "child of the Wall." Her parents were separated when it was constructed. Her father was Swedish, and her mother was East German. The East German government had denied them the right to marry. So Anna's mother left her son to travel to Sweden, and eventually decided return to East Germany without her Swedish fiancé. But she returned pregnant with Anna, who never met her father who died in the early 1980s. It would be nine more years before the Wall would come down. As she grew up, Anna wondered what became of pieces of the obliterated Wall. She discovered that more than 80 countries on every continent had pieces of the Wall. The discovery led her to write a book called The Berlin Wall in the World.[3]

WHO COULD CROSS AND HOW

Rules would evolve over the years of who could cross through the Berlin Wall and how they would get permission to do it. And the rules for West Germans and citizens of other Western nations were far different than the rule for East Germans and citizens of East German countries.

At first, West Berliners were not allowed in to visit East Germany at all. These Westerners would face closed border crossings up and down the line between August 26, 1961, and December 17, 1963. It was not until 1963 that leaders from East and West Germany reached an agreement that allowed limited visits by Westerners during the Christmas season of that year. The same arrangements were made for the Christmas seasons of the following three years. Things improved dramatically in 1971 with the beginning of the "era of rapprochement," when East Germany sought official diplomatic recognition from the West. To achieve that, the GDR leaders agreed to sign the Four Power Agreement on Berlin. Part of that agreement was to allow West Berliners to apply for visas to enter East Germany with regularity. When it came to East Germans, however, border guards would still refuse their entry permits to the West.

So, in general, Westerners could travel into East Germany by the mid-1960s by applying for a visa at an East German embassy in their country several weeks before their planned travel. The East Germans also granted visas for day trips by Westerners, restricted to East Berlin, without requiring a previous application. Those visas could usually be obtained right at the border crossings. There was a caveat, however: the East German border guards reserved the right to refuse entry permits to anyone, and they didn't have to offer a reason for it. During the 1980s, visitors from West Berlin had to exchange at least 25 Deutsche marks (DMs) into East German currency at the rather poor exchange rate of 1:1 since a DM was worth more than East German money. And it was illegal to export East German currency into the West, although unspent money in East Germany could be left at the border crossing and used in subsequent visits. Tourists crossing from the West had to pay 5 DM for the visa, but West Berliners were exempt from this charge.

As noted earlier, the situation was much more difficult for East Germans. In the initial years, no citizens of East Berlin or East Germany were permitted to travel to the West at all; not even into West Berlin itself. While this prohibition actually remained in effect until November 9, 1989, when the Wall fell, GDR leadership did allow for some exceptions to this ban on Western travel. Four of the more important exceptions were:

- Elderly retirees could cross into the West beginning in 1965.
- Visits were allowed to relatives for important family matters.
- Easterners whose professions required travel to the West were allowed to cross the border.
- Some day passes for shopping trips were allowed, but family members usually had to remain behind to help ensure the return of the person granted the visa.

Even with these exceptions, however, East German citizens had to individually apply for visas for each planned visit, and approval was sometimes not granted. As an added precaution, the GDR required that travelers from the East could exchange only a small amount of East German currency into West German currency. West Germany recognized this situation, however, and began giving small travel grants to GDR citizens visiting the West to help them stay longer.

As for citizens of other Eastern European nations, they faced the same ban against visiting countries in the West as the East

Germans did. Each country did have its own list of allowable exceptions, which varied from nation to nation. Over time, Hungary became a country where the rules were a little more relaxed than East Germany, so some East Germans escaped via the "southern route" through that country.

THE SHADOW OF THE STASI

The following scene from an important motion picture depicts accurately what life was like in Communist-controlled East Germany during the time of the Wall.

The year is 1984, and the occupant of the elevator is a severe and profoundly intelligent senior functionary of the East German security service named Wiesler. A stray word about the inhumanity of Stasi interrogations, or a joke about the dictator Erich Honecker, is all Wiesler needs to hear to make a simple mark on a piece of paper that will ruin someone's life.

A soccer ball rolls into the elevator, followed by a towheaded boy. The elevator begins to rise.

"Do you work for the Stasi?" the little boy asks.

"What do you know of the Stasi?" Wiesler says.

"My dad says you're a bad man who throws people in jail."

Wiesler's lips twitch slightly, and as is his habit, he asks the question intended to destroy the boy's happiness: "What is the name of—" The audience tenses, expecting the boy to answer with his father's name.

Then, unaccountably, Wiesler pauses before finishing his sentence: "—your ball. What is the name of your ball?"

The boy protests that his ball doesn't have a name. He looks oddly at Wiesler, not knowing that the Stasi man, who has spent decades destroying families without a second thought, has just spared him unimaginable pain.[4]

This is a hypnotic scene in an elevator from the German film *The Lives of Others*, which is set in the year 1984 but which won an Oscar in 2007 for Best Foreign Language Film. It depicts the potential power—often realized—that the East German police, the Stasi, had over the lives of everyday citizens of the GDR living behind the Iron Curtain. The film focuses on moral questions that even some hardened Stasi agents faced in carrying out their often harsh responsibilities that resulted in arrest, imprisonment, and sometimes death of East Germans found disloyal to the GDR.

Government surveillance was a way of life for individuals living under Communist regimes, and East Germany was no exception. While personal liberties in Russia were even more restricted than in the GDR, the Stasi (short for Staatssicherheitsdienst, or Ministry of State Security) were still relentless in their monitoring of people deemed to be threatening to the Communist movement.

The Stasi was the most dreaded aspect of life in East Germany for most people living there. The organization infiltrated many other groups, associations, and even churches, always looking for those individuals deemed disloyal to the state or the Communist Party. By the time it was disbanded when Communism fell in East Germany, the Stasi had generated probably more paper than any other government agency in the world. Estimates have been placed at a billion pages, which include surveillance records, accounts from Stasi informants, reports on espionage—real and imagined—monitorings of stories appearing in the foreign news media, personnel records, and a cornucopia of other kinds of records and documents. For example, there was a record for every time anyone drove across the East German border.[5]

The Stasi was the muscle of the German Democratic Republic's Communist Party, the SED. Opinion is divided on whether it took its orders from SED leadership or was an autonomous unit within East Germany. In any case, the results were the same. These agents were the enforcers of the laws, rules, and regulations of that party after the partitioning of Germany and Berlin following World War II. In 1989, the Stasi employed 91,000 people, plus many more informants, to provide surveillance for a country of 16.4 million inhabitants. The organization was immense and triple the size of Adolf Hitler's infamous Gestapo.

But the Stasi has been described as subtler than the Gestapo or its counterpart, the KGB, in Russia. While the former secret police groups were either sending prisoners to concentration camps, gulags, or executing them outright, the Stasi exerted more of a psychological set of restraints, although it was not averse to imprisonments and even executions themselves. In fact, according to records in the Stasi Museum in Berlin, more than 200,000 East Germans were imprisoned during the Cold War, and the most common offense was either attempting to flee from East Berlin to the West or expressing a repeated desire to do so. According to Konrad Jarausch, a historian at the University of North Carolina at Chapel Hill, "They (Stasi) beat people up less often, sure, but they psychologically trampled people. Which is worse depends on what you prefer."[6]

Says journalist Andrew Curry, "That finesse helped the Stasi quell dissent, but it also fostered a pervasive and justified paranoia.

And it generated an almost inconceivable amount of paper, enough to fill more than 100 miles of shelves. The agency indexed and cross-referenced 5.6 million names in its central card catalog alone. Hundreds of thousands of 'unofficial employees' snitched on friends, coworkers, and their own spouses, sometimes because they'd been extorted and sometimes in exchange for money, promotions, or permission to travel abroad."[7]

THE CASE OF ULRIKE POPPE

Curry tells the following story to illustrate the methods the Stasi used in spying on East German citizens.

Ulrike Poppe used to be one of the most surveilled women in East Germany. For 15 years, agents of the Stasi (short for Staatssicherheitsdienst, or State Security Service) followed her, bugged her phone and home, and harassed her unremittingly, right up until she and other dissidents helped bring down the Berlin Wall in 1989.

Today, the study in Poppe's Berlin apartment is lined floor to 12-foot ceiling with bookshelves full of volumes on art, literature, and political science. But one shelf, just to the left of her desk, is special. It holds a pair of 3-inch-thick black binders—copies of the most important documents in Poppe's secret police files. This is her Stasi shelf.

Poppe hung out with East German dissidents as a teenager, got black-balled out of college, and was busted in 1974 by the police on the thin pretext of "asocial behavior." On her way out of jail, Stasi agents asked her to be an informant, to spy on her fellow radicals, but she refused. ("I was just 21, but I knew I shouldn't trust the Stasi, let alone sign anything," she says.) She went on to become a founding member of a reform-minded group called Women for Peace, and was eventually arrested 13 more times—and imprisoned in 1983 for treason. Only an international outcry won her release.

Poppe learned to recognize many of the men assigned to tail her each day. They had crew cuts and never wore jeans or sneakers. Sometimes they took pictures of her on the sidewalk, or they piled into a white sedan and drove 6 feet behind her as she walked down the street. Officers waited around the clock in cars parked outside her top-floor apartment. After one of her neighbors tipped her off, she found a bug drilled from the attic of the building into the ceiling plaster of her living room.[8]

THE STASI'S EVOLUTION

To the committed Communists who made up the leadership of East Germany's ruling Socialist Unity Party (SED), the ends justified the means. And the end was that utopian state that Marx and

Engels envisioned when they declared the ideals of Communism in the nineteenth century. The main threat to that utopia was the West and its capitalist structures and ideology. So the SED leadership reasoned that it had to ensure its cause remained true and uncompromised or contaminated by capitalist (Fascist, in their thinking) thought and the corruption it saw in the West. "Protection" was the order of the day for East German citizens, and the goal was to protect them from the evils of the West. That is why the Berlin Wall was called the anti-Fascist protectionist rampart by leaders of the ruling SED in East Berlin.

The unit assigned that protective function was the GDR's Ministry of State Security (MfS) or simply, the Stasi. Its founding leader was Wilhelm Zaisser, who was assisted by Erich Mielke, until the latter took over from 1957 to the fall of the Wall in 1989. Mielke was a faithful Communist who had pressed his beliefs to the extreme when he killed two East Berlin police officers in 1931 because he saw them as a threat to Communism. To avoid local prosecution, he fled to Russia, where he was trained as a spy and then brought back to East Berlin following World War II.

The official symbol of the MfS was a sword crossing a shield, depicting this secret police as being the Sword and Shield of the Party. Said Mielke of the mission: "State Security: That means, first of all, protecting and defending the political balance of power and the political and socio-economic foundation of the Worker-Farmer State from, above all, subversive elements from without and from enemies within so that our Socialist State and social order is kept from harm and danger, from negative influences and impairment."[9]

But the Stasi was much more than a spy organization focused on Western threats; it was just as focused on threats from *within*. From its own people. Leaders of the SED and the Stasi remembered vividly that, in June 1953, a popular uprising against party rule arose in East Germany and had to be put down by Soviet tanks and troops. And they were abundantly aware that, between 1945 and 1961, some 2.5 million East Germans fled to the West, choosing freedom over Communism. That, of course, was the reason the Wall was built: to protect East Germans from the influences of the West. Really, the Wall was not built so much to keep other influences out; it was built to keep East Germans in.

So the Stasi was under no illusion about the possible threats posed by dissidents within the East, and it set about on a massive campaign to create a surveillance mechanism that could keep all East Germans in line. In the eyes of the East German leadership, the population of the GDR represented a constant and ongoing security risk for their dictatorial exercise of power. They felt absolute control of the state and society was needed, along with massive amounts of surveillance information. So the SED created the MFS in 1950, which was the successor to the police and security forces already in place since 1945.

Information from the Stasi Museum in Berlin says of the rationale for the MfS: "Since the Party considered its decision universally accepted and presumed an agreement of its interests with those of the state, society and the individual, but at the same time mistrusted the population, it is not surprising that there was not a single area of life in the GDR in which the MfS was not indirectly or, in the form of 'political-operative cooperation,' directly engaged. Maintaining such a presence in a population of 16.4 million in 1989 required, it seems, 91,015 career personnel and at least 189,000 unofficial employees. About 3,000 unofficial employees were in the "area of operations, which meant working in West Berlin and West Germany."[10]

According to Stasi Museum officials, no legally binding set of bylaws or regulations existed for the MfS. Instead, there was just a statute issued by the National Defence Council, primarily made up of members of the Central Committee of the SED. Not surprisingly, the statute was highly classified. The SED funded all MfS operations, the costs of which were high. "In its final decade, the official State budget allocated 3.6 billion marks annually to the MfS alone. That translates to about 1.3% of the East German budget. The actual financial requirement and consumption might have been far higher, however. The total wealth of the Stasi, the whereabouts of which is still unclear, is estimated to have been 65 billion marks."[11]

Zaisser was removed from MfS leadership in 1953 following a landmark uprising on June 17 in East Germany against SED leadership tactics and goals. That is when the SED decided security needed intensifying, and the MfS was incorporated into the Ministry of the Interior. Ernst Wollweber became Secretary of State, and Mielke remained as deputy minister. At that time, the Stasi employed only about 8,000 workers. Wollweber would last only four years, however, and it was in 1957 that Mielke took command and began to build the Stasi into the massive force it became for three decades. By 1972, the Stasi had become an organization able to implement an all-out surveillance of the entire population of East Germany. Virtually every East German citizen had at least one Stasi employee or confidential informer in his or her group of friends (and sometimes within his or her family as well).

Stasi headquarters in East Berlin grew rapidly from a single building to an entire compound encompassing a large city block of more than 40 buildings and houses, a large area of the city bordered by the streets Frankfurter Allee and Ruschestrasse. The Stasi was subdivided into many different departments and subdepartments with authority ranging from international espionage to infiltration of domestic social organizations in East Germany to the surveillance of virtually all East German citizens individually.

HOW THE STASI GOT INFORMANTS

You're a citizen of East Berlin and you're going about your day, minding your own business; doing your job and trying to take care of your family. You've grown accustomed to the austere and often restrictive parameters of your life, defined by officials of the ruling SED Party in East Germany. Over the years, the pain of not seeing loved ones and friends in West Berlin has eased. You just want to do what you can to maintain a relatively happy home life and you're trying to do your job well, hoping for some kind of advancement. One day, this reality is threatened when you are approached on the street by two men, telling you that you are being detained "for clarification of facts." You are handcuffed and blindfolded, and put into a windowless van disguised as a bakery truck or laundry van. You are disoriented, and the drive may take three hours before the van stops and you are removed from it and find yourself inside an interrogation room. You believe yourself to be in another city entirely but are actually only a few blocks from where you were arrested. You wonder what's in store for you—and why.

Your blindfold is removed and you are told by a Stasi officer that you are under suspicion for being an enemy of the state. But when you ask questions, you get no answers. Your paperwork is filled out, you are processed, and you are taken to jail to be put straight into an isolation cell. As you are led there, you are told not to catch the eye of anyone else, especially other inmates. You look down, or away. There is no talking allowed. You enter the windowless cell and the heavy door is closed, and you are alone, mystified, and very afraid. You wonder what will happen; what will become of you and of your family?

You are thinking that surely someone will come the next day to explain things or tell you what comes next. Can you have a lawyer? You've heard that is not allowed. The day passes. No one comes. You receive food through a small opening in the door, but no one comes. The night passes; then the next day, and the next. Finally, three weeks into your isolation, the door opens and you see Stasi guards.

*You are taken into an interrogation room, and you realize you are now
at the point of breaking, if you're not already broken. The Stasi officer is
telling you he knows you are a dissident, that you've been working against
the Party. There are reports on you; there are incriminating photos and
documents. You have no idea what he's talking about, although you fran-
tically search your memory for anything you might have done that could
be misconstrued as treason.*

*The Stasi now have you in the palm of their hand. They let you know
they are the judge and jury, and that you are facing years in prison. The
evidence is that damning. Then, suddenly, they offer a ray of hope: Sign
this document and agree to become an informant for the Stasi, and all will
be forgiven. You can be freed immediately to rejoin your family and get on
with your life. Maybe you won't even be asked to actually inform on anyone but, if you are asked, you will do it. You've been on the edge of madness for three weeks in dark, cold, solitary confinement. You're ready to
do whatever they ask just to see your family again.*

*You've just become an informant for the Stasi, and there are thousands
of others just like you.*

WHY EAST GERMANS INFORMED

The preceding example, detailed by an official with the Stasi
Museum in 2011, was the scenario confronting many East Germans
in the 1950s and 1960s, and it is one reason why everyday East
Germans became "inofficial collaborators," or IMs for the Stasi, willing to betray their friends and even relatives for the Ministry of State
Security. By the 1970s, however, there were other preferred methods
that the Stasi had for recruiting IMs since East Germany was trying
to get international recognition under an official (but deceptive) policy of "rapprochement" and "détente." The GDR gave the impression that it was liberalizing human rights conditions in the country.
But the situation was not quite what it appeared to be. For example,
East Germany announced it was freeing many political prisoners
"for good behavior." The prisoners were being freed, but only
because they were being sold to West Berlin. The practice did two
positive things for East Germany: it made them seem more humane
to the West and helped them get international recognition as a legiti-
mate nation, and it made them a lot of money, most of which was
used to finance the now even more covert operations of the Stasi.
In the early 1970s, some 30,000 East Berlin inmates were sold to
West Germany for a total of 3.5 billion Deutsche marks.[12]

So, with the new profile that East Germany was showing the world, the recruiting methods for IMs would—for the most part—become more subtle, but just as effective. Direct pressure was still used in some cases, but preferred tactics shifted to simply identifying those East Germans who might have personal reasons to collaborate. Among them are the following:

- The Stasi had the power to open important doors for you and your loved ones. You or your children could get a college education, or you and your new wife could get a better apartment.
- You already have an allegiance to Communist ideology and feel yourself to be an ardent anticapitalist. So the Stasi simply gave you a chance to practice what you preach and to join in the movement whose destination was utopia. When that goal is reached, there will be no more need for the present-day restrictions; even the Wall could come down because Communism will have prevailed. And you will be part of the reason. Your chance to become a hero.
- You know the day may come when you will be met by the Stasi, so you've already programmed yourself to say yes when they ask you to join them as an informant, rather than waiting for weeks or months in a dank cell, alone and in the dark. You're a person the Stasi has already identified as one who will likely say yes if just asked up front to help them.

Everyone had their own reasons for saying yes, and those who didn't probably wound up as inmates for months or—at the least—realized they had made themselves prime targets for Stasi surveillance. By the mid-1970s, the Ministry of State Security had done such a good job at this business of obtaining informants that they had created a country where virtually every person had a connection to an informant, whether they knew who that person was or not. In all probability, they didn't. There were some 180,000 of these IMs spread across East Germany; everyday citizens spying on their friends, loved ones, and neighbors. Whatever positive stories former GDR citizens have to tell about life behind the Berlin Wall, there was always the understanding they lived with an informant among their circle of friends and relatives, and that person was probably ready to betray them to the Stasi under the right provocation.

DEPARTMENT 20

If there were ever a unit of government that made the "dirty tricks" of American President Richard Nixon's Committee to Re-Elect the President (CREEP) look like child's play, it was Department 20 of the Stasi. This was the unit that was assigned the task of monitoring and infiltrating the social groups and networks of East German citizens, spreading disinformation and lies in an attempt to splinter the groups and end the perceived threats these groups might pose to the SED Party. These targeted groups ranged from churches to individual marriages, and the tactics used by the Stasi were beyond unethical. Among the groups and networks that Department 20 were assigned: mass organizations, bloc parties, cultural organizations, churches, sports organizations and teams, schools, justice groups, and—of course—political groups.

You are a member of a church congregation in East Berlin, meeting weekly with many others who go to the same church and discuss things that you probably could not discuss in other group settings. The SED, after all, discourages social groups and discussions, fearing they will promote party dissension. But church meetings are somewhat off limits to the Stasi. Or so you think. What you don't realize is that there are Stasi informants— maybe even active Stasi agents themselves—who have infiltrated your church group. In your naiveté you can't help but wonder why some of your fellow church members have been cooler to you the past few weeks. They don't engage you as much or seek out your advice or ask you out for coffee like they used to. Then one day, an appointed committee comes to you and asks you to leave the group because they hear reports that you may be a child molester, and they can't afford to put the children of the church at risk any longer. You object, telling them there is no truth to this rumor, but the rumor—spread by the Stasi operative—has already done its job. Your friends take your side, and then they are also asked to leave, or they decide to go on their own. Before long, this church group is splintered, thanks to tactics employed by Department 20 of the Ministry of State Security.

As fearsome as the Stasi was, one special unit in the organization that infiltrated even the East German border guards was feared the most. This was the Stasi unit assigned to oversee border guards and enforce the restraint measures at the east-west border. Its agents were often harsher in their methods of bringing East Germans into line.

"SHOOT-TO-KILL" ORDER

August 17, 1962: "Eighteen-year-old Peter Fechter becomes the Wall's 50th casualty when he is shot by border guards during an escape attempt.

A dying Peter Fechter being carried away by East German border guards, who shot him down when he tried to flee to the West on August 17, 1962. (AP Photo/files)

His bullet-riddled body is left unattended on the eastern side of the Wall as West Berliners screamed at the 'murderers' on the other side."[13]

As the 28-year-history of the Berlin Wall and its extensions up and down Europe showed, attempts to cross without permission from Communist countries into democratic countries were met with stiff resistance and—in many cases—deadly force. In fact, many of those who were killed met their death even before the wall went up, in the years following the partitioning of East and West Berlin.

If anyone doubts that, all they have to do is make a visit to the Checkpoint Charlie Museum in Berlin that stands at one of the most famous crossing points in the history of Europe. This museum is dedicated to showing the history of the Berlin Wall and to remembering the many individuals living in Communist Europe who tried valiantly to flee to freedom in the West. Several of these stories will follow in a later chapter.

Although former Soviet and East German officials have debated how seriously the Communist government took these escape attempts, the photos and stories of those still living and the depictions at the Checkpoint Charlie Museum show that challenging the border guards was a serious proposition. An order that was discovered in 2007, in fact, provides strong evidence that there were "shoot-to-kill" instructions given to the Communist border guards.

The order "was a license to kill," said Hubertus Knabe, the head of a Stasi victims' memorial. The Stasi has always denied there was such an order.[14] The seven-page document dated October 1, 1973, was found in August 2007 in an archive in the eastern city of Magdeburg, among the papers of an East German border guard.

"Do not hesitate with the use of a firearm, including when the border breakouts involve women and children, which the traitors have already frequently taken advantage of," it reads.[15] The discovered document appears to belie the official East German border regulations that the use of deadly weapons was to be considered an "extreme measure." Nevertheless, the order proves that the Stasi leadership wanted attempted escapees from the East to be killed, according to Marianne Birthler, who directs the government office that oversees archives from the Stasi. Birthler told reporters from the newspaper, the Frankfurter Allgemeine, "The document is so important because the political leaders of the time continue to deny there was an order to shoot. We have a long way to go in reckoning with the past."[16]

Berlin Mayor Klaus Wowereit is one who believes the order was real, stating it exposed the "implacability, arbitrariness and disrespect for human dignity" of the former communist regime."[17]

According to the BBC, "The document, which is unsigned and dated 1 October 1973, is reported to contain an order for a special unit of Stasi operatives, who had infiltrated border guards, to stop soldiers trying to cross the frontier with West Germany."[18]

One of the former East German government officials denying there was such an order is Egon Krenz, the last Communist leader of East Germany. "There was no so-called shoot-to-kill order," Krenz said. "I know that from my own experience."[19]

The document was at first touted as a new discovery, but it was later found that the same text had appeared 10 years before in a research paper that was apparently overlooked by the media.

Whether such an order existed, the fact remains that many died trying to flee Communist countries. One prominent victims group says that at least 1,245 people were killed in trying to escape over the East German border, half of them before the wall even went up in 1961. The official government figures are lower than that (most say "at least 270") but still substantial.

FAMILIES AND FRIENDS CUT OFF

As seen in previous stories, one of the most jarring effects of the Berlin Wall was the way it instantly separated—sometimes forever—family members and friends who, just the day before, may have been laughing and enjoying each other's company. When the Wall went up, East Berliners could not get out of Communist Europe without permission, and West Berliners had trouble getting in.

Holger Kersten, a university professor of American Studies at the University of Magdeburg, grew up in the West German city of Lubeck and remembers the existence of the Iron Curtain through a prism of pain because it took such a toll on people he knew, including member of his own family, some of whom lived in the East.

"When I think of the Wall, I think of arbitrary repression and anger and forced separation of family members," he said. "To me, reunification is more a coming-together of family members and friends. Bringing back together those who should have always been together."[20]

Dr. Kersten's remembrance is shared by hundreds of thousands of other former East and West Berliners who found themselves separated from loved ones. Here is how author Frederick Taylor describes the forced separations that occurred:

> *On the morning of August 13, 1961, the residents of East Berlin found themselves cut off from family, friends, and jobs in the West by a tangle of barbed wire that ruthlessly split a city of four million in two. Within days the barbed-wire entanglement would undergo an extraordinary metamorphosis: it became an imposing 103-mile-long wall guarded by three hundred watchtowers. A physical manifestation of the struggle between Soviet Communism and American capitalism that stood for nearly thirty years, the Berlin Wall was the high-risk fault line between East and West on which rested the fate of all humanity.*[21]

DAILY LIVING CONDITIONS

Most people understand from their daily living experiences at home, in the workplace, or living in a particular state or country that—despite what the official governing philosophy and rules are—the ways they are translated and imposed on individuals are the most important things for most people. Many individuals can get very creative in carving out personal spaces for themselves, even under an authoritarian or collectivist government, finding positives where outsiders might see only negatives. Other individuals living under the same system, however, might not be so creative and attach more of an operational literalness to government philosophies and edicts. For them, personal living space may be more constricted.

Additionally, there are optimists and pessimists everywhere, those who look at the same set of conditions and perceive either opportunities or dead-end streets. All of this can be said about citizens of free countries like the United States as well as about citizens of authoritarian or Third World countries. There are many Americans who look at their governmental system and see corruption, waste, a heavy burden of taxation for public programs or military efforts they don't approve of, and a government insistence that they support it anyway through taxes or face financial penalties or even jail time. They see an America that is more of a challenge than a helper; an insistent father or mother chiding his or her children to either sink or swim on their own. Other Americans perceive the same system as one of boundless opportunities where any individual can determine his or her own fate in life, and that the difference will be how much vision, determination, talent, and luck they have.

Whether people judged life behind the Iron Curtain as good or bad depended, in part, on the priorities they put on certain things in life. For example, a recurring theme among those who say life was pretty good under Communism is that they were "taken care of" by the state. They were given enough money to live and were also given jobs, albeit with salary caps in most instances. Additionally, education was free. These basic needs were the things these people value, and so they gave East Germany and its overseer, the Communist leadership of the Soviet Union, good marks for providing them. This system also tended to minimize creation of different classes— from the very poor to the very rich—in society. Other individuals look at this, however, and see that you could not advance beyond these salary caps and beyond meeting basic needs. If you wanted a better lifestyle, you probably were not going to get it unless—ironically—you became part the party elite or achieved greatness as an athlete or musician.

Additionally, the government's meeting of your basic needs came at another cost: Your freedom to criticize the Communist ideals or party were almost nonexistent. And, as we have seen, personal freedoms such as travel were also restricted. Getting out of the East and into a Western country was extremely hard, even for a short visit. So these two sets of needs or priorities would often fuel one's evaluation of the Communist glass as either half full or half empty. It also seemed that those who spoke in favor of the Communist system did so only as far as the filling of these basic needs was concerned. Those who spoke against it did so with the passion of individuals who wanted the freedom to achieve more for themselves but who could not find it living under a Communist regime.

Peter Claussen, press attaché for the U.S. Embassy in Berlin, was stationed in East Berlin from 1987 to 1990 and noted in a 2011 interview that the average East German did not consider himself or herself a dissenter. He said those living in the East found ways of adjusting to the restrictions the government laid down and that most did not take overt actions to resist. He calls that a "universal" tendency, in fact. Despite the threat of the Stasi and the everyday surveillance that took place, many believed they would not be affected if they did what they were supposed to do.[22] Often it took someone being personally affected, perhaps either themselves or a loved one or close friend being arrested, to turn one into a resister.

A parallel example of the American Revolution comes to mind where colonists lived under British rule for a century before enough of them felt so oppressed that they banded together as patriots and rose up in armed revolt to demand independence. In more recent years, the Patriot Act following the 9/11 attacks gave a near-blank check to the U.S. Federal Bureau of Investigation (FBI) and Homeland Security to engage in surveillance on Americans. Much of the country didn't like that, but they took refuge in the belief that only those who were doing something wrong would be caught and arrested. There was little widespread resistance to that act, other than through political channels.

A VIEW OF HUNGARY

Given the preceding information, it should not be too surprising that various individuals who lived behind the Iron Curtain of Communism would evaluate life differently while commenting on the *same set* of living conditions. Although we don't often hear accounts like the following from a woman, Zsuzsanna Clark, who is now living in Britain but who grew up in Communist Hungary, her perception proves the point about people having different interpretations of daily life behind the Iron Curtain.

When people ask me what it was like growing up behind the Iron Curtain in Hungary in the seventies and eighties, most expect to hear tales of secret police, bread queues and other nasty manifestations of life in a one-party state.

They are invariably disappointed when I explain that the reality was quite different, and Communist Hungary, far from being hell on earth, was in fact, rather a fun place to live.

The Communists provided everyone with guaranteed employment, good education and free health care. Violent crime was virtually non-existent. But perhaps the best thing of all was the overriding sense of camaraderie, a spirit lacking in my adopted Britain and, indeed, whenever I go back to Hungary today. People trusted one another, and what we had we shared.

I was born into a working-class family in Esztergom, a town in the north of Hungary, in 1968. My mother, Julianna, came from the east of the country, the poorest part. Born in 1939, she had a harsh childhood. She left school at age 11 and went straight to work in the fields. She remembers having to get up at 4 A.M. to walk five miles to buy a loaf of bread. As a child, she was so hungry she often waited next to the hen for it to lay an egg. She would then crack it open and swallow the yolk and the white raw.

It was discontent with these conditions of the early years of communism that led to the Hungarian uprising in 1956. The shock waves brought home to the communist leadership that they could consolidate their position only by making our lives more tolerable. Stalinism was out and "goulash communism"—a unique brand of liberal communism—was in. Janaos Kadar, the country's new leader, transformed Hungary into the "happiest barracks" in Eastern Europe. We probably had more freedoms than in any other communist country.

In the Sixties . . . things had changed for the better. By the end of the decade, almost everyone could afford to go away [take a holiday] thanks to the network of subsidized trade-union, company, and co-operative holiday centres.

The government understood the value of education and culture. Before the advent of communism, opportunities for the children of the peasantry and urban working class, such as me, to rise up the educational ladder were limited. All that changed after the war . . . I loved my schooldays, and in particular my membership of the Pioneers—a movement common to all communist countries. Many in the West believe it was a crude attempt to indoctrinate the young with communist ideology, but being a Pioneer taught us valuable life skills such as building friendships and the importance of working for the benefit of the community. "Together for each other" was our slogan, and that was how were encouraged to think.

Like most people in the communist era, my father was not money-obsessed. As a mechanic he made a point of charging people fairly. He once saw a broken-down car with an open bonnet—a sight that always lifted his heart. It belonged to a West German tourist. My father fixed the car but refused payment—even a bottle of beer. For him it was unnatural that anyone would think of accepting money for helping someone in distress.

When communism in Hungary ended in 1989, I was not only surprised, but saddened, as were many others. Yes, there were people marching against the government, but the majority of ordinary people—me and my family included—did not take part in the protests.

Our voice—the voice of those whose lives were improved by communism—is seldom heard when it comes to discussions of what life was like behind the Iron Curtain.[23]

A VIEW OF RUSSIA

While he himself never lived under a Communist regime, Kevin Koehler often discussed Russian living conditions with his parents, who still lived there when he wrote the following evaluation. Their views echoed some of the same themes of Ms. Clark, including the fact that the government took care of most people's basic living needs of food, housing, medical aid, jobs, and education.

It was actually a good place to be for the most part. (My family lives in Russia, and tells me about how it was before the fall of the Soviet Union.) My uncle was a teacher, and they got three weeks every year for rest at Piatagorsk, or where ever they wanted. It was all paid for. Even now, my father-in-law wasn't feeling well. He is a farmer, and went to the hospital, they kept him for observation for 3 days. He never had to pay for anything.

Yes, of course there was some shortages, such as watermelons in winter, but that is more because of location than anything.

People got jobs a little easier than what we have here now. Families are closer. There are caps on salaries. Professors at colleges only get $40,000 a year. So the span from very rich to very poor isn't as severe as here. But remember, Russia is very big. So a person can say it was wonderful living down by the Black Sea (as it really was), but living in Moscow was harder since it costs more.

Education is free. (My wife got her masters from the money of the village.) Personally, I like living there better than in the U.S. But one needs to give up some things like big cars, and big houses.[24]

AN ARDENT ANTI-COMMUNIST

The perception of another individual who grew up in Communist East Europe and who now publishes a web site called simply, "Anticommunism," puts forth a different perception than that of Zsuzsanna Clark. The writer does not reveal his identity, choosing to cast himself as typical of others who grew up under Communism, but talks about the way he came to view Communism differently as he grew older.

Even though I was born in a communist country, as a child I never sensed that anything was wrong with the world in which I lived. All kids are happy, regardless of the economic and political system of their country. Only later did I begin to ask others and myself questions like, "Why do our teachers tell us that communism is the bright future of humankind, but everyone wants to go West instead of East?"

It was very difficult to live in a society where everyone feared that anyone could learn the naked truth, and not the cosmeticized truth we were fed by our teachers. Our parents were afraid to share their thoughts with us, because, like children everywhere, we communicated what we heard at home. Our innocent chatter could threaten our family's safety if we repeated what we heard in the privacy of our own homes. Careless people and neighbors who did this could disappear overnight. We knew what would happen to them: parents would be sent to jail or work camps, their children would be sent to the orphanage. Anytime this happened it was a reminder of how we needed to keep quiet and stay in line.

When the communist regime fell I was a young man full of dreams and I was able to play an active role in the movement. I have never been so happy in my life. Unfortunately fifty years of communism left deep scars, and most people over the age of thirty were not able to readjust to a new life without communism. After so many years of being told what to do and what to think, some people's brains weren't able to make decisions anymore. And, to make things even more difficult, the corrupt government wasn't able to move forward in a positive direction.

Slowly but surely, happiness turned into deep disappointment followed just as surely by apathy. Angry people began to romanticize the years of communism when everyone had a job and a roof over their head. The people who weren't able to adjust, learn more, and change jobs—they were the angriest ones—and the homeless more often than not were older teachers, engineers, and those who are referred to as "the middle class" in a typical democratic society.

I was able to adapt, learn new things, and I struggled to make it. But being honest didn't help much in a country where the entire political and economic landscape had changed. Corruption and dishonesty are powerful tools in a post-communist society. Because of this I chose to leave my homeland and to immigrate. It wasn't as easy as I thought it would be. My first Christmas far away from home was very lonely. I didn't have any money or food, and to make it even worse, on Christmas day I drilled a hole in my thumb while trying to fix something.

I am happy now and consider myself very fortunate to be living in a normal country where hard work is rewarded, and I can see my dreams coming true. It was not easy to break the language barrier and to acclimate to a new and very foreign environment. Since it is such a difficult journey, I don't advise anyone to immigrate, but this was my path. You may have your own path and hopefully it will be easier than mine.

Having had the experience of coming from a communist country, I feel that I need to share this, to make people aware of the dangers of communism.

My name is not important, nor where I am, or where I come from. I will sign all my postings and emails with "Anticommunist."[25]

INDOCTRINATING THE YOUNG

One of the issues Ms. Clark raised was the belief by Westerners that Communist nations spent a lot of time indoctrinating their children into the tenets of Communism. That is not an inaccurate belief, although Communist officials might say that they don't indoctrinate their children any more than capitalist nations indoctrinate their children into the benefits of living under that society. In an article focusing on this and other points, conservative historian John E. Carey asserts about Communism that "Students living in Communist nations are indoctrinated to minimize the self in favor of the group . . . Individuality is not just suppressed, it is eliminated, unless the young person demonstrates some spectacular asset for the state: a wonderful athlete or scientist or musician seems to be emerging, for example. But the fruits of this labor, though there are individual rewards (travel, nicer home, nicer clothes), are always said to be for 'The State.' As far as individual rights go, there really are none. No freedom of speech, religion or assembly. No free and honest elections or media. No expectation [of] or right to privacy."[26]

In Communist states like Russia and East Germany, however, the indoctrination of the population was state policy. Because they based their methods on Russian practices, let's look at how East Germany did it. The GDR carried out indoctrination across the board, from children in the first grade to adults of every age. It started immediately following World War II when a party conference was held in April 1946 and the Communist Party of Germany (KPD) was fused with the Social Democratic Party of Germany into the Socialist Unity Party (SED). That same year, a meticulous method was followed to transform the SED into a new type of party based on the Soviet model. The SED would claim absolute power in the economy, in politics, and in society in general. Party members were indoctrinated to appropriate beliefs in various ways; literature and seminars were always abundant. By 1989, when the Wall came down, some 2.3 million East Germans were members of the SED. Since the fall of the Wall, only 76,000 members remain, and the party has been renamed *Die Linke*, or the Left.[27]

As for the youth of the GDR, two main organizations were established. The first was the Free German Youth (FDJ), also created in 1946. This was an organization for youth and young adults between the ages of 14 and 25. These young adults were seen as "the reserve of the party," from which future leaders would be drawn. Although membership was voluntary, nearly 90 percent of all East Germans of these ages wound up joining, often because their friends did or because of sports and other activities that the organization offered. By 1989, some 2.3 million young East Germans were members of the FDJ.[28] Its credo read: "As a helper of the Party, the youth league's most important assignment is to form the young generation into class-conscious socialists, who work, learn and live socialistically . . . it nurtures new cadres who will be appointed to responsible positions in all areas of social life in the GDR."[29] After the Wall fell, the Free German Youth organization shrank to less than 200 members.

The FDJ was responsible for managing a similar organization for younger children in East Germany. This group was the Young Pioneers (JP), which was created in 1948 for children from the first to the seventh grades. In many respects, it was East Germany's version of the international Boy Scouts organization, only with a different focus and purpose. Its motto of "Be Ready!" even sounded similar to the Boy Scouts' motto of "Be Prepared." In the case of the JP, however, the readiness was targeted to fending off perceived threats of Western capitalism and Fascism. Like the older organization of the FDJ, the Young Pioneers claimed almost total membership of young children in East Germany. The JP was also given the name Ernst Thaelmann by the Central Committee of the SED. The organization was a vital part of the educational system in the GDR and had chapters at every school. According to the 1973 Political Dictionary for East Berlin, the mission of the Young Pioneers was the following: "Its main task is the socialist education of children through a versatile and interesting life based around the collective of groups and friendships; and support for the schools by nurturing upstanding socialist patriots and internationalists." The first line of the "Commandments" of the organization showed where the primary focus was to be: "We Young Pioneers love our German Democratic Republic." After this primary allegiance was laid down, then came the youths' parents and then peace, which were followed by, "We Young Pioneers are friends with children of the Soviet Union."[30]

After the Wall fell in 1989, the Young Pioneers organization was disbanded.

COMMUNISM AND RELIGION

One of the often-heard things about life under Communism is that individuals have no freedom to practice their religious beliefs because Communism is, at heart, an atheistic system. In theory that is true, and it has also been true (to a greater or lesser degree) in some Communist countries—most notably Russia. But it was not uniformly true at all times and in all countries behind the Iron Curtain.

The ideological founder of Communism, Karl Marx, perceived religion to be the "opiate of the people" because it provided them only with the *illusion* of happiness and hope. To Marx, true happiness emerges only in conditions where a worker controls the rewards emanating from his or her own labor. Those conditions, he insists, can exist only in a Communist society. It is to the advantage of the power elite, Marx said, that the workers believe in religion because it distracts them from the poor conditions they work under and convinces them that their real rewards in life have nothing to do with conditions in this life.[31] It was this theory that many Communist regimes used to justify restricting religious freedoms or to try and suppress religious practices altogether, asserting that all religions are suppressive and subversive, and they detract from people's happiness.[32]

But conditions and laws evolve and, as has been noted earlier, often governments realize they need to liberalize some restrictions in the interest of calming the masses and preventing large-scale demonstrations or even revolutions from occurring. So we will take a look at how Communism affected daily religious life in two of these countries: Russia and East Germany.

My (Russian) Orthodox parents are not very observant. When I was born (in Russia), in 1973, my father had just found work in a chain of supermarkets and was afraid that if I were baptized—given the situation of my country in those years—it would endanger the whole family. Whoever requested baptism had to apply for a passport; that information was then passed on to political authorities and the secret police. After weighing the matter, my parents preferred not to have me baptized.

On my own, I was 12 when I started to think about faith. I believed there was "Someone"—not something—to whom I could go. One day I came across a periodical, "Science and Religion," published by the Atheistic Society of the Soviet Union. Nobody read a publication like that, but it was a topic I was very interested in. It seemed to me the only way I could learn something more about religion. I subscribed to it and for five years had to read "between the lines" of what was published in that periodical.

Basically, all the communications media were engaged in a continuous attack on religion. The point was to make people believe that the churches were trying to perpetuate an ancient mythology with no scientific foundation in order to control people's minds and take their money.

. . . It was religion that interested me, not atheism. The articles attacking religion quoted from Scripture and spoke of the Church and of Jesus Christ. Since I had no access to other sources, I had to make do with that. I started by thinking that if bad things are said about something or someone, it may be because that thing or person isn't really so bad. That could be the case with Opus Dei, too. Once I saw a book that strongly criticized the Knights of Malta, as well. The author called Opus Dei a dangerous organization, and yet he described its foundation and even gave the address where its "leader" lived. So I decided to write for more information, but this was after I had become a Catholic.

Looking back, I see that it was Our Lord who was leading me along that path. I knew that I couldn't speak about these matters, and so I didn't bring them up with anyone; but my interest kept growing. When I got to be 15, I told my father I wanted to be baptized into the Orthodox Church. He didn't oppose it, and even contacted a friend of his, an Orthodox priest who worked as a mechanic in Leningrad. That way, I could be baptized secretly.

—Father Alexey Yandushev-Rumiantsev, ordained to the
Catholic priesthood in 2007[33]

This priest's account gives a grassroots view of what it was like to come to a point of religious conversion while living in Russia in the 1970s and 1980s. Russia was a country that, as the mother ship of Communism, discouraged its citizens from religious practices, despite international declarations that people should be free to believe what they want and practice those faiths.

As early as 1948, the United Nations saw the importance of religious freedom and belief, recognizing both in its 1948 Universal Declaration of Human Rights. Article 18 of that declaration said, "Everyone shall have the right to freedom of thought, conscience, and religion. This right shall include freedom to have a religion or whatever belief of his [her] choice." However, enforcing that declaration around the world has been largely unsuccessful, and Russia was one of the biggest challenges proponents of that declaration faced.

The 1948 declaration was revised 18 years later when the United Nations approved the International Covenant on Civil and Political Rights, enlarging the 1948 document to address the manifestation of religion or belief. Among the points of that doctrine were that everyone should have the right to freedom of thought, conscience, and religion; no one shall be subject to coercion impairing that freedom; these freedoms should be subject only to those limitations needed to protect public safety, order, health, morals, or the fundamental rights and freedoms of others; and parents should have freedom to engage in religious and moral education of their children in conformity with their own convictions. While other articles of the Covenant on Civil and Political Rights have become parts of legally binding international treaties, provisions of Article 18 were not so codified. Finally, in 1981, the UN General Assembly adopted the Declaration on the Elimination of All Forms of Intolerance and of Discrimination Based on Religion or Belief. It lacks any enforcement process but has become the most important codification of principles regarding freedom of religion and belief.[34]

In point of fact, as of 1970, each of the 22 countries of Eastern and Central Europe that were behind the Iron Curtain was officially atheistic, actively encouraged atheism, and opposed any form of religion.[35] There is an irony here, according to many critics of Communism: How do you try to enhance civility within a society (which Communism asserted that it does) but remove all notions of absolute morality, that is, a higher power from where many feel morality and, hence, civility originate? Additionally, after Communism is installed in a society, history has shown the system becomes totalitarian, creating its own set of classes and becoming more oppressive of the people it was meant to serve.[36]

In Russia, more than in any other former Communist country in Eastern Europe, the official state religion was atheism. It was that way for seven decades following World War I. Oddly, Russia had one of the most detailed and—some say—liberal constitutions in the world in guaranteeing individual freedoms and human rights. For example, its article "guaranteeing" press freedom went on for several pages. The problem with such detailed accounts of freedoms is the old adage that "the devil is in the details." It turns out that so many details were needed because party officials wanted to define these freedoms in their own ways and in ways that did not threaten Communism. In daily life, however, it didn't make much difference what was in the constitution because personal freedoms were often curtailed in practice anyway. This was certainly true with religion. Many faith groups in Russia were undermined because of the fear their members would be arrested and because the KGB (Russian secret police) had infiltrated the leadership of many religious groups and could thus discover who was practicing religion illegally.[37]

In the 1930s, under the reign of Joseph Stalin, members of the old tsarist regimes and families were hunted down and killed. And the relics of the tsarist era were also destroyed. That included churches. One of the most famous was Moscow's Church of Christ the Savior where Tsar Nicholas had dedicated the statue of his father. The Russian Orthodox cathedral stood on the banks of the Moskva River, within eyesight of Stalin's window in the Kremlin. Its construction had been completed in 1861 after Emperor Alexander I declared his intent to build a cathedral in honor of Christ the Savior "to signify our gratitude to Divine Providence for saving Russia from the doom that overshadowed her." He was speaking of the threat that Napoleon Bonaparte's army had posed before retreating from Moscow in 1812. The church was to be a memorial to the sacrifices experienced by the Russian people.

That church became the target of demolition by the Stalin government, even though it was one of the most cherished religious structures in Russia. "I was astonished at this barbarism," said the acclaimed Russian cinematographer Vladislav Mikosha, who had been a young cameraman assigned by the government to photograph the destruction. He didn't want to do it because the cathedral meant so much to him. "How could they do it? I filmed everything. What else could I do?" he asked. Years later, on the site of the church, the Soviet government constructed a gigantic swimming pool. "Every time I would walk by I would remember what happened, and feel it again. It was unbelievable blasphemy," Mikosha said.

It was not just churches that Stalin destroyed. Millions of believers were put on boxcars and transported by rail to the dreaded Gulag camps, many in Siberia. Millions more were executed. It was the most determined effort in Russia's history to rid the country of religious believers, who were seen as a threat to the goals of the Communist Party. That was the low point for religious believers in Russia.

The high point came after the Soviet government collapsed in 1991: the Cathedral of Christ the Savior was rebuilt and consecrated in 2000.

Despite its official belief in atheism, Communist Russia did allow the Russian Orthodox Church to exist as the only permitted religious denomination. It has often been described as a state-controlled religious façade, or other words to that effect, however. Communist Party officials felt it would be easier to deal with one approved church, especially if its leadership was cooperating with the party. By 1939, the government had significantly relaxed some of its more severe restrictions on religious practice, and that increased church leaders' cooperation. When World War II began for the Soviet Union in 1941 with the German invasion, the Russian government reluctantly solicited church support in its efforts to appeal to every traditional patriotic value that might spur on the Russian people for the war effort. That seemed to work, so the government eased its restrictions a bit more and allowed people to celebrate Easter, ending (for the time being anyway) the idea that the observance of religious holidays obstructed social advancement under Communism.[38]

The Russian Orthodox Church breathed new life in that period, and thousands of new churches were opened or reopened during World War II. The moment of freedom passed quickly, however, with the Khrushchev regime during 1953 to 1964. That era saw a reversal in policy and a violent six-year campaign against organized religious gatherings and practices. The Russian Orthodox Church remained in existence, but pews were emptier. The main churchgoers were women and older adults, whom the government usually left alone. When Leonid Brezhnev succeeded Khrushchev in 1964, he retained the atheist ideology but was not as stringent in enforcing antireligious edicts as his predecessor had been. That era lasted until 1982.[39]

The number of operating Russian Orthodox churches had decreased to about 7,000 by 1975, and many of the leading Orthodox clergy and activists were removed from their positions. Some were imprisoned, others just forced to leave the church. In their place, the government put more "cooperative" and docile clergy. It was this new rank of church leadership that was often infiltrated by the KGB. The result was that the Orthodox Church became a partner with the Communist Party in espousing the benefits of Soviet foreign policy and the reunification of disparate populations in the Soviet Union.[40]

It is not surprising that young people in Russia, in testing the boundaries of youth rebellion, latched onto the religious practices that were frowned upon by their more cautious elders and by the state. A similar situation occurred in the United States during the "protest era" of the 1960s when young Americans were questioning all kinds of traditional values and authority. While that took many in the Hippie movement into drugs and antiwar protests, it took others into a "Jesus Movement," embracing evangelical religious values and using them as a means of revolution against a society they felt had grown hypocritical or "plastic."

Although conditions eased greatly for churches and for believers during the Brezhnev era, the Russian Orthodox Church did not play the same activist role in undermining Communism in Russia that the Roman Catholic Church played in Poland and other countries of Eastern Europe. Nevertheless, a spiritual awakening did occur throughout the Soviet Union starting in the late 1980s, fueled by the policy of glasnost under Gorbachev. Under his leadership, believers felt that it was acceptable to practice religious beliefs. And in 1990, the Soviet legislature passed new legislation allowing religious freedom in practice as well as in theory. As a result, more than 8,000 Russian Orthodox churches were opened between 1990 and 1995, doubling the number of active churches at the time.[41] Freedoms were also extended to religious groups other than the Russian Orthodox Church. For example, as late as 1989, there were only two Roman Catholic parishes in all of Russia, and they were maintained only because they were the property of the French government, which demanded they be kept open. But by 2002, there were some 350 Catholic parishes all across Russia.[42]

In the German Democratic Republic of East Germany, religious freedoms under Communism were more liberal than in Russia. For example, Radio Free Europe noted in 1980 that, despite East German government efforts to eradicate the influence of churches— especially in the 1950s and 1960s—"The Protestant and Catholic churches continue to play a vital and active role in the lives of a large segment of the population in the GDR. Although the number of church members has drastically decreased and attendance at regular church services is often sparse, diverse religious activities such as church festivals, youth groups, and weekend Bible retreats, continue to attract large crowds."[43]

Young East Germans especially seemed drawn to the religious scene, seeing in these youth gatherings a need that was not being met by state-sponsored organizations. Altogether, approximately 1.2 million East Germans belonged to Catholic churches in 1977, while 7.9 million belonged to Protestant churches. In 1979, thousands of visitors participated in large youth gatherings in the GDR, and the number increased as the years went on. Approximately 10,000 youths participated in a religious gathering at Eisenach, and in East Berlin alone, more than 40,000 youths attended masses there. A Blue Mass, or special Catholic service held to celebrate or remember important issues, in that city in 1980 filled two churches. A Christmas concert in Potsdam by the Thomas Church performing in the Palace of the Republic was sold out.

Adult attendance at religious events also trended up in East Germany during this same era, reflecting the government's reluctance to restrict the practice of religious liberty for fear of popular uprisings. Indeed, East German legislation provided for special laws allowing church members to gather. Participation in the summer Kirchentage (church convention) drew more than 100,000 Christians at three events in 1978 in Leipzig, Erfurt, and Stralsund. In fact, these church meetings and festivals received state support even though there were gatherings of evangelical Christians designed to strengthen their faith and prepare them for their responsibilities in the church and international Christian community.[44]

It should be noted, however, that the number of non-Christians at such youth and adult events was as high as 50 percent, and that their allure was not religion but the offering of secular rock music and readings by contemporary writers dealing with themes of interest to young people.[45] Many of these participants were ardent Communists and atheists. The value of these mass gatherings organized by the church is that they provided a way for large groups of people to gather without violating state laws against such assemblages. Gatherings organized by churches were exempt from these assembly laws because of a unique legal status provided them by the government.[46]

"Most participants do not think of these [as religious] gatherings at all," according to a Radio Free Europe/Radio Liberty summary report. "Instead, the Church offers a type of sanctuary where youths can congregate to listen to their own music or hear young writers without intervention from the state. Similar to youth in the Federal Republic [West Germany] the GDR youth … exhibit a strong tendency toward introspection and individualism. In contrast to the sociopolitical orientation of the state youth organizations, the Church offers a forum for the discussion of such existential themes as 'The Question of Death,' 'Enduring Suffering,' or 'Dependable Relationships.' Perennial topics as abstract as friendship, love, and existence and their meaning for youth are often discussed."[47]

Different generations grow up under different cultural influences. The same was true in East Germany. While parents of the youths of the 1970s and 1980s grew up under massive antireligious propaganda introduced during the 1950s by East German Communist leader Walter Ulbricht, their children were not exposed to such propaganda. Further, because a GDR Church Federation was founded in 1969 and was recognized officially by the state in 1971, the Evangelical Church was no longer viewed as an "outpost of the imperialist enemy" or the "West German NATO churches," as Ulbricht called them.[48] On the contrary, young East Germans saw an unprecedented era of improvement in church-state relations. New churches were being built, and old churches damaged in the war were being rebuilt, often with the state's support. The Church, as an institution in East Germany, was a bit like an island. It was the only large organization that was not socialist and that was free from state control. That began when Chancellor Erich Honecker agreed to recognize the role of the Church as it existed in contemporary GDR society. In turn, the ministers and laity were called upon to strengthen the GDR, to keep the peace, and to work for the best interest of each person in East Germany.

An unwanted effect, and part of the chorus of growing voices speaking out against East German policy, was that the church in the GDR played an increasingly active political role after 1971. Church leaders would often criticize decisions and policies of the East German government. Eventually, these protests, along with myriad others, would build to the climax that produced a breach in the Berlin Wall on the night of November 19, 1989, a breach that brought the Wall down entirely and for good.

West German Chancellor Helmut Schmidt (left) and East German State and Party Leader Erich Honecker (right) prior to their first talks at Hubertusstock hunting lodge near East Berlin, Friday, December 11, 1981. (AP Photo/Fritz Reiss)

SUMMARY

Life behind the Iron Curtain certainly was not easy for most Eastern Europeans, and that was especially the case for those who resisted the policies of the Communist-controlled countries. Life proved to be harshest for those who tried to escape to the West. Many died in those attempts, while the lucky ones made it. But life under European Communism was more than resistance and escape attempts. For most, it was comprised of learning the rules; accepting the subsidies, education, and jobs the government often provided; and not expecting much more. Personal ambitions were held in check, presumably for the good of the larger group. Happiness for many Eastern Europeans was found instead in ties with family and friends, and in enjoying the holiday breaks they were given. Life falls into a familiar pattern in any society, and so it did for many in Soviet-controlled countries as well. After a time, the familiar becomes home, and many don't want to leave those familiar surroundings and culture they have grown accustomed to. But the events that led up to the breach and ultimate fall of the

Berlin Wall and its extended "Iron Curtain" across Europe also showed that there is danger in a government restricting its people's liberties. No one likes to be caged, even in a large cage, nor told what to do or that their aspirations and dreams are too big and cannot be realized.

A final, telling story shows how the East German people were not fooled by what was going on with the Stasi, despite the efforts of both that organization and the SED Party to keep many arrests and imprisonments under wraps. One of the youth organizations the SED and Stasi founded was a sports club. They channeled the best football (soccer) players in East Germany into that club, and it did extremely well playing in Europe's Premier League. But the team, known officially as the Berlin Dynamo, became better known among East Berliners as "the Stasi team." Despite its success on the field, it never became popular with East Germany's avid sporting fans.

NOTES

1. Richard Carter, " 'Barbed Wire Sunday': The Day the Berlin Wall went up," Agence France-Presse, August 11, 2009.

2. George Clack (Ed.), "The Berlin Wall: 20 Years Later," Bureau of International Information Programs, U.S. Department of State, 2009. Retrieved from http://www.america.gov/publications/ on June 15, 2011.

3. Samantha Fields, "Divided by the Wall: A Family's Tale," ABC News, Abcnews.com, November 9, 2009. Retrieved from http://abcnews .go.com/WN/anna-kaminsky-remembers-life-berlin-wall/story?id=9032 219&page=2 on June 14, 2011

4. John Podhoretz, "Looking Back on East Germany: Police State Nightmare Come True," *Weekly Standard*, March 12, 2007. Retrieved from http://www.crosswalk.com/news/looking-back-on-east-germany-police -state-nightmare-come-true-11531504.html on June 12, 2011.

5. Andrew Curry, "Piecing Together the Dark Legacy of East Germany's Secret Police," *Wired*, January 18, 2008. Retrieved from http:// www.wired.com/politics/security/magazine/16-02/ff_stasi?currentPage =all on June 28, 2011.

6. Ibid.

7. Ibid,

8. Ibid.

9. Stasi Museum booklet.

10. Ibid.

11. Ibid.

12. Ibid.

13. Clack.

14. "East German License to Kill Found," BBC News. Retrieved from http://news.bbc.co.uk/2/hi/europe/6943093.stm on June 20, 2011.

15. Ibid.

16. Ibid.

17. "Remembering Berlin Wall Victims," BBC News. Retrieved from http://news.bbc.co.uk/2/hi/europe/6944885.stm on June 21, 2011.

18. Ibid.

19. Ibid.

20. Interview with Holger Kersten, November 15, 2009, as cited in "So Many Stories, So Little Time," entry of "The Virtual Unknown" blog http://blog.newsok.com/virtualunknown/.

21. Frederick Taylor, *The Berlin Wall: A World Divided, 1961–1989*. New York: Harper Perennial, 2008. Retrieved from http://www.harper collins.com/books/Berlin-Wall-Frederick-Taylor/?isbn=9780060786144 on June 22, 2011.

22. Interview with Peter Claussen, Berlin, Germany, November 10, 2011.

23. Zsuzsanna Clark, "Oppressive and Grey? No, Growing up under Communism Was the Happiest Time of My Life," MailOnline.com, October 17, 2009. Retrieved from http://www.dailymail.co.uk/news/article-1221064/Oppressive-grey-No-growing-communism-happiest-time-life.html on June 23, 2011.

24. "Was Soviet-style communism really that bad?" Retrieved from http://answers.yahoo.com/question/index?qid=20100309145023AAaHesi on June 23, 2011.

25. John E. Carey. "People Living Under Communism: Very Limited Rights (If Any)," Peace and Freedom II blog. Retrieved from http://johnibii.wordpress.com/2007/07/24/people-living-under-communism-very-limited-rights-if-any/ on June 20, 2011.

26. "Anticommunism" website, "About Us" page. Retrieved from http://anticommunism.net/index.html on June 20, 2011.

27. Stasi Museum booklet.

28. Ibid.

29. Ibid.

30. Ibid.

31. Karl Marx, *Economic and Philosophical Manuscripts of 1844*. New York: Prometheus Books, 1988.

32. Ibid.

33. "To Serve Russia as a Catholic Priest." Opus Dei: Personal Testimonies. Retrieved from http://www.opusdei.org.sg/art.php?p=37 746 on June 19, 2011.

34. From the Study Guide for "Freedom of Religion or Belief," 2003, The University of Minnesota Human Rights Library. Retrieved from http://www1.umn.edu/humanrts/edumat/studyguides/religion.html on June 15, 2011.

35. Allen D. Hertzke, *Freeing God's Children: The Unlikely Alliance for Global Human Rights*. Lahnam, MD: Rowman & Littlefield, 2006, p. 12.

36. Jeff Haynes, *Routledge Handbook of Religion and Politics*. Oxford, England: Taylor and Francis, 2009, p. 183.

37. "Communism and Amorality." Retrieved from http://www.allaboutphilosophyorg/communism.htm.

38. "Religious Intolerance and Oppression: Russia." Retrieved from http://www.religioustolerance.org/rt_russi.htm on June 18, 2011.

39. "The Russian Orthodox Church." U.S. Library of Congress. Retrieved from http://countrystudies.us/russia/38.htm on June 16, 2011.

40. Ibid.

41. Ibid.

42. "Religious and Political History of Modern Russia." Mary Mother of God Mission Society. Retrieved from http://www.vladmission.org/history/religiouspoliticalhist.htm on June 16, 2011.

43. Sharon L. Kegerreis, "A Church within Socialism: Religion in the GDR Today." RAD Background Report, Radio Free Europe/Radio Liberty, October, 8, 1980. Retrieved from http://www.osaarchivum.org/files/holdings/300/8/3/text/26-10-22.shtml on June 24, 2011.

44. Ibid.

45. Ibid.

46. Ibid.

47. Source is "A Church Within Socialism: The GRD Today," by Sharon L. Keggereis, RAD Background Report/240, Oct. 8, 1980, Radio Free Europe Research retrieved on Aug. 22, 2012, at http://www.osaarchivum.org/files/holdings/300/8/3/text/26-10-22.shtml

48. Kegerreis.

5

MANY RESIST AND PAY THE PRICE

The Stasi, East Germany's dreaded secret police, tried to murder Wolfgang Welsch three times.

The first attempt was a car bomb, which exploded but somehow failed to kill him. Next, they stationed a sniper on an English hillside next to a motorway they knew Welsch would be driving down. He missed.

The third time, in 1981, a "friend" poisoned Welsch, his wife and daughter by putting the toxic heavy metal thallium in their hamburgers during a family holiday in Israel. Against the odds, they survived, though Welsch lost his hair and spent weeks in hospital.

The friend, it turned out, was a Stasi killer, working for an assassination squad codenamed "Scorpion." As a former East German dissident who was helping smuggle people to the West, Welsch was a prime target.

Now a writer, Welsch was dismissed as a crank until Stern *magazine picked up his story. In 1994, he was vindicated when the friend, whose real name was Peter Haack, was sentenced to six years in jail for attempted murder.*

The 65-year-old Welsch got his justice. But like many victims of the Stasi and the East German communist regime, he remains unsatisfied. Twenty years after the fall of the Berlin Wall, there are dozens of lobby groups and support networks for victims. Most trumpet the message that there has never been a true reckoning of the crimes and human rights abuses that occurred in the German Democratic Republic's (GDR).[1]

Many Europeans living in Communist countries refused to accept the oppressive policies of these governments during the days of the Iron Curtain. Some of these stories, forgotten by history in the years following the 1989 collapse of the Berlin Wall, came to light as a result of the 1999 and 2009 commemorations of the fall of the Wall. Among the many stories remembered were of those who lived east of the Iron Curtain and who defied Communist authorities in ways both small and large. These dissidents often faced death or long-term imprisonments or exile in defying the Communist regimes of Eastern Europe. Some also faced the tragedy of discovering they had been spied on—and turned over to authorities—by loved ones or friends. Some were lucky and received short sentences, although they lost their jobs in the process. Others were sent to prison for longer terms; some were sent to Siberia, and some were exiled with orders never to return to their homeland and families. Some emerged after the fall of the Iron Curtain to become national and international leaders. Some, in countries like Lithuania, Hungary, and Czechoslovakia, were tortured and murdered.

The stories of the many who tried to resist by escaping over, under, or through the Berlin Wall are recorded in Chapter 6. The stories in this chapter are a few of the many tales of courage that came out about some of those who dared to resist and stage demonstrations within the borders of their Communist countries. Some names, like Lech Walesa and Vaclav Havel, have become known the world over. But many others, like Wolfgang Welsch and Carl-Wolfgang Holzapfel, are stories of everyday people who risked their lives in pursuit of greater freedoms for themselves and their friends. We will begin with their stories. They are followed by several others, chronicling the tribulations faced by others who tried to resist oppressive Communist measures.

Many of the most dramatic stories of resistance occurred on the frontier of Communism in Europe in the country of East Germany, or the German Democratic Republic (GDR). It was here that the temptation to flee Communism was the greatest since only the Berlin Wall and the infamous "death strip" separated people from the freedoms of West Berlin. For that reason, much of this chapter's discussion will focus on East Germany and the key enforcement obstacle facing would-be resisters: the Stasi. Although Chapter 4 introduced this East German secret police force, this chapter and Chapter 6 show how they carried out their policies on actual or would-be defectors from Communist territory.

RESISTANCE WIDESPREAD

Wolfgang Welsch was one of hundreds of thousands of individuals who resisted the heavy-handed abuses of the Communist governments in Eastern Europe during the days of the Iron Curtain. An index of how widespread the consequences were of such resistance is found in this chapter-opening story by German reporter David Wroe, who wrote about Mr. Welsch.

The Forum for Education and Rehabilitation is one of several victim groups in Germany. This group reported that in the first decade after reunification in Germany, 79,108 investigations were still underway, probing abuses against East German citizens by the Stasi and the East German Communist government. The bad news is that only 993 prosecutions had resulted from those probes by 2009, yielding fewer than 100 convictions. Says Wroe:

> *Erich Mielke, the Minister for State Security and the notorious head of the Stasi, spent less than two years in jail. He was convicted of The murders of two policemen in 1931, but not for anything he did During the GDR era. And that is simply not enough for hundreds of Thousands of victims of "persecution, false imprisonment, perversion Of justice and countless other crimes," said the forum's chairman, Robert Dobrinski.[2]*

Nevertheless, it is obvious that all of those living under the rules of Communism did not do so willingly. In East Germany alone, resistance had been underway for decades, although after 1953 those who would stand up against GDR laws and policies knew they were also confronting the threat of Russian countermeasures as well as the Stasi. For it was on the morning of June 17, 1953, that thousands of East Germans marched from the outskirts of Berlin into the city center. From the town of Hennigsdorf alone, approximately 1,200 workers from a steel mill marched to Strausberger

Platz and through to West Berlin. When, at 11 A.M., the protestors took the red Russian flag off the Brandenburg Gate, the first gunshots were heard. Many more would follow.

What angered these resisters and triggered this "people's uprising" were widespread feelings that workers' needs and working conditions were being ignored by the SED. Following Joseph Stalin's death in Russia in June 1953, the SED announced there would be an increase in the work quota, which resulted in cutting workers' wages by half. Worker strikes across East Berlin began almost immediately after the announcement was made. Then approximately 3,000 protestors marched to the House of Ministries on Leipziger Strasse, demanding a reduction of the work quota and the resignation of the government.

At noon on June 17, with hundreds of thousands of workers and other East German citizens marching through the streets, Soviet tanks appeared at Potsdamer Platz and Unter den Linden, near the Brandenburg Gate where the Russian flag was torn down by protestors. Within the hour, the Soviet military commander declared a state of emergency and imposed a 9 P.M. curfew on the streets of East Berlin. Protestors realized they could not fight Soviet tanks and the Russian army, and the protest was quelled. For several more weeks, however, Soviet troops were present at all key street intersections, government buildings, and other key facilities. Some arrests were made, and the SED struck back with an exhaustive propaganda campaign trying to misrepresent the uprising as being inspired by fascist-imperialist agents of the West. The Communist Party leadership framed the suppression of the uprising as being in the best interest of East German workers. As added insurance, however, the SED agreed to reduce the work quota that had led to the demonstrations and to increase workers' wages.

Nevertheless, the SED and the Stasi refused to allow this kind of dissidence to go unpunished. More than 1,400 participants in the uprising were sentenced to jail terms.[3]

CARL-WOLFGANG HOLZAPFEL

Carl-Wolfgang Holzapfel, now in his 60's, spends at least a few moments every day remembering his time spent in an East German prison, convicted of crimes against the state.

Holzapfel became a symbol of resistance when he stretched out prostrate on the ground at the infamous Checkpoint Charlie, his body spanning both East and West Berlin as they met at that border crossing. He would return to the place of his incarceration, the notorious Hohenschonhausen Stasi Prison for seven days in the fall of 2009 to reenact his imprisonment for the world to see as the 20th anniversary of the fall of the Berlin Wall approached.

For Holzapfel, however, the memories of his confinement remain vivid, although more than two decades have passed since his release with the fall of European Communism.

But Holzapfel still explains that to this day he cannot stand being in a room with the door shut.[4]

And Holzapfel was not even an East German. He was a West German who was arrested on the other side of the Berlin Wall for political activism. He was thrown into prison and stayed there until the West German government negotiated a deal to buy back his freedom.

This was not an uncommon outcome for the time, nor is it today in other repressive regimes. For example, two American hikers, Shane Bauer and Joshua Fattal, were released from an Iranian prison after two years on the condition that Iran receive $1 million in payments for them. Those payments were made by an unknown source.

In East Germany alone during the Cold War era, more than 200,000 citizens were imprisoned for political reasons, which meant there was always dissent, usually in the form of expressing repeated desires to leave the country or actually attempting it. As noted elsewhere in this book, the Stasi freed some 30,000 of them in the early 1970s as a show that it was reducing its prison population of political prisoners in an effort to win the international community's recognition of East Germany as an official state. What the Stasi didn't reveal was that it had actually traded these prisoners to West Germany for some 3.5 billion Deutsche marks and then put that money into beefing up covert Stasi operations to oppress East Germans even more.

Holzapfel was one of an untold number of persons held as political prisoners in Communist prisons during the Cold War era when the Berlin Wall stood tall and impenetrable to most Europeans. He was one of five such men interviewed in 2009 by an Agence France-Presse (AFP) reporter. They all spent varying times behind bars, from 13 months to eight years. The common thread was they all had been arrested on various political charges, including "hostility to the regime," "spying," and "attempted flight from the East German republic."[5]

SECRET STASI FILES OPENED

As the end drew near for the Communist regime in East Germany—and therefore the ruling SED Party and the Stasi—agents of both set about trying to destroy as many Stasi files as possible in an effort to safeguard those responsible for carrying out these crimes against humanity over the years. It was a gargantuan task because of the massive amount of paperwork that filled many rooms. Paper shredders burned out in the process, and an army of Stasi agents took to tearing up pages by hand into small pieces. By the time the Wall came down and the SED regime came to an end, the Stasi had managed to destroy only a *third* of the incriminating paperwork. That still left a huge number of files untouched, and the East German people wanted those files preserved and opened for viewing by the public, or at least by those who had suffered imprisonment or loss of jobs and esteem under the weight of Stasi oppression.

So on January 15, 1990, approximately 1,000 East German demonstrators gathered at the main gate of Stasi Headquarters on Ruschestrasse. They built a symbolic wall to prevent Stasi employees from entering and removing documents. In the evening, the gate was opened and the demonstrators entered the Stasi compound. The goal was to keep the remaining files safe from destruction. A wax seal was made and put on the doors of buildings and rooms housing Stasi files. But the Stasi copied that seal and, under cover of darkness, some agents broke into the rooms, destroyed more documents, then put their own copied seal back on the door. That practice was discovered, and security was increased on the buildings.

The Federal Commission for the Stasi Records, made up of East German citizens, was established to protect the records and, in September 1990, civil rights activists occupied the Stasi archive building and demanded the legal right for people to be able to inspect their records. That was granted, and those files were opened for people who applied to see their files.

An example of how painstaking the effort was to preserve those files can be seen in what the Federal Commission for the Stasi Records has done with the bags of files that Stasi agents tore up by hand. Some 15,000 large bags of those scrapped papers were discovered in 1990, and commission workers started going through each bag, matching up the scraps of paper and piecing individual pages back together to form complete records. By 2007, documents from approximately 320 of those 15,000 bags had been restored, and work was continuing on the remaining bags.

That is how important the East Germans feel it is to bring Stasi abuses into the open. In fact, the former Building 1 of Stasi Headquarters in Berlin, where operations were directed by Erich Mielke and his staff, has been turned into the Stasi Museum, open to visitors from all over the world. This is a story that Germans want told.

JUSTICE UNDONE

Many of these former prisoners feel abandoned by the German government today, as their captors and those who ordered their imprisonment or who otherwise harassed them have often been able to evade justice. The Stasi destruction of many records, plus the German statute of limitations on crimes, plus the desire by some politicians to leave the divisive past behind have resulted in few prosecutions of former Stasi officials and the actual imprisonment of even fewer. In place of prosecutions, victims of Stasi abuse must take refuge in knowing that the records are open, stories of hardships and suffering have been made public, and victims can know who their betrayers and persecutors were.

SATISFACTION SHORT-LIVED FOR SOME

The idea behind opening Stasi files was to allow survivors and families to get more information on what had happened to them, why, and who was responsible for it. For some, though, this made the horrible memories only more vivid.

"The worst shock came from reading the file," says 74-year-old Edith Fiedler, who spent 20 months in prison because of a jealous sister-in-law informed falsely on her to the Stasi. "I only found that out when I read my file," she told an AFP reporter. Not only did the East Germans imprison her, but they took away her nine-year-old son and put him in a foster home.[6]

As this AFP interview with Fiedler was being conducted, her son Daniel Fielder—now a grown man—recalled how authorities had lied to him and said his mother had suffered an accident and was in a long-term coma.

"The Stasi took my life away," he said.[7]

He was not alone. Tatiana Sterenberg, 57 at the time of her 2009 interview with reporters, was arrested when she and her Italian boyfriend tried to flee to the West.

"In jail, I didn't get enough to drink, I didn't get enough to eat, I was given psychoactive drugs. They put me in a straightjacket," she recalled.[8] *She was held, as was her boyfriend, for three years in an East German prison before being "bought" by the West German government. But their mental and emotional imprisonment went on. Unable to overcome their depression, the couple, who married after their release, divorced in 1996. She entered a hospital with a diagnosis of clinical depression.*

Like others interviewed for this 2009 AFP story, she felt justice has never been served for the victims of Communist East Germany. "We are victims of the Stasi, but we have a credibility problem," Sterenberg said. So she and others have formed support groups where they can relate to others who experienced the same kind of abusive treatment.

Another person in the support group was 59-year-old Adam Lauks. He agrees that the support group is helping him cope, long after being freed from the physical prison walls. Lauks was once married to an East German who he fears may have betrayed him to the Stasi. The former dissident spent seven years in prison on trumped-up charges of smuggling. "I'm sure of it," he said. "But there's no proof. It's killing me."[9]

HOW THE STASI WORKED

Many feel the Stasi constituted a "state within a state" in East Germany, although opinions depending on whether you get the description of the Stasi's power structure from a former Stasi agent or a leader of the SED Party from which, officially, the Stasi took its marching orders. Former GDR Chancellor Erich Honecker tried to distance himself from the Stasi operations when the end came for his regime, while former Stasi Chief Erich Mielke said the Stasi was only following SED orders. The answer probably lies somewhere in between, according to those who were close to operations. In any event, the German Democratic Republic of East Germany followed the Russian model of its own secret police in creating the Stasi (officially known as the Ministry of State Security, or MfS) in 1950. The Russian model was the Bolshevik Commission for Combating Counterrevolution and Sabotage, or Cheka, established in 1917. It was renamed the State Political Directorate (GPU) in 1922 and by 1954 was called the KGB (Committee for State Security). The first leader of the Cheka (1917–1926) was Felix E. Dzerzhinsky. Both he and the Cheka became role models for early Stasi members who called themselves Chekists and utilized Chekist methods in their surveillance and oppression of East Germans—and in some cases targeted West Germans.

BARBEL BOHLEY

It is not uncommon to find artists and musicians at the forefront of the dissident movement among Communists in Eastern Europe during the days of the Iron Curtain. One such artist whose work led first to her arrest and then helped to lead to the collapse of the Berlin Wall was Barbel Bohley, who passed away in September 2010.

The reporter who wrote her obituary for the London newspaper the *Guardian* described her as someone who was "small and delicate-looking" but who "gave an impression of intense earnestness and latent toughness, qualities that stood her in good stead when she dared to challenge the most intrusive communist society in Eastern Europe."[10]

Born Barbel Brosius immediately following the Russian army's takeover of East Berlin when World War II ended, Bohley would often remember growing up in a city where seven out of 10 buildings were destroyed by Allied bombs and Soviet artillery shells, their bricks and mortar strewn throughout the streets. It was an image that older Germans recall vividly. She grew up with her father's narratives about the war in the snow and cold on the eastern front. So terrible were those stories that Bohley decided to become a pacifist, working for human rights causes later in life and helping young victims of warfare in the former Yugoslavia.

Bohley pursued her artistic talents and became a professional painter in the early 1970s, marrying Dietrich Bohley, a fellow East German artist. But even the world of creative artists—at least the East German world—found her work too threatening when Bohley established the group Women for Peace. Simply following her pacifistic leanings, her efforts were not appreciated by the East German government, and she was expelled from the GDR artists' association.[11]

That expulsion was followed by a 1983 arrest and six-week imprisonment. The charge was suspicion of treasonable supply of information, supposedly to British activists working to curb nuclear weapons proliferation and to members of the West German Green Party. As a result of that episode, Bohley was told she could not leave East Germany and was also forbidden to take commissions for her artwork or even exhibit that work. Her response: she kept painting and kept working for peace.

Five years later came a 1988 arrest by the Stasi after she offered to support a group of demonstrators who were petitioning for the right to exit East Germany. This time, the government gave her a six-month visa to visit the United Kingdom, with GDR officials hoping they'd seen the last of her. Her response: she went but did return in August of that year. A few months later, she signed her name to a petition for internal reform in the GDR and established the political action group New Forum in the wake of a rigged election in East Berlin in 1989. But this time, the glasnost policy of Russian leader Mikhail Gorbachev stood in the way of another GDR arrest of Bohley or her fellow protestors, now numbering more than 200,000. It was not long afterward that East German border guards decided not to stem the activities of East Berliners who, on November 8, 1989, took sledgehammers to the Berlin Wall.

The next September, Bohley led a peaceful occupation of the former Stasi headquarters to pressure the unification government to open the files of the dreaded security police. She died in 2010.

WERNER FISCHER

Another East German activist was Werner Fischer, but the story of his arrest is even more tragic than many others. The reason is he believes it was his own mother who informed on him to the Stasi. Fischer was one of a few human rights activists from East Germany who planned and led the weekly demonstrations that helped result in the breach and downfall of the Berlin Wall on November 9, 1989.

After many Stasi documents were released to the public following official reunification, Fischer discovered 67 files had been kept on him. Among their revelations: his own mother, Erna Fischer (operating under the Stasi alias as Ursula,) spied on Werner for four years and was even decorated for it. The Stasi felt she had done such a thorough job probing the activities of her son and others that they gave her the East German Service Cross, an honor reserved for informants whose information proved valuable.

"I decided to go public with this story because it reveals something important about the nature of East Germany," Fischer told the London newspaper the *Telegraph* in 2002. "I was an enemy of the state to my mother. As far as I am concerned, whatever relationship I had with her is now over. I do not intend to see her again."[12]

As for her thoughts, Mrs. Fischer wrote the following in one of her reports to the Stasi: "I have concluded that my son is basically a coward. He is easily led, he fantasizes and dreams."

Telegraph writer Tony Patterson notes: "In another report she denounces her son as a potential anti-Communist agitator: 'Werner Fischer thinks of the peace initiatives of the German Democratic Republic [East Germany] as wrong and hypocritical,' she states."[13]

Even more tragically, this was not an aberrant case. The formerly secret Stasi files showed that the secret police used approximately 180,000 "inofficial collaborators," or IMs, to help monitor the country's 16.4 million citizens. While some of them were paid for keeping tabs on their friends and even loved ones, other methods (noted earlier in this chapter) were used to recruit many other IMs. Stasi files indicate Mrs. Fischer did it simply out of loyalty to Communism.

Another known case of an East German dissident being turned in by a close relative was Vera Wollenberger who in 1990 disclosed that her husband, Knud, had likewise informed on her to the Stasi. Unlike Fischer, however, Mrs. Wollenberger said she had agreed—at last—to forgive her husband after he wrote a detailed letter explaining his reasons.[14] Mrs. Wollenberger will be profiled in the next section.

As for Fischer and Barbel Bohley, they were both arrested by the Stasi and received temporary expulsions from East Germany for acts deemed traitorous to GDR principles. Their crime was to help organize a 1988 march in East Berlin that protested the lack of free speech in the GDR and demanded that East German citizens be given the right to speak and write freely. It was only when the East German government saw that Communism was nearing an end in Eastern Europe and that the Wall would soon fall that Fischer and Bohley were allowed to return to East Berlin. Five years after reunification, in 1995, the two activists were awarded Germany's Federal Order of Merit for protesting the GDR's system of totalitarianism.

VERA WOLLENBERGER

"From the moment Vera Wollenberger left home at the age of 18, she was the prototype of an East German rebel." So wrote Stephen Kinzer in 1992 as he reported on the life and contributions of Wollenberger.[15]

Ironically, Wollenberger's own father was a Stasi officer, but she grew up with an independent mindset that favored the ideals of Communism over its oppressive realities. After rising to become a leader in the party, she was expelled for views that were considered too liberal by East German rulers. For one thing, she was adamantly opposed to the placement of Russian nuclear missiles on East German land and helped lead protests against them. Then she assisted in organizing a human rights organization called the Church from Below.

As a result of her dissidence, she was spied upon and harassed by the same Stasi that her father worked for, arrested, sent to prison, and released but then fired from her job at a government research institute. Through it all, Wollenberger adhered to her principles of pacifism and human rights—two things not on the GDR rulers radar—and became a leader in the dissident movement that ultimately brought down the Berlin Wall and Communism in Europe. After reunification, she was elected to the German parliament in Bonn at the age of 38.

While in parliament and feeling the need to right some wrongs of the Stasi, she was instrumental in helping create a unique law to provide victims of the Stasi with at least some degree of justice. Provisions of this act forced the opening of the secret Stasi files so that victims of Stasi harassment could read the files kept on them and also possibly discover the identities of those who informed on them. The revelations from those files proved to be anything but comforting for many former East Germans who discovered that people they thought were trusted friends and loved ones had actually betrayed them to the Stasi. Such was the case with Wollenberger who, as noted in an earlier section, discovered her own husband had informed on her to the feared and hated secret police of East Germany.

She told the *New York Times* in an interview, "What I have had to go through, I wouldn't wish on anyone. Not even my worst enemy."[16]

Among her discoveries: More than 60 different Stasi agents and informers, some whom she had trusted, had reported on her to the secret police. One was a man named simply Donald. From the information in the file and by process of elimination, Vera realized to her agony that "Donald" was actually her husband Knud, the father of her two children. After this revelation surfaced, the couple separated and then divorced.

Stephen Kinzer wrote of this in a 1992 story, "Vera Wollenberger has described the case of Donald as 'above all, my own personal tragedy.' But it is a tragedy being played out, with greater or lesser intensity, across eastern Germany. Almost every day, the Stasi files reveal new details, new cases, new conspiracies. Information from the files has already ruined several promising political careers, destroyed countless friendships and plunged many eastern Germans into crises of anger and depression. All of Germany is transfixed by the drama emerging from what the magazine *Der Spiegel* calls 'the horror files.' "[17]

Kinzer continued that the "sheer volume of paper" was astonishing to the groups that began poring through the Stasi files when there were opened. Those files filled 125 miles of shelf space, with each mile containing about 17 million sheets of paper and weighing nearly 50 tons.[18]

Kinzer's *New York Times Magazine* article shows how exhaustive, revealing, and often trivial the information was that found its way into Stasi files. For example, there was this report, filed by one of the many informants. The subject was a writer named Lutz Rathenow who was being spied upon for some unspecified reason:

Rathenow then crossed the street and ordered a sausage at the sausage stand. The following conversation took place:

Rathenow:	"A sausage please."
Sausage seller:	"With or without roll?"
Rathenow:	"With, please."
Sausage seller:	"And mustard?"
Rathenow:	"Yes, with mustard." Further exchange of words did not take place.

Another entry focused on another artisan, Wolf Bierman, who was a West German folk singer and poet who spent most of his life in East Germany until the GDR expelled him in 1976. Kinzer notes that the Stasi amassed some 40,000 pages on Bierman, much of which was taken up with trivia like the following: "Wolfgang Bierman had sexual relations with a woman. Afterwards he asked her if she was hungry. The woman said she would like a drink of Cognac. She is Eva Hagen.

Then it was quiet inside."[19]

Kinzer's conclusion, after discovering so many reports on so many East Germans, was, "That a Government agency would feel compelled to gather so much information about so many citizens reflects the frightening pathology of the men who led East Germany. They considered each citizen a potential subversive, and wanted to know as much as they could about anyone who expressed even the slightest political or social criticism. With a meticulous efficiency almost unknown outside Germany, they ordered every detail typed and filed. They accumulated far more information than they could possibly analyze or use. Ultimately, they drowned in their sea of minutiae, so consumed with detail that they failed to recognize the changes sweeping through their country."[20]

In the case of Stasi victims like Vera Wollenberger and Werner Fischer, the heaviest price they paid for protesting oppressive GDR measures was not in a long-term incarceration, but in living with the betrayal of loved ones who were either pressured into spying on them or did so willingly as they put their political beliefs ahead of family ties.

GENOCIDE IN THE BALTICS

In 1997 and again in 2001, the *Baltic Times* reported on the unearthing of hundreds of corpses and body parts found beneath a recreation field in Vilnius on the bank of the Neris River. The place is known locally as Tuskulenai Manor. But the name took on a new meaning after the Lithuanian Security Department discovered that this land contained the traces of Soviet genocide. The deceased had been killed after the Soviet Union occupied Lithuania at the end of World War II. Anti-Soviet partisans, priests, and politicians of independent Lithuania were placed in trenches there, most buried in banana boxes. The executor was the People's Commissariat for Internal Affairs (NKVD), the former name of the notorious KGB.[21]

According to the *Times*, in 1994, the Security Department discovered KGB files documenting the killing of 766 people by the Soviets in Vilnius' KGB headquarters. The victims were later buried secretly at this site, which came to serve as a football field. After the discovery of the KGB files, searchers uncovered hundreds of human skeletons.

"Tuskulenai is just a fragment of the mosaic of Soviet genocide against the Lithuanian people. We expect to find up to 1,000 skeletons in Tuskulenai," said director general of the Security Department, Jurgis Jurgelis, during a press conference at the Lithuanian Academy of Science on Jan. 23. During excavations in 1994–1997, archaeologists found the remains of 706 people.[22]

The government promised to build a memorial to the victims in Tuskulenai. On Jan. 29, the government created a commission for the commemoration of the Tuskulenai victims. One of the members of the commission is Dalia Kuodyte, director general of the Center of Genocide and Resistance and editor of the journal Genocide and Resistance.

As of 2001, however, the government had set aside no money for such a memorial, and the bodily remains were being kept in the Museum of Genocide Victims, which is under the patronage of the Genocide and Resistance Center.[23] A few years later, however, the Memorial Complex of the Tuskulėnai Peace Park was finally built and stands today as the permanent resting place for the bodies of the 724 victims of Soviet genocide found there up to 2010.[24]

"Lithuania suffered from Soviet and Nazi occupations as did other countries," Kuodyte said. "It lost one-third of its inhabitants due to killings, deportations and forced emigration. The Tuskulenai story is strongly tied with the Lithuanian partisans' war against the Soviets. Mostly partisans are buried there."[25]

Leading the partisan forces were Lithuanian soldiers, many of them officers. They all wore Lithuanian army uniforms, and they used aliases instead of their real names because there was always the danger of infiltration by Soviet spies. Although the major cities in Lithuania were controlled by the Soviets, the forested areas were the stronghold of the partisans. It is estimated that about 20,000 Lithuanian partisans died in combat with the Soviet army and NKVD (or KGB) units. Most of this fighting took place up to 1956, although some partisans continued the fight, and the last of them didn't come out of the forests until the 1980s.[26] The partisans were ever-hopeful that America and other Western allies would join their fight and drop troops and support to help them. In most cases, they waited in vain.

The Vice Minister of National Defense Edmundas Simanaitis, then a high-school student, took an active part in the anti-Soviet resistance. He belonged to the Tauras military district of the partisans' army in the southwestern town of Marijampole. He remembers blowing up railways and spreading underground literature. He also remembers spending years in Soviet concentration camps for it.

"The remains of many of my friends were found in Tuskulenai," Simanaitis told a reporter for the Baltic Times.[27]

According to archaeologist Vytautas Urbonavicius, the Forensic Medicine Center said the skeletons show marks that could be the result of torture.

Some peoples' hands and legs were cut off. Some skulls reveal that heads of living people were put into machines that slowly squeezed them. Some skulls were crushed. Others are scarred with knife and axe marks. Usually victims were shot from a short distance. Some skulls show the marks of up to six bullets.

Historian Arturas Dubonis told the Baltic Times *"Such tortures are rather gentle for the NKVD."[28]*

HUNGARIAN DISSIDENTS PAY THE PRICE

In ceremonies across the country on February 25, 2011, Hungarians remembered the victims of Communism. The estimated number of victims of Communism worldwide nears 100 million;

in Hungary, this number is 500,000. The numbers include victims that died in concentration camps, detention centers and during deportations. Many of these died while resisting oppressive measures of local Communist governments.

"Millions have survived but remained psychologically scarred, unable to put their lives back together," according to the organization Hungarian Ambiance.[29]

The Hungarians picked February 25 as the day to memorialize these victims because on that date in 1947, the Soviet-controlled government arrested Bela Kovacs, the first secretary of the Smallholders Party. Kovacs, born in Hungary in 1908, joined this party as a young adult. It drew most of its support from Hungarian peasants who made up more than half the country's population. However, the large landowners were able to force most peasants into voting for the government party, applying economic pressure and other threats. Leaders of the Smallholders Party were mostly members of the middle class. Their political views varied from liberal to socialist.

The Soviets invaded Hungary toward the end of World War II, in September 1944. Budapest came under their control in 1945, and they set up their own government. Although the Smallholders Party won 57 percent of the vote, the Soviet leadership refused to allow it to form a government. Instead, the leadership set up its own Soviet-controlled government, giving Kovacs a post as minister of agriculture from 1945 to 1946 because of the threat posed by so many members of the Smallholder Party in Hungary. As the Soviets became stronger and made more and more political arrests, that threat waned. At that point, in 1948, the government dissolved the Smallholders Party and its leaders, most notably Kovacs, who was arrested and charged with treason against the occupying Soviet forces. He was found guilty and sentenced to life imprisonment in Siberia.[30]

The ruling Hungarian Workers Party, controlled by Soviet influence, demanded total loyalty from its members. Laslo Rajk was one of those highly placed members, serving as Hungary's foreign secretary. But when he became critical of Joseph Stalin's efforts to impose his own policies and laws on Hungary, he was arrested and summarily executed. With the Soviet-controlled leadership now imposing authoritarian rule on the nation of Hungary, approximately 2,000 dissidents were executed and another 100,000 or more were sent to Siberian labor camps and other prisons.[31]

After the Hungarian Uprising began on October 23, 1956, Kovacs was released from prison in a partial attempt to defuse the situation and calm hard-core dissidents. The uprising was a peaceful attempt, mostly by students in Budapest, to demand that Soviet occupation of Hungary come to an end and that "true socialism" be put into practice by the government. In other words, they were demanding that the realities of Communism match its ideals. The government of the Hungarian Worker's Party fell and after a few days of sporadic fighting, Soviet military forces, which had entered Budapest on October 24, withdrew to garrisons outside the city. A de facto cease-fire lasted until the Soviet Union decided to crush the rebellion on October 31.

Active Soviet military intervention began on November 4 and continued until the final Hungarian resistance ceased on November 11. The Soviets refused to leave Hungary and continued to impose oppressive rules on the country for years to come. Kovacs would live until 1959 and wrote a book called *The Hungarian Revolution*. The Soviets, still fearing his influence with the country's many peasants, let him remain in parliament while he lived.[32]

Here is how *New York Reporter* writer Leslie Bain described meeting Kovacs after his release from prison in 1956:

Late in the evening of Sunday, November 4—a night of terror in Budapest that no one who lived through it will ever forget—I met Bela Kovacs, one of the leaders of Hungary's short-lived revolutionary government, in a cellar in the city's center.

Kovacs, as a Minister of State of the (Imre) Nagy regime, had started off for the Parliament Building early that morning, but he never reached it. Soviet tanks were there ahead of him. Now he squatted on the floor opposite me, a fugitive from Soviet search squads.

A hunched, stocky man, with a thin mustache and half-closed eyes, Bela Kovacs was only a shadow of the robust figure he once had been. Now in his early fifties, he had risen to prominence after the war as one of the top leaders of the Hungarian Independent Smallholders Party.

Back in 1947, when Matyas Rakosi began taking over the government with the support of the Soviet occupation forces, Kovacs had achieved fame by being the only outstanding anti-Communist Hungarian leader to defy Rakosi and continue open opposition. His prestige had become so great among the peasantry that at first the Communists had not molested him. But then the Soviets themselves stepped in, arresting him on a trumped-up charge of plotting against the occupation forces and sentencing him to life imprisonment.

After eight years in Siberia, Kovacs was returned to Hungary and transferred to a Hungarian jail, from which he was released in the spring of 1956, broken in body but not in spirit by his long ordeal. After what was called his "rehabilitation," Kovacs was visited by his old enemy Rakosi, who called to pay his respects. Rakosi was met at the door by this message from Kovacs: "I do not receive murderers in my home."

So long as Nagy's government was still under the thumb of the Communist Politburo, Kovacs refused to have anything to do with the new regime. Only in the surge of the late October uprising, when Nagy succeeded in freeing himself from his former associates and cast about to form a coalition government, did Kovacs consent to lend his name and immense popularity to it.[33]

RELIGIOUS DISSIDENTS

Helping to undermine the credibility of Communism in Eastern Europe were religious dissidents, and some of them fell victim to the same kind of punitive measures (imprisonment, expulsion, or even death) that faced political dissidents. Keep in mind that for many years, the only "religion" allowed in most Communist states was atheism. Defying the bans against organized religious could and did produce serious negative consequences for those found guilty. For more than half a century, Communist leaders tried— and failed—to eradicate religion from their countries, even though their means included intimidation to the point of terrorism, executions, and long-term imprisonment of dissenters. The heaviest of these measures came under the regime of Joseph Stalin, who labeled most religious followers enemies of the state. After Stalin fell from power, Communist rulers realized that political support depended on softening their policies toward followers of organized religion and gradually, the harassment of these people lessened. However, according to some leaders of the Russian Orthodox Church, some of these repressive measures continued under the heading of "psychopolitics."[34] This type of intimidation took the form of the government's simply declaring religious dissidents as insane and sending them to psychiatric facilities where "therapists" would bring them back to reality or else never release them from the institution. One such facility was Orel Hospital, dubbed a "special psychiatric hospital."

It should be noted, however, that much evidence, including the firsthand testimony of former Soviet psychiatric prisoners, shows this kind of treatment was also meted out to political dissenters as well as religious dissenters in the Russian-controlled Communist states.

A pastor delivering a simple church sermon could be accused of "anti-Soviet agitation and propaganda" in the 1950s and 1960s.[35] This, despite the fact that Article 52 of the Soviet constitution guaranteed "freedom of religion." Countering these arrests and prosecutions with their own study of the law, religious leaders fought back and often cited Article 52. Facing potentially losing battles in court, government officials might simply declare these religious zealots as insane and ship them off to places like Orel Hospital. The signature of a psychiatrist was all that was needed. There was no hearing, no appeal.

According to an article titled "The Cry of the New Martyrs: Psychiatric 'Treatment' of Christians," there is plenty of evidence for this kind of Soviet harassment of religious followers. Among their sources are the memoirs of Vladimir Bukovsky (published as *To Build a Castle*) who, like Alexander Solzhenitsyn, spent many years in a Soviet Gulag in Siberia. In Bukovsky's case, his imprisonment included time in prisons, labor camps, and psychiatric facilities. Several of these institutions sprang up across the Soviet Union under the regime of Nikita Khrushchev.[36]

Several sources cite the contributions of Bukovsky, a neurophysiologist, in revealing the warped psychiatric treatment of political and religious dissenters in the Soviet Union. Bukovsky smuggled more than 150 pages to the West in 1971. These documents provided evidence of the abuse of psychiatric institutions for political reasons in the Soviet Union. The documents proved a rallying point for human rights activists around the world and also resulted in Bukovsky's arrest in the Soviet Union for slandering the psychiatric profession, making contact with Western journalists, and possessing, reproducing, and distributing censored publications. The offense normally carried a sentence of one to seven years in prison plus five years in exile. In 1974, Bukovsky and another jailed offender, psychiatrist Semyon Gluzman, coauthored a *Manual on Psychiatry for Dissenters* to provide any future victims of "political psychiatry" a manual on how to act during an official hearing so that they might not be diagnosed as mentally ill.[37,38]

In 1976, after 12 years of imprisonment and time spent in psychiatric hospitals, Bukovsky was deported to the West and exchanged for an imprisoned Communist leader. He settled in Great Britain, where he wrote his memoirs.

Another victim sentenced to a psychiatric prison was a Russian Orthodox nun named Valerya Makeeva. She was first arrested by Soviet authorities in 1949 at the age of 20, apparently on the instigation of her own mother, who was not a religious believer.[39] Makeeva was assigned to the Serbsky Institute for psychiatric examination and was judged to be mentally ill. The official diagnosis was schizophrenia, and she was then transferred to the Kazan special hospital for four years. Not swayed from her religious beliefs, she was finally released and went straight into a Russian Orthodox convent for 10 years. When the Khrushchev regime closed that convent, Makeeva moved to Moscow and founded a movement to support other homeless nuns by making prayer books and embroidering belts with words from Psalm 90. That Psalm reads in part:

> Lord, you have been our dwelling place
> throughout all generations.
> Before the mountains were born
> or you brought forth the whole world,
> from everlasting to everlasting you are God.

But the oppressive measures of the Soviet government were still in force, the group had to disband, and Makeeva was sent back to an institution, this time Psychiatric Hospital Number 5, for seven months. She was released but was then rearrested in 1975 and again in 1978, both times being sent to psychiatric hospitals. Her latter sentencing was on the basis of Article 162 of the Soviet Criminal Code: "Being engaged in a prohibited trade." Doctors at the Serbsky Institute pronounced Makeeva insane, and she was sent back to the Special Psychiatric Hospital in Kazan in 1979. There she received such high doses of medication that her right arm became paralyzed and her overall health deteriorated.[40]

Richard Wurmbrand was a Lutheran pastor from Romania who lived 14 years of his adult life in different Romanian prisons for preaching against the oppression and unfairness of Communism in his country. Wurmbrand and his wife Sabina distributed Gospel tracts to Soviet soldiers and put up posters, usually under the cover of darkness, urging people to turn to God and have faith during their trying times under Communism. The posters became the object of scrutiny by Communist forces, who would go around and tear them down during the day. The following night, Wurmbrand and his wife would put them up again. The couple, along with other family members, would also urge others to protest "show trials" of unjustly accused believers who articulating their own religious beliefs. It has been said that the Wurmbrand family was one of the strongest voices of opposition to the oppressive measures of Communism in the 1950s.[41]

Lazlo Tokes was a Hungarian Reformed Church leader who defied Communist authorities at great personal risk. The stands he took and his personal protests gave rise to the 1989 revolution in the Romanian city of Timisoara. It was under the regime of Nicolae Ceausescu that Tokes protested the displacement of people caused by the government's systematic destruction of villages just so that more room could be made for block apartments (high-density living units) in the city.[42] He also continued to sponsor organized activities for youths in the city, despite orders from even his own bishop to cease that activity. When Tokes refused to leave his own church that was targeted for destruction in 1989, his congregation and other students and neighbors stood by him, and stopped authorities from evicting him. He became known as a defender of Christians who were being unfairly targeted by the Hungarian and Romanian governments. However, violence broke out at a protest, held in support of Tokes, and Romanian police fired into the crowds of gathered students. At this point, the crowds ceased protesting just for Tokes and began a larger protest against the Romanian government's oppression of all dissidents. So what began as a demonstration in support of a church turned into a revolution against the Ceausescu regime that was often seen as the most Stalinist regime in the entire Communist bloc of countries.[43]

LECH WALESA

One of the names of dissidents under European Communism has become legendary not just in his native Poland, but around the world. That name is Lech Walesa, the Gdansk shipyard worker who rose to become president of Poland during the tumultuous times of the Iron Curtain and afterward. The story of Walesa's struggle and triumph is a model that others have followed in the quest for freedom from oppression around the world.

Walesa, born in 1943 in Popowo, Poland, began his adult years as a car mechanic and became an electrician who worked in the shipyards. From his humble beginnings, great things were to result from his courage and dedication to helping his fellow Poles. *Time* magazine described his contributions as follows: "Walesa . . . shaped the

Lech Walesa, leader of the former Solidarity Union, reacts to cheers by his fellow workers as he leaves the Lenin Shipyards in Gdansk, Poland, on June 17, 1983. (AP Photo/Langevin)

20th century as the leader of the Solidarity movement that led the Poles out of communism. It is one of history's great ironies that the nearest thing we have ever seen to a genuine workers' revolution was directed against a so-called workers' state. Poland was again the icebreaker for the rest of Central Europe in the 'velvet revolutions' of 1989. Walesa's contribution to the end of communism in Europe, and hence the end of the cold war, stands beside those of his fellow Pole, Pope John Paul II, and the Soviet leader Mikhail Gorbachev."[44]

Walesa and other worker activists in Gdansk began to organize free non-Communist trade unions in 1978 and participated in several worker demonstrations seeking greater freedoms along the seacoast. Walesa was always a target of surveillance by Polish state security forces, and he was often arrested and detained. In August 1980, he led the Gdansk shipyard strike, which opened the door to many other strikes across Poland. At the center of the demands were workers' rights. Because Walesa had organized hundreds of thousands of workers (a movement that became known as Solidarity), he became a powerful force for Polish authorities to reckon with, and they gave into the key demands of the workers in the Gdansk Agreement of August 31, 1980, allowing workers the right to strike and to establish their own independent workers union. Walesa's popularity and notoriety grew, and his causes became supported by the Catholic Church. This support was so great that in January 1981, Pope John Paul II received Walesa at the Vatican. Walesa had always said the source of his inspiration and strength arose from his Catholic faith. Later in that year, Walesa was elected Solidarity chairman at the First National Solidarity Congress in Gdansk.[45] The future looked bright for the workers of Poland.

That bubble of optimism burst, however, when General Wojciech Jaruzelski, head of Poland's Military Council, declared martial law in Poland and suspended the Solidarity movement. The general feared armed Soviet intervention if "order" weren't restored and labor brought back under Communist rule. So in December 1981, several Solidarity leaders, including Walesa, were arrested. He was interned in a remote country house under guard. In November of the following year, he was released and given his job back at the Gdansk shipyards, where he was kept under constant monitoring by security forces. Despite this surveillance, he was still able to have regular contact with underground Solidarity leaders.[46]

Martial law was lifted in 1983, but many of the former civil restrictions on workers were reimposed. In the face of this, the rest of the world was bestowing its highest honors on Welesa, and he was awarded the Nobel Peace Prize. It was an honor that the state-run Polish media criticized, but that did nothing to dampen Walesa's popularity and respect.

Once again, the Polish government was forced to negotiate with Walesa and his Solidarity Party, and the outcome included allowing parliamentary elections, which would lead to the creation of a non-Communist government in Poland. This was against the backdrop of Mikhail Gorbachev's policy of openness (glasnost) and his refusal to continue using military troops to keep the Soviet states in line. In 1990, Walesa was elected chairman of Solidarity, and later that year he was elected president of the Republic of Poland, a position he kept until he was defeated at the polls in 1995. Walesa has continued to lecture at universities and elsewhere, and serves on the international advisory council of the Victims of Communism Memorial Foundation. In 2009, he was spotlighted in Berlin's twentieth-anniversary celebration of the fall of the Berlin Wall.

VACLAV HAVEL

Born in the city of Prague in 1936, Vaclav Havel grew up in a way that Poland's Lech Walesa didn't. Although each man rose to become president of his country, Walesa grew up in a poor working-class family, while Havel was the son of wealthy and intellectual parents who were in the midst of cultural and political events of Czechoslovakia from the 1920s to the 1940s. His father owned Barrandov movie studio, and his mother was the daughter of a journalist and ambassador. The young Havel was prevented by the ruling Communist Party from entering any humanities-oriented university because he came from a capitalist-oriented family of successful entrepreneurs. He was allowed to enter technical school, however, but he wanted more of an artistic career, so he dropped out after a couple years. He worked on the edges of the theater, as a stagehand and in other jobs, then found his way into acting and writing plays. Two of his best-known plays are *The Memorandum* and *The Increased Difficulty of Concentration*. He became known in the United States when *The Memorandum* premiered in New York.

Because his plays presented viewpoints and issues that ran counter to Communist ideals in his own country, Czech officials banned his plays there after 1968. Havel was not permitted to leave Czechoslovakia, so he didn't get the chance to attend performances of his plays in other countries. It was also in 1968 that the Czech government banned Havel from theatres entirely. This only served to deepen his anti-Communist activism, and it also put him in the crosshairs of ruling Communist leaders in Prague. He continued to write plays and see them distributed internationally, however, and the Communist regime increasingly saw Havel as a leading revolutionary. Relations between Havel and his government became most acute after he wrote the *Charter 77* manifesto, which he did in support of band members from a group called The Plastic People

The last Czechoslovak Communist prime minister Ladislav Adamec (right) attends a demonstration during the Velvet Revolution with former dissident and later the first post-Communist president Vaclav Havel (left) in Prague on November 26, 1989. (AP Photo/CTK, Zuzana Humpalova, file)

of the University, who were arrested and sent to prison.[47] He continued to agitate Communist officials when he cofounded the Committee for the Defense of the Unjustly Persecuted in 1979.

As a result of these activities, Havel himself was arrested numerous times and jailed just as many, once for four years. Even when he was not in prison, he was under constant surveillance—a common practice in all Communist countries for those suspected to be dissidents.

When he was not writing plays, Havel was writing essays and books, including *The Power of the Powerless*. Havel's dissent was in the mode of a Martin Luther King or Mahatma Gandhi, both of whom used nonviolence as an effective means of protest that gained worldwide attention. As the dissent against Communism grew louder in Europe, Havel became a leader in the "Velvet Revolution," which brought about a bloodless end to Communism in Czechoslovakia in 1989.[48]

Havel often said that "Truth and love must prevail over lies and hate," and it was that motto—along with his immense popularity over the years—that led him to be elected president of the new Czech Republic by a unanimous vote of the Federal Assembly in 1989.[49]

NOTES

1. David Wroe, "East German Victims Lament Lack of Justice," *Local*, November 5, 2009. Retrieved from http://www.thelocal.de/national/20091105-23067.html on July 29, 2011.

2. Ibid.

3. "Stasimuseum Berlin: Information and Explanations" (English version), distributed at the Stasimuseum, Ruschestrasse 103, Haus 22, Berlin, Germany.

4. "Stasi victims still searching for peace after 20 years," *The Local*, October 5, 2009. Retrieved from http://www.thelocal.de/national/20091005-22353.html on September 23, 2011.

5. Ibid.

6. Ibid.

7. Ibid.

8. Ibid.

9. Ibid.

10. "Barbel Bohley Obituary," *Guardian*, September 19, 2010. Retrieved from http://www.guardian.co.uk/world/2010/ on September 28, 2011.

11. Ibid.

12. Tony Paterson, "My Mother Spied on me for the Stasi Secret Police," *Telegraph*, Retrieved from http://www.telegraph.co.uk/news/worldnews/europe/germany/1390090/My-mother-spied-on-me-for-the-Stasi-secret-police.html on September 29, 2011.

13. Ibid.

14. Ibid.

15. Stephen Kinzer, "East Germans Face Their Accusers," *New York Times Magazine*, April 12, 1992. Retrieved from http://www.nytimes.com/1992/04/12/magazine/east-germans-face-their-accusers.html?pagewanted=all&src=pm

16. Ibid.

17. Ibid.

18. Ibid.

19. Ibid.

20. Ibid.

21. Rokas M. Tracevskis, "Terror Unearthed in the Heart of Vilnius," *Baltic Times*, 1997. Retrieved from http://vip.latnet.lv/LPRA/TerrorVilnius.htm on September 28, 2011.

22. Ibid.

23. Rokas M. Tracevskis, "Victims of NKVD Get No Peace," *Baltic Times*, May 17, 2001 as retrieved from http://www.baltictimes.com/news/articles/4957/ on Sept. 30, 2011.

24. Ibid.

25. Museums of Lithuania. Retrieved from http://www.muziejai.lt/vilnius/tuskulenai.en.htm on September 28, 2011.

26. Tracevskis, May 17, 2001.

27. Ibid.

28. Ibid.

29. Ibid.

30. Bela Kovacs: *"The Hungarian Revolution."* Retrieved from http://www.spartacus.schoolnet.co.uk/COLDkovacs.htm on October 8, 2011.

31. Ibid.

32. Ibid.

33. Ibid.

34. "Orthodox America: The Cry of the New Martyrs: Psychiatric 'Treatment' of Christians." Retrieved from http://www.roca.org/OA/5/5e.htm on October 1, 2011.

35. Ibid.

36. Ibid.

37. Vladimir Bukovskiĭ and Semyon Gluzman, *A Manual on Psychiatry for Dissidents.* Hoboken, NJ: Keuffel and Esser, 1976.

38. Hanfried Helmchen and Norman Sartorius. *Ethics in Psychiatry: European Contributions.* Munich, Germany: Springer. 2010, 495.

39. "Orthodox America."

40. Ibid.

41. "Religious Dissidents under Communism in Eastern Europe." Retrieved from http://iemima-ploscariu.suite101.com/religious-dissidents-under-Communism-in-eastern-europe-a359502#ixzz1ZwVyXNLQ on October 9, 2011.

42. Ibid.

43. Ibid.

44. Timothy Garton Ash, "Lech Walesa," *Time,* April 13, 1998. Retrieved from http://www.time.com/time/magazine/article/0,9171,988170,00.html on October 3, 2011.

45. Ibid.

46. "A Force More Powerful: We've Caught God by the Arm." Retrieved from http://www.aforcemorepowerful.org/films/afmp/stories/poland.php on October 2, 2011.

47. "Vaclav Havel: Biography: The Official Website of Vaclav Havel." Retrieved from http://vaclavhavel.cz/index.php?sec=1&id=1 on October 4, 2011.

48. David Remnick, "Exit Havel," New Yorker, February 10, 2003. Retrieved from http://www.kirjasto.sci.fi/vhavel.htm on October 2, 2011; Petri Liukkonen (author) and Ari Pesonen. Kuusankosken kaupung inkirjasto 2008. December 4, 2008.

49. Ibid.

6

"WE'RE GETTING OUT OF HERE!": ESCAPE ATTEMPTS FROM THE EAST

I want to tell you something, Comrades. When you shoot, you have to shoot so that the guy you hit doesn't get away, but stays here with us. Yes, it's something to fire 70 shots and the guy still gets over there and makes a big fuss.

—*Stasi head Erich Mielke*[1]

This border scenario, played out many times during the Iron Curtain era, was the reality facing anyone in East Berlin who wanted to escape to West Berlin between the years of 1961 and 1989. The Berlin Wall stood in between, and it was well guarded in many ways. If any doubt exists that conditions in East Germany were all that bad, all those doubters need do is to take time to listen to stories like the following:

The night was pitch black, but that was just the way this young artist wanted it. For he had chosen this night to get out of East Berlin. Enough was enough. He craved freedom to live; freedom to create. He had thought about this for some time: how to get past this "monster" separating him from West Berlin. He had heard stories of tunnels, but he didn't have enough people he trusted to try to dig his way to freedom. Wasn't there a simpler way?

His answer lay just overhead as he looked up. Suppose he were able to cross over the Wall on the power lines after dark? It was winter, and it was cold—would be even colder at night—but it might work. So he picked out his spot and then saw where the lines went, how far he might have to travel on the wire, and how he would get down on the West side. He tried it out on a homemade cable to see if he was up to the task of dangling from a wire for that long. He knew he would need protective gloves and boots and that, even then, he might be electrocuted. But, to him, it was worth it.

So on this night, he put on his gloves and boots, climbed the electrical tower to the 11,000-volt transmission line above, uttered a silent prayer, reached out, and touched it. So far, so good, but the journey had just begun. He swung his body out onto the high-voltage line and began going hand over hand in the frigid night air. After a short time, he could see the "death strip" below and the Wall approaching; seconds seemed like minutes; minutes seemed like hours. But the Wall passed beneath him, and he knew he was dangling over freedom in West Berlin.

He still had problems, however. His arms were about to give out, and his grip was weak. The western electrical tower was too far for him to make, so he knew he would have to drop to earth. He judged it to be 40 feet, which was too far in normal conditions. But the wintry night had produced big snowdrifts below, so he gave it a chance. He loosened his grip on the power line and fell to earth. It seemed farther than he had thought, but he did land in the drift he was aiming for. Pain jolted through his body when he hit, however, and he soon realized he had broken both his arms in the fall.

It was a small price to pay, though. He was free at last.

The name of this escapee was not used in the brief description of his attempt at the Checkpoint Charlie Museum, possibly because the museum went up long before the Wall came down, at a time the Stasi was very interested in the names of escapees who may have left family members—and an escape helper—behind. The lack of names is not uncommon in several of the escape descriptions found in the museum, though most *are* named.

At the Allied and West German Checkpoint Charlie, and the East German guard station a hundred meters to the east, life-and-death drama was played out every day during the Cold War. The stakes were as high as anywhere along the East–West border. West and East Berliners would have their papers examined before being granted passage from the free world to the Communist world, or vice versa. Today, Berliners walk through that intersection at Friedrichstrasse and Zimmerstrasse at will, and the only reminder of the past is a replica of the wooden border-crossing shack with spotlights and protective sandbags still in place. There are no American or Soviet tanks facing off as they did in 1961, and instead of convincing the guards inside that they are okay to cross, tourists

People gather to take part in a ceremony in front of the original first passport control house of the former U.S. Army Checkpoint Charlie in Berlin on Monday, August 13, 2001. (AP Photo/Jan Bauer)

line up on the intersection, smiling for friends who take pictures like they were visiting Disneyland.

A secondary reminder consists of two large photos of soldiers— one American and one East German—hanging from tall lamp posts. You see one or the other, depending on whether you are traveling east or west across the Checkpoint Charlie intersection. There is also a large sign, in four languages, still there that lets travelers know they are either entering or leaving the "American Sector." Again, a photo opportunity for tourists.

But in another era—one that ended in November 1989—it was a much different story. The border stations at this intersection were very real, very functional, and very intimidating for anyone without the right paperwork or with the thought of somehow escaping across the border to the West. Shoot-to-kill orders were in place, and the infamous death strip that separated East and West Berlin claimed many lives during the 1960s, 1970s, and 1980s.

This chapter will chronicle some of those escape attempts, some successful and some not. Much of the data comes from the Checkpoint Charlie Museum that stands at the former border crossing of the same name. This museum, situated on the west side of Zimmerstrasse, which divided East and West Berlin, was established by Rainer Hildebrandt, who wanted to build a memorial to those Germans suffering from the injustice of the German Democratic Republic (GDR). The museum was begun in a two-room apartment shortly after the Wall went up. It now occupies two entire floors of a large retail building in Berlin.

Hildebrandt knew something about German oppression. During World War II, he was imprisoned by the Nazis for 17 months. In founding the Checkpoint Charlie Museum, he wrote, "I have learned to fight against injustice. My real joy about Hitler's end was soon followed by great worry about the fate of occupied and divided Germany. This is why I founded the Taskforce Against Inhumanity in 1948 and this museum after construction of the Wall."[2]

Some stories of escapees are relatively obscure, while others have been told so many times that the names of the escapees have become well known in households of Berliners who remember the days of the Wall.

THE BARRIER-BREAKERS

Some 4,000 visitors a day pass through this Checkpoint Charlie Museum, according to museum officials, and the first exhibit they see is a Volkswagen 1200 sedan that we all know simply as "the bug." In this and two other bugs just like it, an "escape helper" named Kurt Wordel from West Berlin successfully smuggled 55 East Germans out of East Berlin to freedom in the West from 1964 to 1966. Wordel simply cut through the perimeter of the front "boot" (trunk), put hinges on it, took out the spare tire beneath, and in would climb an escapee willing to twist himself or herself into a pretzel. The fact that so many made it out this way is attributed to the quality of the hiding place that Wordel built, the absolute secrecy of his escape helpers, and his own examination of those asking him to get them out of East Berlin. After all, the Stasi had "IMs" or inofficial collaborators, as they called them, everywhere.

But this WV 1200 was only one means Wordel used to spirit refugees out of East Germany. He also created fake passports, allegedly from Monaco and Andorra (he even created diplomatic passports), and documents for another 400 East Germans who found freedom using them. Good as his system was, it was not foolproof. Only eight out of every 10 of his clients made it to freedom.

A total of 40,101 "barrier-breakers" (East Germans without exit visas who fled to the West) risked their lives as they successfully escaped to freedom. Sadly, well over 200 lost their lives trying to get over, under, or through the Berlin Wall. More than 700 others lost their lives at other border crossings in Germany. The actual numbers vary from source to source, but at least this number perished from 1961 to 1989. The means of escape were as many and varied as the East German citizens trying to make a run for it. They included tunnels, automobiles, busses, trucks, trains, boats, homemade submarines, homemade airplanes, balloons, ladders, ropes, pulleys, cables, high-power electrical lines, electronic speaker boxes, and many others. Sometimes refugees just walked or drove across, stopping at the guard stations to show their fake passports. Sometimes that worked, sometimes it didn't. Sometimes there were ingenious and elaborate schemes worked out to fool the border guards. Sometimes they worked, and sometimes they didn't. Usually there were escape helpers, who facilitated escapes either for money, out of friendship, or because of their idealism. Often West Germans would help friends or relatives in the East. Sometimes they would help total strangers.

WHO WERE THE ESCAPEES?

Most of the refugees fleeing to West Berlin were everyday citizens (although some were high-profile figures) who were angry over being cut off from relatives, loved ones, and friends in West Berlin. Others felt that risking death was better than living under the constant surveillance of the Stasi. Others just wanted more freedom of movement. Many were university students and young idealists. In fact, probably more refugees came from this group than any other. But there were also middle-age family members, often a father or mother trying to spirit his or her spouse and children out to the other side—sometimes to meet loved ones with whom they had been denied contact for so long. But there were also elderly East Germans among the escapees. One story, detailed later in this chapter, tells of a group of eight of them who tunneled their way to freedom.

WHEN DID THEY ESCAPE?

Surprisingly, perhaps, many escape attempts were made in broad daylight. If a mother was going to try and get her child out in a shopping cart, she had to cross during daytime shopping hours. If an escapee needed the light of day to navigate his way out, that meant a more daring crossing. But most escapes seem to have occurred at night, under the cover of darkness. That was especially so for those who tried to flee East Berlin in the most dangerous way: overland through the infamous death strip that contained automatically triggered machine guns, guard towers, land mines, and attack dogs.

Altogether, according to figures posted at the Checkpoint Charlie Museum, 959,914 people living in the GDR left East Germany to go to West Germany from 1961 to 1989. The vast majority of those left with valid exit visas, while 31,775 were ransomed political prisoners for whom West Germany paid an average of $100,000 to $120,000 each. The rest were those 40,101 barrier-breakers

Arial view of Berlin border wall, 1978. (AP Photo)

somewhere along the European path of the Iron Curtain. It is significant that more than half of those escapees (about 23,000) made their attempts from 1961 to 1965, that is, during the first four years after the Wall was built. That was when the shock of being cut off from loved ones in West Germany was the strongest, and it also took years for the Stasi and their border guards to catch on to the various schemes East Germans were using to get across the border and to add more effective counter-measures to keep East Germans home.

That turned out to be an ongoing effort as the escape attempts kept mounting. One new and deadly device, for example, was installed on each watchtower along the long Wall, which actually encircled West Berlin. Each tower was equipped in 1971 with automatic guns at three different heights that were triggered unwittingly by the escapees themselves as they crossed the death strip separating the inner East German border and the main wall to the west that we know as the actual Berlin Wall. These guns were often heard at night, mowing down anyone in their path. Many would-be escapees were injured, and at least eight known attempted escapees were killed by them.

The years of 1973 and 1974 seemed to be the point when the number of escape attempts diminished radically from the years before, and from 1980 to 1989, only a total of 2,700 escape attempts was recorded, or an average of 300 each year. This is still a large number, but less than a tenth the number of attempts made during each of the first several years of the Wall's existence. Certainly word began getting back to East German citizens about the fatalities among refugees and the number of failed attempts caused by increased defenses along the East–West border. So one would have to be very upset to risk his or her life and the lives of loved ones in making a break. But there were other factors contributing to the decreased numbers of attempts. There was the new avowed policy of "rapprochement," starting in 1971, by East Germany when the GDR allegedly curbed its human rights violations (although that attempt was only superficial). That era also ushered in at least some easing of travel restrictions to the West, especially for older East Germans who had grandchildren in the West. More East Germans were allowed to go across to West Berlin on a day pass for shopping, although they usually had to leave family members behind in the East to ensure their return. Then in the 1980s, Mikhail Gorbachev came to power in the Soviet Union and began his policy of *glasnost* that resulted in greater openness and freedoms in the

Soviet Union. East Germans figured it would just be a matter of time before Erich Honecker's government in the GDR would have to follow suit. Many felt that the days of the Berlin Wall might be numbered, after all, and maybe they should just wait it out a little longer.

But the 1960s and first part of the 1970s were years that were especially rife with daring attempts to escape to West Berlin. Some of the most daring ones are the following.

NOT A TYPICAL MODEL PLANE

One Prague University student from Czechoslovakia decided he would put his engineering talents to use to get him out of the oppression he felt in the East. So, piecing together a variety of parts, most of which weren't designed to be made into an airplane, the student built the first homemade escape airplane that would take him high over the Wall. There would be other such attempts. The key elements of this aircraft were the motor, wheels, and gas tank from a Trabant automobile. The rest of the parts he made himself or scavenged from surplus yards. The contraption wound up flying him 100 kilometers, over the Wall to freedom in the West.

*****

Inspiration for other would-be escapees could be found in a note found attached to an old brown Opel P4 that five East Germans used on November 14, 1961, as their escape car through the Chauseestrasse Gate of the Berlin Wall. The sides of the car were fortified with armor plating and poured concrete. Nevertheless, four bullets pierced the windshield, glove box, and one tire, but all five escapees made it to the West unhurt and with a story to tell their grandchildren. The note on the car reads, "The testimony of artists and poets has enabled us to understand the hopes in the past and so to recognize the potentials of the future."

BY BOAT, TRAIN, OR CABLE

Since the Stasi, which was in charge of securing the East–West border, had worked so hard to keep East Germans home, those people wanting to escape often had to find ingenious ways of doing so. The following are three such examples.

While most young East Berliners were just starting to enjoy the warm summer months on June 8, 1962, thirteen of them were planning something else. Something more daring. It was early on that morning that these young dissidents hijacked the most popular of the East German excursion boats and steamed their way to freedom. The boat they stole

The escape car used by artists fleeing from East Berlin. It is one of many exhibits at the Checkpoint Charlie Museum of escape mechanisms in Berlin. (Photo by Jim Willis)

was the Friedrich Wolf, *the largest and most modern passenger boat in East Berlin's White Fleet.*

Some of these fugitives had been drinking with the captain and mechanic the night before, trying to get them drunk. The plan worked and, as the two of them lay unconscious, the students locked them in their cabins and took the ship for the Eastern Harbor. When it reached the Landwehr Canal, just a few hundred yards from the Oberbaum Bridge, the hijacked boat suddenly turned left and headed full throttle toward the upper water gate, located in West Berlin territory.

The change of course did not go unnoticed by East German border guards, however, and they opened fire on the boat. Guards on the Oberbaum Bridge also opened fire. Under a hail of gunfire, the Friedrich Wolf *reached the West Berlin riverbank. A West Berlin police officer who had been alerted to the planned escape in advance by a friend of one of the escapees, protected the East Berliners from Stasi gunfire as they exited the boat on free soil. The captain and engineer, however, chose to remain on the boat and return it to East Berlin waters.*

As a result of the successful escape, border guards began implementing new security measures. All passenger ships were guarded at night, and their steering wheels were removed at the end of each business day. The captain of the Friedrich Wolf *was demoted to a freight shipping position.*

*****

In 1964, eight university students, alone or in pairs, leaped from a hiding place near the Friedrichstrasse border crossing onto the heavily guarded Moscow–Paris Express and into freedom, all within a few days of each other. A ninth student didn't make it, tripping while jumping onto the train, falling short of the mark, and injuring himself. He was left behind, arrested by the Stasi, interrogated, told of the other eight who had managed to escape, and sentenced to eight months in prison for "attempted escape from the Republic."

*****

A year later, a family managed to flee from East to West Berlin using a suspended cable. The south wing of the House of Ministries near Niederkirchnerstrasse in Berlin-Mitte stood directly at the Berlin Wall. The engineer and economist Heinz Holzapfel, from Leipiz, locked himself, his wife, and his daughter in a restroom of the government building after hanging an "out of order" sign on the restroom door. As the business day ended and the building emptied, Holzapfel waited for dark and then threw a hammer attached to a rope over to the far side of the Wall, where some relatives from West Berlin attached a cable to the end of the rope. Holzapfel then pulled the heavy cable back up and over the Wall to his building. Rigging a carrying strap and pulley, his family escaped up and over the Wall to Berlin-Kreuzberg and to freedom.

The curious thing about this attempt, other than the way it was done, is it was witnessed by Soviet soldiers stationed on the roof of the heavily guarded government building in which the family was hiding. They saw the whole escape but didn't sound an alarm because they thought they were watching Stasi agents being smuggled over the Wall as spies sent to the West.

LOVE CONQUERS WALL

Some couples and families were just too much in love to let a thing like the Wall or the Stasi keep them apart for long. There were many cases of loved ones who had been separated by the building of the Wall when one of them was out of East Berlin. They faced the prospect of never seeing each other again, or maybe just on a limited basis if the GDR would give them temporary travel visas. For them, the chance to be together was worth the risk of getting caught and going to prison. Some of them came up with creative plots to fool the East German border guards into reuniting them. Two of those cases follow.

They were sisters, and people often said they looked alike. One was blonde and one was brunette, but that was easily fixed. The problem is the brunette and her family didn't make it out of East Berlin before the Wall went up, so she couldn't make it to West Berlin to be with her sister, who wound up on that side of the Wall. Leave it to sisters to come up with a scheme, though. Realizing not only that they looked like, but their husbands resembled each other too, they hatched a plan and carried it out. They applied to Czech authorities to have the two couples meet in the Czech Socialist Republic (CSSR,) each driving their own car. But they switched cars and passports in Czechoslovakia. Then, after giving her sister and brother-in-law time to get across the border to the West, the East German sister and her husband reported to the Czech police that their car and their papers had been "stolen." When the car was found abandoned in Austria with no sign of the "thieves" in sight, the Czech authorities went so far as to apologize to the West German couple, believing the thieves to have been Czechs. The couple retrieved their car and passports, and drove back to freedom. The result: both families wound up reunited in West Berlin.

*****

Peter Selle longed to see his wife again. She was trapped in East Berlin, and the Wall had separated them for too long. It was 1966, and Peter had a plan. It may not have been very ethical—maybe even illegal even as far as

West Berlin was concerned—but he was determined to bring his wife to freedom. To get her out of the GDR, he found a woman in West Berlin who looked like his wife, made friends with her, and talked her into going on a day trip to see East Berlin.

Although the rest of this sounds hard to believe, it happened. While Selle and his "girlfriend" were in Berlin, he stole her papers, went and found his wife, and took her out of East Berlin using the other woman's travel documents, leaving her behind to fend for herself. She was arrested by the Stasi and put in jail for two months before the press picked up on the story and she was released. Back on the other side of the Wall, Selle and his wife were finally together but had to be separated for another seven months because he was arrested by the West Berlin police, tried, and convicted of deprivation of freedom.

A WELDING MACHINE AND SUBMARINE

From 1971 to 1973, a total of 29 East Germans escaped alone, in pairs, and sometimes with children, to West Berlin while twisted up like pretzels in the hollowed-out belly of a four-foot-tall welding machine box on wheels. The machine, which weighed 260 kilos, had been specially prepared for the refugees. The internal fittings had been removed, although the electrical fuses and cable were left in place along the inner wall, behind which the refugees hid. The escape helpers who gutted the machine designed two ways to open it: one official way that the border guards were to use and another secret way that only the escape helpers knew about. The only visible way to open the side panel of the machine was via two screws that would drop the outer panel for the guards to inspect. The guards didn't know there was a false wall hiding the fugitives, however. It was hoped that when they saw the cables and electrical fittings, they would be satisfied.

And that's exactly how it worked for the 29 who escaped. The real way of opening the internal cavity from the outside was via two simultaneous mechanical movements, followed by an electrical relay. There was no way the guards could have done this. From inside, if something happened to the relay outside, the fugitive could pull a single lever, dropping the wall down.

*****

Twenty-eight-year-old Bernd Boettger escaped 15 miles across the Baltic Sea, navigating the heavy swells by traveling beneath the surface, holding onto a homemade submarine, and using a scuba tank he fashioned out of an oxygen bottle and other spare parts. His aquatic adventure took him in range of the Danish lightship Gedser five hours after he shoved off from Communist shores. After reaching freedom, Boettger secured a piece of the capitalist dream when the manufacturing firm ILO-Werke bought his submarine and made a commercial model that sold well.

DIGGING TO FREEDOM

Of course many refugees from Communist Eastern Europe chose not to try to go over the Wall or through any of the border crossings or via swimming across a river. Instead, they chose a subterranean route by digging tunnels from East to West Berlin. Before the Wall came down, many escape tunnels were dug. Several of them were successful. Others were discovered by the Stasi, sometimes while escapees were either in or entering the underground passageways. This section will look at three of those tunnel efforts.

It would be called Tunnel 57, not because it was the fifty-seventh tunnel dug by escapees but because that is how many refugees would use it to find freedom in West Berlin. It was built by six West Berlin university students who started it in the fall of 1963 and finished it a year later, and it was actually the thirteenth successful tunnel to be dug to that date, three years after the Wall went up. The student engineers found their names carved in history for what they accomplished in freeing so many East Germans. They were Hans-Jorg Buhler, Wolfgang Kockrow, Christian Zobel, Reinhard Furrer, Hubert Hohlbein, and Joachim Neumann.

The tunnelers wanted to go deep enough to avoid any street level cave-ins of the kind that proved disastrous for some other would-be escapees who didn't make it. So they went down 12 meters before going west. Finally it was finished and, on October 3 and 4, 1964, they took 57 Eastern Europeans to West Berlin, and they didn't even make them exert the effort of crawling through the tunnel. Anyone who has seen the movie from the 1960s called The Great Escape *will know what these students did in constructing a small wooden wagon connected to a rope and pulleys. It was on this vehicle that the 57 escapees rode to freedom. The escapees were not just individuals but, in some cases, entire families. The parents of one girl believed their daughter might worry if she knew the family was going to attempt an escape, so they simply told her, "We're all going for a little walk." Fifteen minutes later, they were in the tunnel and a few minutes after that, they were in West Berlin, where she saw her grandmother for the first time in three years.*

More refugees would have been able to use it, but the tunnel was betrayed by a Stasi spy who had infiltrated the group of clients. East German soldiers, accompanied by Stasi agents, hurried to the tunnel site at

55 Strelitzerstrasse and found four of the students, who had armed them-
selves with pistols. The Stasi opened fire, and the students returned it in
what became a pitched battle. One of the students was hit and wounded,
but one of the East German border guards, Egon Schultz, was killed. The
Stasi said he was killed by the student escape helpers, a "fact" that the
leaders of the GDR publicized, calling it murder by those loyal to
Western fascism. In truth, Schultz had been hit by nine bullets, and only
one was shot from a pistol, striking him in the shoulder. The other eight
came from East German Kalashnikovs, and some of them came from
behind. It is unclear whether the shots were errant ones by the Stasi and
if Schultz just got in their line of fire, or whether they were intentional,
perhaps a kind of execution because the border guards failed in their duty
by letting the refugees escape.

The West German students who dug the tunnel managed to get back
through it to safety. Sometime later, they composed an open letter to the
mother of Egon Schultz, which they copied and put in balloons that they
released over the Wall to East Berlin. The letter expressed regret for the
killing of her son but explained, step by step, how the fatal bullets could
not have come from their own weapons and had to have come from the
East German border guards. They said that was one of the reason East
Germans were fleeing in the first place, because their own government
had turned on them, using bullets to keep them from going where they
wanted.

The leadership of the Socialist Unity Party (SED) would often
attempt to justify shooting escapees and those assisting them by
framing the shootings as a response to the fascist threat from the
West that was infiltrating and undermining the safety of the good
citizens of East Germany. They said it took armed action to ward
off this corrupting Western influence, put down treason, and protect the populace of the GDR. For example, on October 18, 1963,
the East German newspaper *Volksarmee* had this to say: "Each shot
fired from the machine gun of one of our border guards saves the
lives of thousands of GDR citizens and secures millions of marks
of national assets. Showing mercy to traitors means being inhu-
mane to the entire people."

Yet another story of a tunnel escape showed some of the com-
plexity—and unexpected challenges—faced by many escapes and
those who attempted to make a break to the West.

It was not uncommon for neighbors to be constructing tunnels simulta-
neously. Such was the case in 1962 when Erwin Becker, who had a house
on the border, began digging a 40-meter tunnel with the help of his rela-
tives and friends. The plan was to have 22 of them use it to get to West

Berlin. But just a few houses away, his neighbors had thought about doing the same thing before Becker invited them to go through his tunnel instead. That idea worked okay until his neighbors got into an argument with him about how tall the tunnel should be. The interesting thing about Becker's neighbors is that they were a group of eight, and all but two were over the age of 55. In fact, three of them were over 70, and the oldest was 81.

The five men in this group told Becker they wanted their women to be able to walk to freedom standing up proud, not hunched over. His tunnel was too short to allow for that. Becker took the criticism of his tunnel as an insult, so the two groups parted company and the 81-year-old took charge of his group's own tunnel project, which was 1.75 meters tall. His group finished the project in just 16 days. All but the eldest actually worked in the tunnel, while he stood guard, pretending to tend his garden while transporting and hiding the dirt that came up from the tunnel in a hen house and compost pile.

The elderly group of friends made it safely through their tunnel to freedom. There is a large picture of them t the Checkpoint Charlie Museum, gathered around a table having dinner. The caption from one of them notes, "It made us all feel ten years younger!" Meanwhile, Becker's group wasn't having as much luck. Shortly after the fourth escapee made his way through the tunnel, it was discovered by an East German border guard who prevented the remaining 18 from fleeing. They were all arrested and jailed.

SOME PLANS WERE SIMPLE

Not every plan of escape involved creative engineering, a complicated scenario, or a tunnel. Some plans were so simple it is surprising they worked at all. Following are a few of those direct approaches.

One East German young woman decided she knew how to get her three male friends across the border in 1963. She was talented as a seamstress, so she spent some time inspecting the uniforms of Soviet officers she saw on the streets of East Berlin. Then she bought some material, made some insignia, and fashioned uncanny copies of uniforms of officers of the Soviet Union. Her friends donned them, got into a car, and hid her underneath the dashboard. When they got to the East German guard station, they each shot well-rehearsed officer salutes to the guards, who let them pass in deference to their rank. They simply drove across the border.

*****

One young couple put a wreath on the roof of their car to show they were going to visit the Soviet cenotaph (war memorial) in West Berlin.

They knew Soviet cars with wreaths could pass without a border check of paperwork. They were half right: the first set of border guards let them through but, when they were ordered to stop at the second barrier by the guards there, the driver floored the gas pedal and stormed through in a hail of gunfire. Shaken but unhurt, the couple were welcomed to safety on the West Berlin side by military police of the American Army.

*****

Another East German man had a helper who convinced the East German border guards that a huge plastic model of a cow was needed for exhibition purposes in West Berlin. What he didn't tell the guard was that his refugee client was curled up inside.

*****

What could be more simple than getting a big balloon, hanging on to the string, and floating to freedom over the wall? Well, it wasn't that simple for a group of East Germans who decided to go that route, and its simplicity never belied its danger.

It was a risky plan that two East German families hatched when they chose to work together to build a homemade hot air balloon. The project took months, with Peter Strelzyk and Guenter Wetzel collaborating in their basements to construct a flamethrower and gas burner powerful enough to propel them out of Communist East Berlin. This "engine" would be attached by ropes to a multicolored 65-foot-wide, 75-foot-high balloon that their wives were patching together from curtains, bedsheets, and random scraps of material.

One curious thing about this escape was that, given the simplicity of the idea, it's a wonder that the Stasi wouldn't have had a preventive measure designed to stop it. Because this escape would occur not during the first few years after the Wall was constructed, but on the night of September 15, 1979, some 17 years after the Wall was completed. And by this time, the border guards had become experts on escape plots. Nevertheless, on this September night, the Strelzyks and the Wetzels and their four children all climbed aboard and launched their hot air balloon from East Berlin. Because of the weight and the relative size of the balloon, they couldn't carry much fuel and found—happily—that they had just enough of it to float them safely for 28 minutes across the 40 kilometers (about 25 miles) to freedom into West Berlin at a height of about 8,300 feet. The refugees were very cold in the night air at that altitude, but they were also out of sight of the border guards below. The escapees considered that discomfort a small price to pay for floating to freedom.

THE "SOUTHERN ROUTE"

"Two dangling strands of barbed wire have haunted Olaf Hetze for more than a quarter-century, since his failed attempt to escape from the Communist bloc, not by going over the Berlin Wall but around it, by a little-known route through Bulgaria."[3] So wrote Nicholas Kulish in a 2008 *New York Times* story chronicling the unveiling of a new escape route many East Germans took by going around the wall, to the south through Bulgaria. All told, some 4,500 refugees from several Communist countries attempted to find freedom in the West by going over the Bulgarian border, according to Stefan Appelius, a professor of political science at the University of Oldenburg, located in the German city of that name. Some 100 of them were killed by border guards, but there has never been an official investigation into those deaths or the number of them.[4]

Hetze said he believed that he and Barbara Hille might have made it if he had managed to cover their tracks better, trimming the loose ends after cutting the top wire of the border fence. If he had, Hetze said at their home in Munich, he might never have seen the shooting stars of tracer bullets arcing across the night sky, or had to watch his girlfriend twist in the air and fall to the ground, blood rushing out of a life-threatening wound to her shoulder. Olaf and Barbara Hetze, now married and with two grown sons, had decided their escape would be easier where the attention of the security forces in their native East Germany was not fixed. They would make their getaway in Bulgaria, a choice vacation destination in the east, with sunny Black Sea beaches and breathtaking mountain scenery.[5]

The popularity of the Bulgarian route was due to the relatively lax defenses these border guards had in place, compared with the more sophisticated defenses of the East Germans, and especially the Stasi-led guards who patrolled the Berlin Wall. It was not long before word got back to would-be escapees in East Germany that this might be a way to do what seemed more and more impossible in East Berlin: get to West Berlin. The full extent of this route was not known until Appelius began investigating it and published his findings in 2007 and 2008. According to the *New York Times*, he came upon this part of history in 2005 while doing research in German government archives. He discovered the case of a young German man who had been killed trying to escape in Bulgaria, began digging deeper, and found out many others had used this route as well. The stories were as many and varied, it seemed, as those of East Germans trying to get over, through, or under the

Berlin Wall itself. For example, one young couple from Leipzig were slain in 1975 as they tried to flee amid a hailstorm of bullets. The man was hit 37 times and the woman 25 times, all of the bullets coming from close range. The escape attempts and shootings went on for a long time, and the last was recorded on July 7, 1989, about four months before the Wall came down. By 2008, Appelius noted he found evidence of 845 escape attempts, involving 18 identified escapees who were killed. He says there were many more fatalities—possibly as many as 100—based on other interviews and evidence he has obtained. Overall, as is mentioned earlier in this text, more than 1,000 people died while trying to flee East Germany during the Cold War era.[6]

NOT ALL ATTEMPTS WORKED

By 1989, approximately 5,075 people had managed to cross the Berlin Wall and escape to freedom in West Berlin, sometimes in unusual and dangerous ways, as the previous examples have already shown. Numbers of those who were killed at or near the Wall varies from source to source. In his book *The Divided Berlin: 1945–1990*, Oliver Boyn writes, "At least 136 people died at the Berlin Wall."[7] Others put the figure at around 270. However, in the information posted at the Stasi Museum in Berlin, the number of dead is much higher. "About 1,000 people were killed on the Wall or the inner German border (that corridor just inside the Wall known as the 'death strip.') The SED (ruling Communist party in the GDR) tried to keep the East Germans locked in by any means including mines, barbed wire, dogs, and the order to shoot on refugees."[8]

Clearly, many potential escapees did not make it. One failed escape attempt occurred on May 12, 1963, at the border crossing on Invalidenstrasse. In this dramatic effort, eight young men and women, all between the ages of 20 and 28, attempted to use a stolen bus to make a run across the border to West Berlin. East German border guards opened fire using every weapon at their disposal. The bus was hit many times, but the young barrier-breakers had taken precautions by installing armor plating along the inside walls of the vehicle. Nevertheless, three of the would-be fugitives who were sitting in the cabin were hit and seriously wounded. Disaster for all ensued when the bus took a tight turn into the border crossing and got stuck in a narrow opening in the Wall just meters from the border. All eight escapees were arrested and sentenced to prison terms of between three and ten years. As always happened following an escape attempt, the border guards intensified the defensive structure and security at the border blockades.

PETER FECHTER

One would-be escapee deserves special recognition because the death of this 18-year-old man did so much to spur protests in West Berlin, gave courage to some in East Berlin, and put pressure on the leadership of the GDR to consider some reforms.

His name was Peter Fechter, he was a bricklayer in East Berlin, and he was shot by a hidden border guard as he attempted to make a run to West Berlin only about a year after the Wall went up. He made the escape run across the death strip with his friend Helmut Kulbeik. The two young men hid in a construction workshop near the Berlin Wall along Zimmerstrasse, then jumped out the window into the death strip with plans to run across it and enter the Kruezberg district of West Berlin near Checkpoint Charlie. Kulbeik managed to make it to the Wall and scampered over it, but Fechter was shot in the pelvis while scaling the Wall. In pain, he was unable to complete the climb and fell back into the death strip on the eastern side, all in plain sight of hundreds of witnesses, many from West Berlin.

Although he was shot and lay bleeding, his wound was not immediately fatal. In fact, it took 50 minutes for Fechter to bleed to death as he repeatedly cried, "Help me! Help me!" East German citizens who witnessed the shooting were silent, fearing reaction from the guards. West Germans who witnessed it were vocal and screamed repeatedly, "Murderers!" to the East German guards. Protests went on for days in West Berlin. Any Soviet vehicles entering the city were stoned. A large cross, dubbed the Peter Fechter cross, was paraded through the streets. But nothing changed in the immediate future in the East. In fact, when West Berlin photographer Heinz Grimm entered East Berlin to cover Fechter's funeral, he was arrested for "collection of news," was convicted, and served two years in a Stasi prison.

There is, however, a postscript to this story. Thirty-five years later, the border sniper who shot Fechter was tried for the killing but received a suspended sentence because of the amount of time that had passed.

SIEGFRIED NOFFKE

While some loved ones were reunited due to successful escape attempts, others were not so lucky. One ill-fated attempt occurred on June 29, 1962, when Siegfried Noffke wanted to reunite with his wife and child, who were in West Berlin. To this end, he began tunneling. Although he built his tunnel well, he didn't know that two East German students were building their own tunnel only two houses away. At one point, the tunnels came so close together that they caused the earth to weaken above. When border guards noted a hollow appearing in the ground, they used a jack to break through it. Noffke was shot dead as he came out, and his two helpers were arrested and sentenced to life in a Stasi prison.

SUMMARY

The risks taken by the many dissident citizens of Communist countries shows that, while many chose the safe path of finding some level of peace in the midst of oppression, others could not. For them, freedom was everything, and it was worth the possible loss of life to achieve it. Their courage and ingenuity stand as fitting memorials to freedom-loving people, down through history, throughout the world.

NOTES

1. Oliver Boyn, *The Divided Berlin: 1945–1990: The Historical Guidebook.* Berlin: Christopher Links Verlag, 2001, 52.
2. Display information posted at the Checkpoint Charlie Museum, Friedrichstrasse at Zimmerstrasse, Berlin, Germany.
3. Nicholas Kulish, "Decades Later, Stories Emerge of Another Escape Route out of East Germany," *New York Times*, March 24, 2008. Retrieved from http://www.nytimes.com/2008/03/24/world/europe/24iht-bulgaria.4.11 382073.html?pagewanted=all on November 22, 2011.
4. Ibid.
5. Ibid.
6. Boyn, p. 53.
7. Ibid.
8. Display information posted at Stasi Museum Berlin; Gedenkstatte Normannenstrasse, Ruschestrasse 103, Haus 22, Berlin, Germany.

7

DEPICTIONS OF EUROPEAN COMMUNISM IN MOVIES

Much of what the world sees of international events comes to them from the movies. We are restrained by distance and economic resources from traveling the world ourselves, so we gain many of our impressions from the depictions of countries and people of the world from the big screen and from television. Like all mediated depictions, the impressions conveyed by them may be accurate or inaccurate depending on the purpose of the film, the intent of the filmmaker, and the amount of research done on the subject matter. Even the best commercial films, however, must bow to the needs of entertainment. Movies are not documentaries and often must omit some things, add others, or rearrange the sequencing of historic events to get the most out of the dramatic elements of the story. The films presented and discussed in this chapter are ones that have succeeded both as entertaining movies and as accurate chronicles of countries and people caught up in the web of Communism and, for those depicting life in this era, the shadow of the Iron Curtain. They show what a skilled and committed set of filmmakers can do in enlightening moviegoers about countries and lifestyles alien to their own. The films are presented in no particular order, although they are generally from the most recent to the older films.

THE LIVES OF OTHERS (DAS LEBEN DER ANDEREN)

One of the latest significant movies about life behind the Iron Curtain is one of the best films about what it was like to live in a society where privacy from the state was virtually nonexistent. It is a German film that premiered in 2006 and won an American Academy Award as the Best Foreign Language Film of the Year. It tells the story of life in East Germany where the agents of the dreaded Stasi, or state security force, were employed to keep tabs on everyday citizens in the GDR.

So it is not surprising that when director/screenwriter Florian Henckel von Donnersmarck set about making a film depicting the fear that gripped GDR citizens living behind the Berlin Wall, he chose as his title *The Lives of Others*. For the Stasi, which held East Germany in its grip from 1950 to 1990 and which was established with help from the Soviets shortly after World War II, engaged in rampant political surveillance and espionage. The intent of the organization was to monitor "politically incorrect behavior among all citizens of East Germany."[1] At full strength, it employed nearly 100,000 officers and hundreds of thousands of informants. At any one time, about a third of the entire East German population was being monitored.[2]

In writing about his film, Florian Henckel von Donnersmarck explains that "German movies produced after the reunification generally and strangely depict the GDR as funny or moving."[3] Although that seems odd, it may be because the relationships between former

Still from *The Lives of Others* (2006, Germany) aka *Das Leben der Anderen*. Directed by Florian Henckel von Donnersmarck Shown: Ulrich Muehe (as Gerd Weisler). (Sony Pictures Classics/Photofest)

East Germans and West Germans are still a bit fragile, and few seem to want to dredge up memories of what conditions used to be like. But von Donnersmarck is in a good position to dredge up those memories accurately. Both of his parents came from Eastern Europe, and he often traveled with them as a child to East Germany to meet with relatives and friends. He writes the following:

> *A cousin of my father has been named chief of protocol of Erich Honecker, the East German head of state and boss of the ruling S.E.D. Party (Sozialistische Einheitspartei Deuschlands, or the Socialist Unity Party of Germany). Other people we knew had very normal jobs, yet one could see the fear in all of them, right up to the end of the regime. Fear of the Stasi, fear of the 100,000 highly trained employees whose sights were trained on one thing: "The Lives of Others," the lives of those who thought differently, who were too free-spirited and above all, the artists and people working in the arts. Every aspect of life was recorded.*[4]

The Lives of Others starts in 1984 East Berlin, or five years before the fall of the Berlin Wall. It spans a seven-year period to 1991, after East and West Germany were reunified. The story follows the disillusionment of a loyal Stasi operative, which continues to grow deeper over the time of his surveillance of an East German couple, both professionals in the artistic world. The operative is Captain Gerd Wiesler, and his assignment is to monitor the lives of Georg Dreyman, a well-known playwright, and Christa-Maria Sieland, a celebrated actress. Wiesler orders the bugging of Dreyman's apartment and also sanctions a personal threat delivered to one of Wiesler's neighbors who accidentally witnesses the wiretapping as it is being done.

Dreyman is atypical of other artists in the GDR who were more open in their criticism of the East German government and the SED Party. He remains reserved and seems a loyal GDR citizen until his girlfriend, Christa-Maria, and another close friend are harassed by the Stasi. After these incidents, Dreyman sets in motion a plan to write a critical article for the West German publication *Der Spiegel*. All the while, Wiesler is monitoring conversations between Dreyman and Christa-Maria, which include discussions of this article. Although he finds he has the evidence needed to arrest Dreyman, he has become so involved in Dreyman's life and the couple's relationship that he develops second thoughts about revealing the information, even though hiding it could cost him his career and, probably, his life. In short, his humanity kicks in and he begins to question what his own life and career are all about.

This, of course, is the point of the film—asking how loyal a person can be to an ideology that goes against personal principles and essential traits of most human beings who long for personal freedom and who respect the need others have for that freedom as well.

The film drew strong critical praise among reviewers, with more than 90 percent of critics applauding it for its accurate depiction of life in East Germany behind the Berlin Wall and for its gripping story. Said Terry Lawson of the *Detroit Free Press*: "Few would deny that *The Lives of Others* is true to its self, and in its depiction of human nature and human spirit."[5] And Roger Moore of the *Orlando Sentinel* said, "Florian Henckel von Donnersmarck's film is a melodrama in a minor key, quietly affecting, quietly chilling, quietly quiet. It captures the drab architecture of totalitarianism, the soul-dead buildings of a soul-dead state."[6]

Some film buffs will find a parallel between the plight of Wiesler, as he grows a conscience, and the plight of Harry Call in a 1964 American film classic, *The Conversation*. That film, where Call is a professional snoop for hire, depicts what happens when a wiretapper gets too emotionally involved with the people he is monitoring.

GOODBYE LENIN

When people speak of the fall of the Berlin Wall, it is usually with a sense of pride that the repressive regimes related to European Communism finally fell and that the people of East Germany were now liberated to pursue personal freedoms denied them under the previous regimes. But that is definitely not the premise of the 2003 film *Goodbye Lenin*, which is one of the few successful, lighthearted looks at the fall of Communism. In this story, a woman ("Mrs. Kerner") who is a proud socialist, falls into a coma in October 1989 after she discovers her husband is having an affair with a woman who is officially an "enemy of the state." She doesn't awaken until eight months later, after the Communist-named "anti-Fascist protectionist rampart" (the Berlin Wall to the rest of the world) had fallen and capitalism had begun to replace Communism.

Mrs. Kerner's son, Alex, is told by doctors that his mother's condition is fragile and that any shock or excitement could send her back into the coma, or worse. Realizing how much shock she would feel if she knew about the fall of the Wall, Alex sets about keeping his mother cloaked in the fantasy that nothing has changed, that the Wall is still up, and that Communism still reigns. Alex recreates, within the walls of his mother's apartment, the same somber and Spartan environment of former East German life, keeping her away from any outside news that the world on the other side of her apartment walls has changed dramatically.

It is not an easy task, especially in the age of television and the myriad news publications being sold outside by street vendors. Alex also wants to get on with his new life in this freer, post-Communist atmosphere. After all, while Mrs. Kerner was in her coma, Alex took his first trip to the West, and his country experienced its first free elections. Further, his sister Ariane has quit her university studies and gone to work at the very Western Burger King.

Goodbye Lenin is directed and cowritten by Wolfgang Becker, who was born in 1944 Berlin and who has a great grasp on the history of the country and its encounter with the divisions of East and West at the foot of the Wall. The film received much critical acclaim, both as a sophisticated comedy and as a slice of life showing former East Berliners who were saddened when their way of life ended with the breaching of the Berlin Wall. Says *Arizona Republic* writer Richard Nilsen, "It is a sweethearted comedy about the fall of Communism and the lingering nostalgia for an East Germany that no longer exists."[7]

Although the idea of someone having nostalgia for the GDR seems unusual to many, it is not an uncommon feeling among former East Berliners who were loyal socialists and who appeared to want only the freedom to travel to West Berlin to shop as well as see relatives and friends. However, anyone visiting the Checkpoint Charlie Museum, which stands adjacent to the infamous border crossing, will get the strongest impression that many East Germans wanted much more than that. Nevertheless, in the onslaught of the new capitalist life and the tough task of finding jobs, many East Berliners did slip into periods of nostalgia for the days when at least the basics of life were taken care of by the ruling Communist Party.

Writing about the film, *Washington Post* writer Mark Jenkins said simply, "Beneath the family saga and easy digs at the tackiness of Western consumer culture, Becker presents a serious critique of authoritarianism and propaganda."[8] It is thus another classic example that comedy is not a bad vehicle for delivering provocative thoughts, much the same as the American film *Dr. Strangelove* did decades earlier.

SUNSHINE

A film that received only limited release in the United States is a film produced in 1999 and released a year later, called *Sunshine*. Written by Israel Horovitz and Istvan Szabo', produced and directed by Szabo'. It traces the lives of three generations of a Jewish family, from the start of the twentieth century to just after the 1956 revolution in Hungary, who carried the original name of Sonnenschein, the German word for "sunshine." The family later changes its name to Sors, the Hungarian word for "fate."

The story is fictional, but it weaves in many events that actually occurred, and the sources for the story are impeccable. Ralph Fiennes, who stars alongside Rachel Weisz, plays three different roles, one of which is based on the life of Attila Petschauer, a Hungarian Olympian. There are also various mentions of other well-known Hungarian Jews who suffered from anti-Semitism under both Nazism and Communism. It is an ironic role for Fiennes, given that he played a Nazi death camp commander in the earlier film *Schindler's List*.

Sunshine involved international collaboration by filmmakers from Germany, Hungary, Austria, and Canada, and it won the Genie Award as the best Canadian film in 2000.

The film begins when Hungary was under the rule of the Austro-Hungarian Empire. The family became wealthy in manufacturing and distributing a successful herbal tonic. They decided to change the family name to Sors and ostensibly become Catholics in an attempt to survive the Nazi anti-Semitism in the decade preceding World War II. Although managing to survive that era, the Sors family ran headlong into the specter and reality of Communism after the war.

The film shows that changing one's heritage and religion is not as easy as it might seem at first. Following the liberation of Hungary from Nazis by Russian Communists, a young Ivan Sors is hired by the Communist regime to interrogate presumed conspirators. Born into the Sors family, he is a loyal Hungarian, but he is loyal to a country and its causes that had earlier caused the Sonnenscheins so much trouble because of their Judaism. So the two realities of who Ivan is— a Sors and a Sonnenschein—are bound to collide and do.

Writer Jordan Hiller says of the film, "*Sunshine* is the definitive Jewish Experience movie. Beautifully told with heartbreaking eloquence, it is mandatory viewing if one intends to understand what it means to be a Jew living in the world. It weighs equally the balance between the two—being Jewish *and* living in the world."[9]

NIGHT CROSSING

In 1982, the Walt Disney Motion Picture Company released a film based on the true story of two men who dared to escape over the Berlin Wall in a hot air balloon, taking their families with them. It was one of many attempts, some successful and some not, made by those living in the East who wanted to leave and head west for freedom. This film mixes in some real-life footage of the Wall and the no man's land surrounding it where many East Berliners met their death. One of those courageous people was Lukas Keller, a teenager from the village of Possneck, Thuringia. In 1978, Keller jumped aboard a bulldozer and rode it into the danger area known as the Inner German Border Zone. He didn't make it, as he came under heavy automatic machine gun fire and was shot. The East German border guards left him for dead, and the Stasi went after his parents, who were on a picnic with two families, the Strelzyks and the Wetzels. The police informed the Keller family of their son's death and then arrested them. This episode was enough to convince Peter Strelzyk to conceive a harrowing escape plan and present it to his friend, Gunter Wetzel. The two men had been chafing under GDR control of their lives and their families' lives, but they needed an extra spark to spur them to action. Young Keller's death provided it.

The plan was simple enough: construct a hot air balloon to airlift themselves and their six family members to freedom over the Berlin Wall. Carrying out the plan proved anything but simple, however. They start by buying more than a thousand yards of taffeta, saying it was for making tents for a camping club. While Wetzel uses a sewing machine in his attic to stitch the fabric together, Strelzyk tries various experiments to build a burner that will hoist the balloon from earth and help bring it back down again. Fearing the worst, Wetzel bows to the wishes of his wife Petra and backs out of the plan, but Strelzyk goes ahead. He eventually builds the burner and inflates the balloon with the help of his older son Frank.

On July 3, 1979, one day before Independence Day in America, the four members of the Strelzyk family take off and can smell freedom, only to have cloud moisture dampen both the balloon and burner, bringing the whole escape ship down in the border zone just short of the fences. They get off safely and manage to elude border guards, but the balloon floats away.

The family is still not safe, however, because East German border guards locate the derelict balloon, and the Stasi swings into action to discover who built it. With the security police closing in on their identities and nothing to lose, the Strelzyks decide to try again and start building another balloon and burner. This time, Wetzel agrees to go along, helps construct the apparatus, and convinces his wife to come, too. The Stasi is getting closer each day, so there is no time to test the new balloon. About ten weeks after the initial failed attempt, the two families climb aboard the new balloon on September 15, 1979. However, by this time the border guards have been alerted to the possibility of a new balloon escape attempt, so the journey is even more fraught with danger.

The two families—eight members in all—climb into the basket as the balloon inflates and lifts off. They are discovered by guards, however, who are searching the skies, and a helicopter is dispatched to bring them down. After a while, the burner's propane supply is depleted, the balloon starts to descend, and it comes down in a clearing. Neither family knows which side of the border they are on but are ecstatic when they are informed by police that they have landed in West Berlin.

Like another Disney film of that era, *The Girl Who Spelled Freedom*, the movie *Night Crossing* tells the universal story of people caught under repressive governments who long to be free and find a way to escape to that freedom. Unlike the previous films discussed in this chapter, *Night Crossing* was an American-made film from Hollywood director Delbert Mann. Although it was made to appeal to a large commercial audience, the film stayed close to the grimness of the Berlin Wall era when such escape attempts carried the very real possibility of death to those who would seek freedom.

REDS

This epic film came from the book by John Reed called *10 Days That Shook the World*. During the World War I era, radical American journalist Reed is covering the rise of unions among American laborers and feeling the plight of the common worker more and more personally. This perception—that a society of classes works against the *everyman*—fuels Reed's interest in the Communist revolution taking place in Russia in 1917. Reed meets and falls in love with another liberal American writer, Louise Bryant, who shares his views, and they travel to Russia to cover—and in Reed's case become a part of—the October Revolution of 1917 when the Communists take control. Both Reed and Bryant feel invigorated and hope they can light similar revolutionary fires back home in America through their writings. They find they are facing an uphill battle, however.

While they are in Russia, Reed and Bryant have front-row seats to the October Revolution in which the Russian Social-Democratic Labor Party (or Bolsheviks) led by Vladimir Lenin, ousts the Russian Provisional Government led by Prime Minister Alexander Kerensky. The "Kerensky Government" was the interim administrative body that governed Russia immediately after Tsar Nicholas II abdicated his power on March 15, 1917.[10] Kerensky's government would exist for only eight months, and this regime was ended by the Bolsheviks who took over shortly after the October Revolution. Both Reed and Bryant were present at the fall of the Winter Palace when the Bolsheviks, who sought a total socialist government and an end to Russian participation in World War I, effected a power transfer from Kerensky to a Congress of Soviets. This was an elected group of workers and soldiers' deputies. The power was supposed to transfer to the people, but Russian politics would eventually get in the way, keeping Communism from reaching its ideals.

Reed crossed the line that separates reporters striving for objectivity from those journalists who join the causes they are writing about. He became an ardent supporter of Lenin's government and even became an employee of the new People's Commissariat for Foreign Affairs. In that role, he translated official documents and actions of the new socialist Russian government into English. The Russian's found Reed, as an American, useful to their cause of spreading propaganda. He became a kind of ex-officio member of the power elite in Russia, meeting both Trotsky and Lenin in 1918.

When he returned to America, Reed used his writings and speeches to whip up support for the Bolshevik revolution, and wound up facing sedition charges. His health deteriorated, and he returned to Russia, where he died in Moscow of spotted typhus. The Russian government gave him a hero's funeral and laid his body to rest at the Kremlin Wall Necropolis.

As Vincent Camby of the *New York Times* wrote, "The focal point of 'Reds,' . . . is the love affair and marriage of John Reed, the flamboyant American journalist and radical sympathizer, and Louise Bryant, the Portland, Oregon, dentist's wife who, in 1915, fled from her husband and middle-class conventions to follow Reed to Greenwich Village and her own desperately longed-for emancipation."[11]

The two find the cause they are seeking in the Russian Revolution, although the idealism that leads them into that adventure is fraught with the perils of reality. Things just don't work out with that revolution as the two envisioned they would.

Camby continues, "Most astonishing is the way the movie, which abounds with great moments of history including the Bolshevik takeover of the Winter Palace in Petrograd, avoids the patently absurd, even as Reed and Louise, drunk on the excitement of the successful revolution they've just witnessed, make love in a cold Petrograd flat to the strains of 'The Internationale.' The secret, I think, is that the film sees Reed and Louise as history's golden children, crass and self-obsessed but genuinely committed to causes they don't yet fully understand."[12]

The movie drew near-universal praise from top critics around America and remains one of the definitive films about the Russian Revolution and its immediate aftermath. The movie's credibility is greatly enhanced by the inclusion of interviews with actual survivors of the events being depicted in Russia and the United States at the time.

DR. ZHIVAGO

This lavish spectacle, released in 1965, was written by acclaimed Russian author Boris Pasternak and directed by David Lean, who had previously awed audiences and critics with his other major cross-cultural films, *Lawrence of Arabia* and *Bridge on the River Kwai*. Having tackled the Middle East and Burma in those two films, Lean this time turned his attention to Russia and the era punctuated by the Russian Revolution of 1917. The times are focused and articulated through the individual characters of Yuri Zhivago (Omar Sharif), his wife Tonya (Geraldine Chaplin), and his lover Lara (Julie Christie). The movie opens when a top Russian general, Yevgraf Zhivago, shows up at an industrial site, looking for his niece who is the daughter of his half-brother, Yuri. Finding a skeptical woman who appears to be her, he begins to relate the details of her father's life. This becomes the story of the film from that point on.

The general tells the young woman that her father Yuri was an orphan who was raised by wealthy stepparents in Moscow. This is the Gromyko family, which was living in tsarist Russia, and they had a daughter Tonya, who is the same age as Yuri. As Yuri grows into a young man, he becomes a doctor but also distinguishes himself as a poet. As he is out one evening, he witnesses the merciless slaughter of a group of socialist protestors by a cavalry unit of the tsar's army. The event changes him, stirring his poetic passions and ideals of humanity.

He marries Tonya, although he is distracted by a new woman he encounters named Lara. In time, his affections turn to her instead of Tonya. World War I breaks out, however, and Yuri is posted to the Ukraine to treat patients coming from the battlefields. There he re-encounters Lara, who is now a nurse.

The war winds down in Russia, and the summer of 1917 produces the October Russian Revolution, which alters almost everything in Russia. When Yuri returns to his home in Moscow, he finds the city in the grip of the Bolsheviks, and the process of collectivism (Communism) has started. Yuri is now a published poet as well as physician, but the new Bolshevik leadership find his writings at odds with their own ideals and target him for arrest. He is spirited out of the city by Yevgraf, his half-brother, and Zhivago travels to Yuriatin, a small country town near his family's estate. On his way, he is kidnapped by a Red Army unit and pressed into service as their medical officer for 18 months before he deserts. He later suffers from the effects of ill health, but not before fathering Yevgraf's niece who is the daughter of Lara and whom his half-brother finds in the opening scene of the film.

Dr. Zhivago is, at its heart, a love story but one set against the historical backdrop of the Russian Revolution and the emergent Communism that will lead to the formation of the Soviet Union. As such, the story provides a grassroots perspective of what that era did to individuals and families who were caught in its grip. The film drew critical praise and was nominated for 10 Academy Awards, winning five.

THE SPY WHO CAME IN FROM THE COLD

When the famed writer John le Carré spins a yarn about espionage agents, there's usually more to it than meets the naked eye. Among other things, the reader is never sure whether the British are the good guys or whether they rival the Communists as the bad guys. There's never a guarantee of a happy ending, either. Such is the case with his 1963 seminal thriller, *The Spy Who Came in from the Cold*, which was made into a motion picture two years later starring Richard Burton as an aging British spy experiencing a career's worth of angst.

Le Carré is actually David John Moore Cornwell, born in Great Britain in 1931. He changed his name to le Carré when he started writing spy novels in the 1950s and 1960s. He was in a good position to know about espionage since he himself worked for the British intelligence services, MI5 and MI6. He retired from intelligence work to become a full-time author following the success of his early novels.

The Spy Who Came in from the Cold is set, as are many of le Carré's novels, in the shadow of the Berlin Wall in the 1960s. This 1965 film tells the story of Alec Leamas, a British intelligence operative and head of a failing West Berlin branch of the British Secret Intelligence Service. When the last of his agents is killed, London dispatches a tired and burned-out Leamas to Communist East Germany for one last mission, seemingly to defect. His real mission, of course, is anything but that. He is to become a double agent, and his task is to sow the seeds of disinformation in Communist Europe. The London office of "the Circus," the name given the intelligence service, prepares Leamas's cover story well, ostensibly firing him for an alleged theft and giving him barely enough of a pension to live on, whereupon Leamas goes to work for a library but loses that job because he drinks too much.

While at the library, however, he meets a young woman named Liz who is the secretary of her local Communist Party cell in England. Leamas falls in love with her and she with him. Fearing for her safety, should she try to follow him into East Berlin, he exacts a promise from her that she will not try to find him after he leaves Britain. He also exacts a promise from his superiors that they will not interfere in Liz's life. At this point, the next part of the plan is to have Leamas get arrested for assaulting a local grocer in a drunken stupor.

Leamas is now seen as a bitter ex-spy for England who might be ripe for defection and turning by the Communists. So after his jail stint is up, Leamas is approached by a "recruiter" from East Germany who takes him there to meet with members of the Abteilung, which is the East German equivalent of MI5.

Back home, Leamas's superiors do not keep their word and instead go to see Liz. They say they are Leamas's friends, ask her questions, and even offer her financial help because she is struggling. The plan is to use her as part of Leamas's mission, without letting him know, at least initially. Leamas continues to make inroads with the East German spy network. Before long, the Communists invite Liz to East Germany as part of a program to exchange information with leaders of Communist cell groups.

A power struggle ensues within the East German Communist Party, and Leamas, along with a colleague, are arrested. It is at that trial that Liz is called as a surprise witness in defense of Leamas's colleague. She winds up putting herself in jeopardy because she is taking money from the British Intelligence Service for her apartment. Leamas realizes his cover is now blown and that he might be able to save her if he confesses to his own true mission. However, he discovers that what he thought was the true mission is not; British Control actually sent him to East Germany so that this trial would take place and put Liz's life in danger, all with the goal of having another agent arrested by the East Germans. A friend is able to spirit Leamas and Liz to the Berlin Wall, and show them a way to escape over it, but the plan goes awry and both Liz and Leamas are shot and killed while trying to cross the barrier.

This gritty film gives a sense of the dark days of the Cold War between Communist Eastern Europe and the West, and of the perils existing in issues confronting the Wall and the intersection of these two ways of life. East Berlin is a dank, dark, and treacherous place for political ideologues and, particularly, spies for both the East and the West. Both sides can be equally brutal in their treatment of people, and the blacks and whites of West versus East become grayer as the plot of this film thickens.

ONE DAY IN THE LIFE OF IVAN DENISOVICH

Ivan Denisovich is a World War II hero from Russia who is captured by the Germans. When the war ends and he returns to his native land, he is arrested and sentenced to 10 years of hard labor at a Siberian prison camp. The reason: he let himself be captured by Germans instead of fighting to the death. This 1971 film chronicles one day of Ivan's life at the Gulag to which he is assigned in Siberia.

The film is from the novel of the same name by the late Alexander Solzhenitsyn, himself a Russian Gulag survivor who spent eight years in the camps because authorities felt his writings were disrespectful to Stalin. He would later write a novel based on his experiences, *One Day in the Life of Ivan Denisovich*. In 1979, Solzhenitsyn won the Nobel Prize for Literature.

The story depicts the brutal life that prisoners of Russian labor campus had to endure. It is the 1950s, and Ivan Denisovich is serving year number eight of his 10-year prison term in Siberia. He is content with the small achievements of each day, and it is through these small victories that he is able to retain most of his humanity. A day without sickness is an achievement, for example; so is getting an extra cigarette; so is doing a good job working on a wall and not suffering a beating at the hands of the prison guards. It's a stark and harsh life under Communist rule, especially so for those sent to these Siberian labor camps for things that are not really crimes at all. They are just actions that are deemed to fall short of the Communist ideals of what a person should be; they reflect badly on the Party.

Solzhenitsyn knew what he was writing about in creating the novel on which the film is based. He knew the possible consequences of writing to show how oppressive the Stalin-led Soviet government was. One writer noted, *"One Day in the Life of Ivan Denisovich* did more than expose the horrors of the vast system of labor camps for political enemies; it also revealed the author's belief in the common man's ability to survive with dignity and integrity."[13]

ONE, TWO, THREE

On the funny side of a serious subject, filmgoers can find a 1961 Billy Wilder comedy called *One, Two, Three* that pokes fun at the differences between Communist East Europe and the West. Veteran actor James Cagney plays an American executive with the Coca-Cola Company in West Berlin. He loves his career but finds it may be in danger if he can't keep his boss's American daughter, played by Pamela Tiffin, from falling in love with and marrying a young East German Communist, played by Horst Buccholz.

Cagney's C. R. "Mac" MacNamara is the director of the West Berlin offices of Coca-Cola. Not content with that level of responsibility, Mac wants to become the chief of all European operations for the soft drink company, a post that would land him in London instead. West Berlin becomes even stranger turf to him as his German staff insists on relating to him as they would (and some probably did) to Adolph Hitler. After all, only 16 years have passed since the fall of the Nazi Party and the collapse of Hitler's Germany. Memories are still fresh in the minds of Germans, although a new threat has arisen that they can practically see from their office windows: the guardhouses and checkpoints between East and West Berlin. The Berlin Wall has not yet been built, but the city and its ideologies are nonetheless divided into Communism and capitalism.

Despite the divided city, country, and world, Mac is working on a trade deal that would take Coca-Cola into the Russian market. Differing ideologies are not going to stop this businessman from succeeding in climbing the corporate ladder.

Standing in his way is not Russia, but Scarlett Hazeltine, the 17-year-old extroverted and pretty daughter of his Atlanta boss. She is on a European holiday, so Mac decides to host her in West Berlin, assuming he will score points with her dad. Mac starts getting concerned, however, when Scarlett decided to prolong her stay in Germany, and he is even more concerned when he discovers the reason: she has fallen for—and married—a young and committed East German Communist, Otto Ludwig Piffl.

The clock is ticking for Mac because Scarlett's mom and dad—unaware of these developments—have told him they will be in Berlin within 24 hours to pick up their daughter. Mac sees his career slipping through his fingers unless he can do something about Scarlett's romance and, hopefully because of her age, somehow have the marriage annulled and stricken from the public records. Then comes the kicker: he finds that Scarlett is pregnant and that he must reverse course. After finding a way to get Otto out of his daughter's life, he must find a way to make him accepted by his boss, Scarlett's dad.

With the exception of a few films like *Goodbye Lenin, The Russians Are Coming, the Russians Are Coming,* and the dark American comedy *Dr. Strangelove* there haven't been too many attempts by producers and directors to release comedies about the Cold War. But Wilder manages to pull it off in this classic comedy and, before long, filmgoers of the 1960s could smile and even laugh at the divide between Communism and the free world.

One reviewer noted that Wilder has the gift of reducing the complexities of Communism to the absurd, and he does so here. "Buchholz is a kid who's real good at spouting all kinds of left wing slogans without delving to deeply into their meanings," he notes.[14] In doing so, his character Piffl is not that much different from other young zealots of the 1960s, many of whom were fired up more by the rhetoric of Communism than the reality of it.

DR. STRANGELOVE

If the main title of this dark comedy weren't strange enough, the subtitle is even quirkier: *How I Learned to Stop Worrying and Love the Bomb.* This 1964 film, which has developed a large cult following, premiered as a dark and controversial film—although it is extremely funny in places—at the height of the Cold War standoff between the United States and Russia. The Wall had been up only three years, and the Cuban missile crisis was fresh in Americans' minds.

The tensions that gave rise to the Wall's construction were palpable in America, and many Americans were flat-out scared. This was also the first year of America's major commitment of troops to what would become the unpopular and little-understood Vietnam War, so many Americans—especially young ones—would soon be at odds with the power brokers in Washington, DC. Antiwar and anti-bomb rallies and demonstrations were beginning to appear and would soon spread across the country.

Into this volatile American environment comes director Stanley Kubrick with a dark comedy poking fun at, while still remaining deadly serious about, the nuclear arms race between the United States and Russia. The film is set in America, so this movie doesn't technically qualify as a film that peels back the curtain to show life under Communism in Europe. But it does show a lot about the tension that existed between East and West as well as the paranoia that gripped some Americans about the need to build bigger and better nuclear kill systems to stave off the Communist threat.

Dr. Strangelove focuses on a U.S. Air Force general, Jack D. Ripper (pun intended, as is the case with most names in the movie), played by veteran actor Sterling Hayden, who goes mad and one day surrenders to that madness by issuing orders that send a flight of B-52s to drop thermonuclear bombs on Russian targets. He has been given no orders to do so, although he has been given the authority to release the bombers from his Strategic Air Command base when and if he should receive such orders. He just decides to fast-track the decision and release the bombers without such orders. He has grown paranoid about the threat of Communism invading America; about as paranoid as his fear that fluoridation is a Communist plot to drain Americans of their "precious bodily fluids."

Because of built-in complexities of the Strategic Air Command (SAC) alert system, no one else other than General Ripper possesses the secret code that would abort the bombing mission, and the B-52 pilots have been instructed not to return until such a code is given them. And General Ripper is not giving it up, even under orders from the president of the United States, one of three roles played by the late British comedian Peter Sellers, of Inspector Clouseau fame. Sellers also plays British RAF Group Captain Lionel Mandrake, who has the misfortune of being locked in an office with the mad Ripper while American troops are raiding the general's base to enforce the president's order of retrieving the recall code.

The third role Seller plays is the enigmatic Dr. Strangelove, a former Nazi nuclear scientist the president calls upon to help get the

British actor Peter Sellers during a break in filming *Dr. Strangelove* at Shepperton Studios in Middlesex, near London, England, on March 3, 1963. Sellers is wearing a bald piece for his character in the movie. (AP Photo/Bob Dear/file)

United States and Russia out of this mess. Indications are that Strangelove is translating his hidden disappointment over the downfall of Hitler to planning a takeover or a makeover of the planet by America, using this catastrophe as a way to do it. After making it painfully clear that there is little chance of recalling the bombers, Air Force General Buck Turgidson (George C. Scott) urges President

Merkin Muffey to launch an all-out first strike against the Soviet Union, noting that it would be so devastating that a retaliatory Soviet strike could kill only 10 or 20 million Americans. President Muffey brings Russian Ambassador Alexi de Sadesky into the Pentagon War Room to confess to the Soviets what has gone wrong. But Sadesky drops his own bomb on things when he announces the Soviets have built a "doomsday machine" that will activate automatically if Russia is attacked. This machine can wipe out everyone on the planet. Sadesky's job is to convince Soviet Premier Dimitri Kisov not to retaliate, a job that President Muffley has to undertake himself in a hilarious conversation with Kisov over the War Room's hotline phone.

Nothing works, however, and the final scene is of one of the American bombers hitting their primary target inside Russia. Is mutual annihilation next?

Dr. Strangelove received near universal praise from movie critics and was nominated for four Academy Awards. It probably would have garnered more nominations had it not been for its controversial nature on a subject that scared the living daylights out of many Americans. Latter-day audiences—such as today's critics—are nearly unanimous in their praise of this five-decade-old film, although audiences of 1964 were divided over its antiwar message. While some Americans found release from their fears in a comedic presentation of the somber topic, others realized their fears did not go deep enough. What if some deranged SAC officer could simply push a button that scrambled bombers to attack the Soviet Union without cause?

Reviewer Jonathan Rosenbaum of the *Chicago Reader* writes, "Like most of his work, Stanley Kubrick's deadly black satirical comedy-thriller on cold war madness and its possible effects has aged well: the manic, cartoonish performances of George C. Scott, Sterling Hayden, and Peter Sellers . . . look as brilliant as ever, and Kubrick's icy contempt for 20th-century humanity may find its purest expression in the figure of Strangelove himself, a savage extrapolation of a then-obscure Henry Kissinger conflated with Wernher von Braun and Dr. Mabuse to suggest a flawed, spastic machine with Nazi reflexes that ultimately turns on itself."[15]

THE RUSSIANS ARE COMING, THE RUSSIANS ARE COMING

Depending on how you classify films about Communism, several other films have been made that look at the tensions between the United States and the Soviet Union, For example, 1966 brought us a very funny film called *The Russians Are Coming, the Russians Are Coming* about the comedic chaos that follows when a Russian submarine, *Sproot,* has the misfortune of running aground on the New England shoreline near a small island village populated by Americans who wrongly perceive it as a Soviet attack. The film also features a Russian sea captain who makes frequent runs to this American seaport, often stocking up on goods as a capitalist (but not a Communist) would, and befriends the Americans in the process. The film features an all-star comedic lineup with Carl Reiner, Alan Arkin, Jonathan Winters, Theodore Bikel, Ben Blue, and Paul Ford.

Unlike the dark comedy of two years earlier, *Dr. Strangelove,* this film presents more of a zany look at Americans and Soviets who really mean each other no harm, but who have trouble getting past stereotypes. They're supposed to be enemies, aren't they? If so, why do they find it so hard to get angry at each other? In a sense, *The Russians Are Coming* reminds filmgoers that just because political systems are at odds is no reason individual Americans and Russians can't learn to get along and treat each other as humans.

OTHER FILMS

The foregoing are most of the significant films that have addressed the East–West divide during the Cold War era. Some deal with life behind the Wall; others deal with how those tensions were felt in America as well as Europe. Certainly other films have probed especially the American impact of the Cold War. Who could forget the punch that the historical drama *Good Night and Good Luck* (2006) packed for audiences? This film recounted the standoff between Senator Joseph McCarthy, the right-wing extremist on a Communist witch hunt in 1950s America, and veteran CBS newsman Edward R. Murrow, intent on exposing the McCarthy sham to Americans. Among the paranoid era's restrictions on many Americans was signing loyalty oaths and giving up friends to the House Un-American Activities Committee, which ruined the reputations of innocents just to get names of people who might have Communist leanings.

Other films, like Woody Allen's *The Front* (1976), Irwin Winkler's *Guilty by Suspicion* (1991), and Sydney Pollack's *The Way We Were* (1973), focused on the infamous "blacklist" era of the early 1950s as well, showing how little difference there was in that kind of state surveillance and summary legal proceedings and the oppression of Communism itself.

Still other films, like the 1959 big-budget melodrama *The Journey*, tried to bring a story about people caught up in the in 1956 Hungarian Revolution into the arena of epic Hollywood films of that era. The film had a stellar cast with Deborah Kerr, Yul Brynner, Jason Robards Jr., Robert Morley, and E. G. Robinson. But the Hungarian revolt was treated as only background material while the main event was the relationship between Kerr, who played an English aristocrat trapped in Hungary, and Brynner, a Hungarian army officer who was charged with ferreting out revolutionaries.

Why Not More Films about Communism?

One might think that the struggle of Eastern Europeans against the totalitarian regimes of Communism would make for the kind of drama Hollywood is looking for. If that were true, however, there would be more films to talk about in this chapter instead of the few discussed. The fact is, there haven't been that many movies made about what it was like for everyday people to live under the shadow of Communism. The reasons are many, but certainly one of the main ones is that films dealing with life in other countries— especially depressing lives in other countries—are not big box-office draws in the United States. Indeed, serious dramas themselves are on the decline in the United States, as the demographics of the average moviegoer dictate the production of more CGI (computer graphic imagery) action films, light romantic comedies, and graphic horror films. None of these genres fit the profile of a historically based film on individuals struggling against the oppressions of Communism.

Kenneth Lloyd Billingsley, author of *Hollywood Party: How Communism Seduced the American Film Industry During the 1930s and 1940s*, wrote in 2000 that "Indeed, in the decade since the Berlin Wall fell, or even the decade before that, no Hollywood film has addressed the actual history of communism, the agony of the millions whose lives were poisoned by it, and the century of international deceit that obscured Communist reality. The simple but startling truth is that the major conflict of our time, democracy versus Marxist-Leninist totalitarianism, is almost entirely missing from American cinema."[16] He continues that this void is even stranger given the many individual dramatic stories that the Cold War era produced. "The conflict encompasses millions of dramatic personal stories played out on the grand tapestry of history:

courageous Solidarity unionists against a Communist military junta; teenagers facing down tanks in the streets of Budapest and Prague; writers and artists resisting the kitsch of obscurantist materialism; families fleeing brutal persecution, risking their lives to find freedom."[17]

Given the realities of the American motion picture industry and its heavy dependence on moviegoers out to find escape on Saturday nights, it is unlikely that many more films will be produced illuminating the courage of those who resisted Communism. The nexus of America's moviegoers is the 20-something ticket buyer who has only a cloudy notion of what the Iron Curtain was all about, anyway.

SUMMARY

Some might ask, "Why spend a chapter discussing how movies have depicted Communism over the years? Movies aren't real, are they?" The answer is that some films come very close to depicting the eras they portray, while still managing to deliver an entertaining and artistic movie in the process. Further, although even the best of commercial films take some artistic liberties with sequencing of events and characters, the *impact* these films have on filmgoers is very real indeed. In America, as in so much of the world, much of our view of what happens—and what has happened—in the world is provided us by the news and entertainment media. Films become powerful influences in how we perceive the world and its different eras of history. The Cold War was such an era in world history. It affected Americans to the core, and many films—such as the ones described in this chapter—helped Americans navigate through complex issues and, often, showed the absurdities of both Communism and the paranoia that arose in reaction to what would ultimately be a failed political and economic system. Of course hindsight is often 20/20, and Americans of the Cold War era did not know Communism would collapse in 1989 with the first breach of the Berlin Wall. Any film can only portray conditions as they are and how reactions to those conditions might make sense or—on the other hand—be as insane as the threat itself. Some films did this through serious drama; others did it through comedy; some mixed both in presenting the story. Taken together, the films about the Cold War era provide a pretty comprehensive analysis of the tensions that existed when the Wall separated the world.

NOTES

1. Florian Henckel van Donnersmarck, director, *The Lives of Others*. Retrieved from http://www.sonyclassics.com/thelivesofothers/swf/ on November 1, 2011.

2. Ibid.

3. Ibid.

4. Ibid.

5. Terry Lawson, *"The Lives of Others"* (review), *Detroit Free Press*. Retrieved from http://www.rottentomatoes.com/m/the_lives_of _others/ on November 7, 2011.

6. Roger Moore *"The Lives of Others"* (review), *Orlando Sentinel*. Retrieved from http://www.rottentomatoes.com/m/the_lives_of_others/ on November 7, 2011; Richard Nilsen, *"Goodbye Lenin"* (review), *Arizona Republic*. Retrieved from http://www.rottentomatoes.com/m/good_bye _lenin/reviews/?type=top_critics on November 8, 2011.

7. Mark Jenkins, *"Goodbye Lenin"* (review), *Washington Post*. Retrieved from http://www.rottentomatoes.com/m/good_bye_lenin/reviews/? type=top_critics on November 8, 2011.

8. Ibid.

9. Jordan Hiller *"Sunshine"* (review). Retrieved from http://www .bangitout.com/articles/viewarticle.php?a=1596 on November 9, 2011.

10. "Announcement of the First Provisional Government, 13 March 1917." Retrieved from www.FirstWorldWar.com on November 7, 2011.

11. Vincent Camby, *"Reds"* (review), *New York Times*. Retrieved from http://movies.nytimes.com/movie/review?res=9406E4DC103BF937A35 751C1A967948260&partner=Rotten%20Tomatoes on November 7, 2011.

12. Ibid.

13. *One Day in the Life of Ivan Denisovich*. Retrieved from www .glencoe.com/sec/literature/litlibrary/pdf/one_day_in_life.pdf on November 2, 2011. Signet Classics: New York City, 1998.

14. "Billy Wilder Gets Hot over the Cold War." Retrieved from http:// www.imdb.com/title/tt0055256/reviews on October 30, 2011.

15. Jonathan Rosenbaum, "Dr. Strangelove." Retrieved from http:// www.chicagoreader.com/chicago/dr-strangelove-or-how-i-learned-to-stop -worrying-and-love-the-bomb/Film?oid=1067167 on October 28, 2011.

16. Kenneth Lloyd Billingsley, "Hollywood's Missing Movies: Why American Films Have Ignored Life under Communism." Retrieved from http://www.freerepublic.com/focus/f-news/939417/posts on January 1, 2012.

17. Ibid.

8

THE NEWS MEDIA'S ROLE UNDER COMMUNISM

Perhaps the best way to start a chapter on how the news media was used by Communist regimes to build and perpetuate their ideology is to read how an early Communist editor framed what the role of journalism should be in a Communist state:

> Long before we started to publish the Daily Worker we were many times admonished by the Executive Committee of the Communist International, and by Lenin personally, that we must take up this heavy task at all costs. Lenin often said that the publication of a national, daily political organ was one of the first prerequisites for the consolidation of a real political party. His maxim that such a paper should be "the collective propagandist, agitator and organizer of the movement" is familiar to most Communists.
>
> The Daily shapes the ideological unity of the party and gives a lead to the entire left wing movement on all decisive questions, even in the farthest outposts of the class struggle and the remotest sections of our vast country.
>
> A stronger staff, from a Communist political standpoint, is one of the first prerequisites to the execution of the decision of the Political Committee. The staff as a whole must be nearer to the party and, for the most part at least, have a stronger background of party experience and political understanding. It is true that newspaper work is a trade for which certain technical qualifications are more or less necessary. It is also true, however, that Communist journalism can be successfully practiced only by those who have a certain minimum of acquaintance with the principles of Communism and the history of the labor movement. Workers can be trained

for these tasks. It is easier, as a rule, to make a journalist out of a Communist than to make a Communist out of a journalist.

—*James P. Cannon*[1]

These words, written about the Communist Party's main newspaper in early twentieth century Russia, captured the essence of how Soviet leaders over the next several decades perceived the role of journalists in Communist societies. As long as Communism was in power in Eastern Europe, the news media were supposed to be tools of the Communist Party in mobilizing support, delivering ideology to the masses, and essentially serve as propaganda instruments of the government. Throughout most of Communism's reign in that region, this is what most of the media did, although some countries were stricter than others about enforcing the boundaries within which the media operated. The means these governments used to control the press came through censorship, as well as managing personnel and the equipment needed for production of newspapers and newscasts. Looking at the news media in these states before the end of Communism and after the fall of the Iron Curtain provides a stark contrast of how journalists operate under oppressive conditions versus conditions of freedom. Since Russia set the tone for the rest of the Communist world to follow in Europe and Western Asia, we will focus on the Soviet stance toward media freedom. First, however, let's look at some ideas about the role of the media in any nation's development.

THE MEDIA AND NATIONAL DEVELOPMENT

The news media serve several important functions in the development and maintenance of any nation. One of those roles is agitator, and it is a role that authoritarian and Communist governments have traditionally had trouble with, unless of course the media were agitating in favor of the ruling party. Media professor and authority John C. Merrill has noted about this agitator role of the press:

When we examine the world media today, we get the feeling that the jangled nerves of the world's populations can hardly be eased by the newspapers—and certainly not by TV. On the contrary, anxieties are crated, magnified, and perpetuated, religion is set against religion, social class against social class, race against race, and nationality against nationality. Instead of being conveyers of enlightenment and harmony, the national media systems tend too often to be mere extensions of factional and party differences and animosities, thus doing a good job of increasing irritations and suspicions among groups and governments and giving distorted pictures of various nations.[2]

Certainly this is one role that is hard to deny. In any society, journalists are seen as a rather unruly lot who are capable of breaking embarrassing news stories before politicians have a chance to put their own spin on events. Further, journalists are prone to focusing on the conflict and the differences between ideologies, organized groups of parties, and individuals. It is the main reason many of those restraints are tight indeed, and the Communist nations of Eastern Europe were no exception. As Merrill points out in his voluminous writings on international media, some media add their own ideological slants to the message they deliver to the public. In Communist Europe, that slant was intentional and was designed to give a larger voice to the socialist philosophy of Communism. The quotation that opens this chapter is a good example of how that was supposed to happen.

Merrill asserts, "There have been few truces in global psychological warfare. As technology pushes mass messages into the more remote regions and saturates ever-growing populations, the world's psychosis is bound to worsen."[3] He adds, however, that even truthful media messages are not guaranteed to enlighten or stabilize the individual recipients of those messages. By their very nature, the media beam their messages to a mass audience that by its nature is diverse and layered, and each of which is influenced by its own subcultures. Added to this group diversity is the individual mindset of experiences that differs from other individual mindsets. So many filters are at work among the audience members, and they influence how the message is received for that individual or for that subgroup. Message intended does not always equal message received. What one takes into hearing a message will influence what one takes away from it.

The leaders of the Communist Party knew this all too well. They understood from their own revolutionary days of 1917 how the press could be used to agitate and coalesce the public around an idea, a cause, or a movement. Now that Communism was entrenched in Eastern Europe, they needed the press to turn from its role of *agitator* and into the role of *stabilizer*, always reminding the populace of their responsibilities in a Communist society and always promoting the tenets and ideas of Communism.

The leadership of the Party understood not only their history but also the history of countries like the United States where the media played such a huge role in the development and stabilization of society, albeit one built around capitalistic and democratic ideas. History shows that the genesis for America is found within an impassioned group of writers, impatient for freedom and separation from the perceived tyrannical and controlling forces of England. Ideas were in circulation long before—and during—the colonial days of America in the work of such English penmen as John Milton, John Trenchard, Thomas Gordon, Richard Steele, and Joseph Addison. Later, American colonial writers like Thomas Paine, Samuel Adams, and Benjamin Franklin contributed their inspiration. Before there was an American nation, there were the stirrings of early-day poets, essayists, pamphleteers, and journalists such as these men. If one were to look for articulation of the freedom of expression that America was built on, one would have to look no further than the writings of these wordsmiths.

Soviet leaders knew that if Communism was going to take root flourish, and dominate thinking in Eastern Europe, they also needed this kind of literary power that enflamed the hearts of the masses and gave wide and articulated voice to their enduring principles of Communist socialism. The difference between the way Communist leaders enlisted support from journalists and the way democratic leaders did it in America was obvious: In America the writers could develop their own thoughts and voluntarily contribute them to the cause. In Communist Eastern Europe, writers would be told what to write, and it was demanded that they contribute their words to the cause. That may well be a key reason why democracy is still flourishing in the West, while Communism has died in Europe.

THE SOVIET COMMUNIST PRESS THEORY

In 1956, a trio of communication scholars—Wilbur Schramm, Fred Siebert, and Theodore Peterson—developed a schema in a book called *Four Theories of the Press*.[4] The four theories were authoritarian, libertarian, Soviet Communist, and social responsibility. Each sought to explain the interplay between the news media and the governments around the world within which each operated. While the libertarian and social responsibility theories fit the nations of the West best, the authoritarian theory fit Third World nations, and the Soviet Communist theory fit the Soviet bloc countries during the years of the USSR. It is this Soviet Communist theory that most Communist nation journalists operated under. To a large degree, it also fits Communist nations still in existence, for example, China, North Korea, and even Cuba.

The Soviet Communist Theory developed in the early twentieth century in the USSR. The essence of this theory is stated by James P. Cannon in the quotation that begins this chapter. It grew out of the philosophy and writings of Karl Marx and Vladimir Lenin, and its purpose was to use the press to support the Marxist Communist system and—in an ideal sense never realized—to serve the people. In theory, the people of the Soviet Union were to own the press and use it; in reality, the leadership of the Communist Party owned the press and dictated its rules of use. Under this system, the news media were controlled by the Communist Party bureaucracy. The media operated under many restrictions, but the main one was that journalists were not allowed to criticize the objectives and ideals of the Communist Party. Criticizing the judgment of that party's leadership was also banned.

Here is how Merrill describes the development of the press under Communism:

> *When the Bolsheviks came to power in 1917, the overwhelming majority of the people that came to be included in the Soviet Union were out of reach of the mass media. Many were illiterate. Poorly developed infrastructure meant that distribution of newspapers was difficult. What became the Soviet Union at the beginning was a primarily rural society whose peasants saw little need for the media. Radio was the first medium to gain an important role throughout society. It was not until the 1960s and 1970s that the printed Soviet word began to reach the broad range of people. The Soviet journalists who wrote for these publications had multiple roles: ideological warrior, literary craftsman, publicist, investigative reporter, citizen's friend, and member of the collective. The most important newspapers were the all-Union papers, such as Pravda and Izvestiya, whose circulations climbed past 10 million. Journalism was designed to serve the party through a complex system of appointments, rewards, party control, and censorship.[5]*

Even after Mikhail Gorbachev began ushering in his openness policy of glasnost in 1985, many journalists were unsure of the degree of their freedom and proceeded cautiously. As it became apparent this was to be a new era of openness, however, the news media began investigating and exposing the warts of corruption and inefficiency in the Soviet Union, and championing plurality and debate among the people. For the everyday journalist,

Gorbachev's new policy translated to expanding the news agenda, acquiring more factual information, doing more human-interest news and—as Merrill calls it—"more moderately negative news."[6] This was true inside Russia; in other Soviet bloc states—like East Germany—the degree of openness lagged behind Russia's and was controlled by local party leadership. Before long, however, the leaders of these countries realized they could not maintain restraints that the Soviet leadership had already loosened.

It was this growing openness, as reflected in newspapers and even on television news, that helped to spur the demonstrators in East Berlin and that eventually led to the breach—and quickly the crumbling—of the Berlin Wall in November of 1989. The Iron Curtain was coming down at last. Before it did, however, many journalists lived under the fear of punishment, imprisonment, and/or exile for writing stories that made the Communist leadership look anything less than ideal and efficient. A few of their stories follow the next section.

THE SOVIET CONSTITUTION AND PRESS FREEDOM

Many people find it surprising to learn that the constitution of the Union of Soviet Socialist Republics (USSR) had a clause in it that sounded much like the First Amendment of the U.S. Constitution. In that clause, ostensibly, was the freedom granted to journalists to report the news without censorship. Although the Soviet constitution underwent three revisions from 1936 to 1977, this clause remained in all versions, although it was moved to different sections in each iteration. The original 1936 USSR constitution put press freedom into Article 50 of Chapter 7 called "The Basic Rights, Freedoms, and Duties of Citizens of the USSR." It read, in part, as follows:

> *In accordance with the interests of the people and in order to strengthen and develop the socialist system, citizens of the USSR are guaranteed freedom of speech, of the press, and of assembly, meetings, street processions and demonstrations.*
>
> *Exercise of these political freedoms is ensured by putting public buildings, streets and squares at the disposal of the working people and their organizations, by broad dissemination of information, and by the opportunity to use the press, television, and radio.*

It doesn't take much to see the additional phrasing, however, that sets this Soviet clause on press freedom apart from the U.S.

Constitution. That added phrasing is "In accordance with the interests of the people and in order to strengthen and develop the socialist system . . . " There is also that subtle phrase asserting that this freedom is guaranteed by the "opportunity" (not right) to use the press, television, and radio. In fact, this was not a right, but was a privilege reserved for those who the Soviet leadership thought would use these facilities in ways positive to the ideals and laws of the Communist Party. In an ironic twist on the Marxist/Leninist criticism of the West, chiding the elite of the West for controlling the means of production and thereby the wealth, the Soviet leadership wound up controlling the means of production of the country's mass media. If the government doesn't give you a printing press or a broadcast tower, then your "opportunity" to engage in journalistic freedoms is somewhat hollow. Add to that the imprisonment one could face for not engaging in journalism that is uplifting to Communist ideals, and you have a system that severely limited freedom of the press. Following are a few brave journalists from Communist countries who tried to report objectively in spite of these conditions.

IVA DRAPALOVA

When the Soviets invaded Czechoslovakia in 1968, becoming a journalist was the last thing on the mind of Iva Drapalova. This Czech mother had already passed the age of 40 and wanted nothing more than to raise her children in peace. But the oppressive changes wrought by the new Soviet rule would actually inspire Drapalova to change her plans and spend the next two decades trying to get news of conditions in her homeland out to the rest of the world.

As *Global Post* journalist Bruce I. Konviser would write in 2009, that was a lonely struggle for this Czech woman.

"Directly after the invasion, there were a lot of western journalists in Prague, and they all needed interpreters," she told Konviser. "Previously there was a whole group of interpreters who were very keen on working for the western journalists. But after the invasion they got scared. It's understandable. After all, none of us knew where it would lead . . . whether we would end up going to Siberia."[7]

Putting those fears aside, Drapalova said yes to working with the Associated Press (AP), serving as an interpreter and enabling them to report what was happening and what was being said about it in and around Prague. "I came to help for a week and I got hooked— and I stayed for the next 20 years," she said. "It was a time when we still hoped that something of the Prague Spring would be preserved. And I felt that perhaps helping these western journalists might help in preserving it."[8]

The Prague Spring was a period of political liberalization in Czechoslovakia, beginning on January 5, 1968, and ending when Soviet tanks rolled into Prague to crush it on August 21 of that year. Even though this time of additional freedoms came in the midst of Soviet-directed rule of the country, Czech leader Alexander Dubcek (first secretary of the Communist Party) took a chance on implementing reforms he felt were needed. Among the reforms Dubcek granted during those eight months were an easing of restrictions on travel, speech, and the news media. These were reforms designed to bring a partial democratization to the country, and they were just too much for the Soviet leadership to tolerate. The liberalization was crushed by force. In a way, however, the Prague Spring became seen by many as "socialism with a human face."

Drapalova felt deeply inspired by the Prague Spring, along with many of her fellow countrymen and -women. It was that inspiration that caused her to risk her life to assist AP reporters in telling the story of the Czech Republic, and later to tell it herself as a journalist. It endured the dismantling of those reforms by heavy-handed Soviet invaders in the late summer of 1968, and it lasted during the Soviet occupation of the country, during which Czech citizens were under the thumb of one of the most repressive regimes in the Soviet galaxy of states the USSR controlled.

As Drapalova told the *Global Post*, "You had to make a conscious decision to do this work because you had to accept certain things. You had to accept that you would be under surveillance all the time; that your phone calls could be listened to; that your letters could be opened."[9] She realized it would be easy for an East-Central European country of 15 million people to be forgotten by the free world, populated by people wrapped up in their own pursuits and distractions. So she made a vow to export news of her country to the world beyond the Iron Curtain, hoping for the day when help might come from outside. As it turned out, however, the help came from inside the Communist states and began with Soviet Premier Mikhail Gorbachev's policies of glasnost and perestroika. In Prague itself, brave Czech citizens would arise in number and begin leading the "Velvet Revolution" on November 17, 1989, which unseated the Communists from the halls of power.

During the two decades Drapalova was telling the Czech story, she realized she was in peril and that both reformers and hardline

Communists might distrust her motives as well as her allegiance. "You were suddenly alone," she told Konviser. "You couldn't belong to either side, and both sides would think that you were working for the other side. You were completely dependent on your integrity."[10]

She said it was often impossible to convince Americans that she wasn't working for the Czech authorities, and there was no way for her to convince the Czechs that she wasn't a spy for the Americans. Due to her hard work and painstaking attention to accuracy, however, most Western journalists who knew her became convinced of her objectivity. That said, Drapalova did acknowledge that she censored herself several times. "Not because I was scared but because there was no point in getting the bureau shut. I might have been a heroine for a few days [if she had been more aggressive at times] but that would be the end of AP. It already happened once in 1952."[11] In fact, the Prague AP bureau did not reopen after that year for another 15 years.

THE MARTON FAMILY

In her book *Enemies of the People*, Hungarian-born journalist Kati Marton discovered many stories of courage while digging through the formerly secret files of the Hungarian Secret Police (AVO). Among the stories she came across were those of her own parents, Endre and Illona Marton. Through her research, Kati found out about the challenges and hardships faced by these two Hungarian journalists who risked imprisonment during the 1950s by writing hundreds of articles about life behind the Iron Curtain as reporters for both the United Press (UP) and the Associated Press, the two premier news agencies of the time.

The legacy of her parents was handed down to Kati, who has written several books and was married to the late Peter Jennings, long-time anchor for ABC News. She later married U.S. Ambassador Richard Holbrooke, so she has accumulated a deep well of information about international affairs. But the seed was planted by her courageous parents.

Kati, who lived her first eight years in Hungary, from 1949 to 1957, has stated that *Enemies of the People: My Family's Journey to America*, is her means of honoring her late parents and other courageous journalists like them who helped in bringing the Cold War era to an end.

Writer Hope Katz Gibbs has included Marton as one of her Truly Amazing Women Who Are Changing the World, which is a study

Acclaimed journalist and author Kati Marton speaks
during a memorial service for her husband Richard
Holbrooke at the Kennedy Center on January 14,
2011, in Washington, DC. (AP Photo/Carolyn Kaster)

of 131 women from different professions who have helped bring
peace and prosperity to the world.[12] About Marton, Gibbs says
she was "opening a Pandora's box" when she decided to dig into
the AVO files to find information about her journalist parents.

Among the things she discovered were that her parents—like
many other journalists and dissidents in Communist countries—
were actually spied upon by close friends, who relayed that information to the AVO. Being a writer for a Western news service while
living in a Communist country was like living in a hall of mirrors,
never knowing which of your friends' reflected personas were real
and which were mere images. In the case of the Martons, the secret

police seemed bent on arresting them if only they could get enough solid information from their informants. That the Martons had made several friendships with Americans and lived an affluent lifestyle only made the job easier for the AVO in perceiving them as traitors.[13]

Marton first visited the AVO archives several years ago and was shown hundreds of pages that had been accumulated on her parents. She has said that "Everybody in your circle, whether your parents trusted or did not trust them, was informing on them. That was just the way it was."[14]

Marton writes that the AVO was the chief instrument of the Sovietization policy that Russia imposed on Hungary. The AVO had been created immediately following World War II and was made up of 17 divisions, each with a special function. It was Hungary's version of East Germany's Stasi or Russia's KGB. In fact, the AVO reported to KGB officers. Its method of operation was brutality, and it had the Soviet army waiting in the wings to help enforce things if they got out of hand with Hungarian citizens. It was, in effect, a Soviet party within the Hungarian Communist Party. One of its most dreaded divisions was Division One, the unit whose function was to infiltrate and control Hungarian life by using a vast network of informants. Again, similarities to the Stasi are apparent. Often these informants were "recruited" through intimidation tactics that included being snatched from their beds while they slept in the middle of the night. They were arrested and offered immediate release if they would inform on their friends, neighbors, and even loved ones.[15]

"Your mother and father were indispensable," an American reporter once told Kati. "They gave us leads that we didn't have. They were models of what journalists should be under difficult circumstances. They were bright, and had such charm and such professional integrity ... We really cared about them. We knew they were on thin ice. But they just kept on reporting."[16]

As Jonathan Yardley of the *Washington Post* wrote, "The ice grew thinner as (Matyas) Rakosi's government gradually expelled all Western journalists, leaving the Martons, in effect, the outside world's only reliable source of information about what was going on in Hungary."[17]

In the introduction to *Enemies of the People*, Kati Marton writes, "All of my life, my parents' defiance of the Communists, their stubborn courage as the last independent journalists until their arrest, trial and conviction as CIA spies, has been at the core of our family identity. On Feb. 25, 1955, at two in the morning following a game of bridge at the home of the U.S. military attaché, my father was abducted by six agents of the AVO . . . His arrest was front-page news in The *New York Times*. Four months later, they came for my mother."[18]

Endre was detained and interrogated for four months by the AVO. He was sentenced to six years in prison. Illona was arrested on a trumped-up charge of "discussing the price of eggs and meat" with American journalists and of being a "permanent" advisor to them. She was sentenced to three years in prison. Marton writes that, ironically, her parents were never traitors to Hungary and they both considered themselves to be loyal Hungarians. They disagreed with the Soviet-enforced policies, however, and wrote about conditions in Hungary for the outside world, which was more than enough for them to be jailed. Thanks mostly to intense Western diplomatic pressure, however, both were released suddenly in 1956, serving only a fraction of their sentences.

During her parents' time behind bars, however, young Kati and her sister Juli were sent by the state to live with a Hungarian couple. But Marton writes that this couple were polar opposites from her parents, and both she and her sister longed for a time when they would be reunited. That would happen much sooner than expected, and the family escaped to America shortly after the state released Endre and Illona. Shortly after their arrival, Endre received a special George Polk Memorial Award for Distinguished Achievements in Journalism for his work in telling Hungary's story to the outside world. Endre continued his work for the Associated Press for many years, based in Washington—and still under the surveillance of AVO agents.[19]

Near the end of her book, Kati writes about the influence that her parents—especially her father—had in her life: "No one played a bigger role in my life than my father, who was so sparing with praise. I think I even chose my life partners with him in mind. In 1977, when I was hired as an ABC News foreign correspondent, Papa told me to observe and learn from Peter Jennings."[20] Kati did and wound up marrying Jennings and, although they divorced, her father still considered him his son-in-law. Marton later married Holbrooke, then an assistant secretary of state.

SOVIET JOURNALISTS

During the Cold War era of the Iron Curtain, most journalists in the Soviet Union belonged to the Union of Journalists, an organization controlled by the Communist Party. Some 74,000 reporters and editors belonged to this union and, as late as 1988, about 80 percent of the membership belonged to the Communist Party. Moreover, all the top newspaper editors belonged to the Central Committee of the Communist Party of the Soviet Union. Clearly, Soviet government leaders wanted to make it clear to journalists that their loyalties lay first with the party; then to journalism. The Communist Party extended control over journalists by controlling journalism schools, such as the large one at Moscow University. In those classes, party history, ideals, and protocol were taught alongside the protocol of writing a good story. By the late 1980s, however, things were changing under Yuri Andropov and Mikhail Gorbachev. Journalists were allowed to cover Politburo sessions and write short articles, and Gorbachev's glasnost policies brought more opportunities for journalists to report on Soviet domestic and foreign affairs. Whereas before Gorbachev came to power the media were not supposed to report on issues involving crime, drugs, natural disasters, injuries suffered in the workplace, official organs of censorship, and so on, the Gorbachev era pushed back these restrictions.

Starting in 1983, American journalist Watson Sims began a nine-year tenure of chairing a committee of the American Society of Newspaper Editors (ASNE) on exchanges with Soviet journalists, working with five Soviet delegations of reporters and editors in the United States and five ASNE delegations in the Soviet Union. In 1992, he directed a Gallup Institute study on Russian journalists' attitudes about the concept of freedom of expression. From his exchanges with Russian journalists, he came to realize that—while there were stark differences between U.S. and Soviet journalists— there were also similarities. For example, there were attitudes toward their profession that intercultural communications might call etic—or universally shared—attitudes across cultures. In describing this, Sims wrote for Nieman Reports in 2003 the following:

> We shared a number of concerns. Among them was the perception and reception our reporting received from our respective audiences. Public image is a concern for all whose work reaches an audience. But it offers a special challenge for journalists, who rarely own the organizations for which they work and are often subject to guidance in their presentation of news. Publishers may demand excessive profits or special treatment for advertisers or sponsors. Governments may restrict reporting on grounds of security. Consumers generally

prefer good news to bad news and can resent those who bring unwelcome messages.[21]

To illustrate his point, Sims cited the following story told to him by Vitaly Chukseev, foreign editor of the Russians' Tass News Agency.

A Russian journalist fell in love with a girl whose father, thinking her too young to marry, sent her to live with a distant relative. Years later, they met again, and the journalist learned that the girl had borne his son. "Why didn't you tell me?" he asked. "Father wouldn't let me," she replied. "He would rather have a bastard grandson than a journalist son-in-law."

Citing a similar story from America that made the same point, Sims responded: *I told Chukseev it reminded me of William Tecumseh Sherman's reaction when the general was told three journalists had been killed during the siege of Vicksburg: "Good! Now we'll have news from hell before breakfast."*[22]

Backing up the anecdotes with statistics, Sims points to a November 2002 study by the Gallup Organization that discovered just 26 percent of Americans surveyed rated U.S. journalists "high or very high" on ethical and honesty scales. A similar study done at Moscow State University revealed only 13 percent of Russian citizens perceive journalists as trustworthy.[23]

The United States–Soviet exchange that Sims chaired took a long time in coming about, and the wariness of journalistic organizations on both sides of the world reflected the high degree of tension of the Cold War era. The exchanges were originally proposed in 1969 by the ASNE but, according to Sims, the Union of Soviet Journalists responded, "We have nothing to exchange in that area."[24] Fourteen years later, the same view was shared by A. M. Rosenthal of the *New York Times*. Rosenthal wrote in a letter to the ASNE leadership that "These are not simply journalists—in some cases not journalists at all—but officials of a society devoted to the repression of any form of free expression, particularly the press."[25]

Other leading U.S. editors disagreed with Rosenthal, however, saying—in effect—nothing ventured, nothing gained. So the exchanges began later in 1984. Even then, top U.S. officials were putting up roadblocks and saying nothing could be gained by conversations between "apples and oranges." But the ASNE persevered, and five different exchanges of 115 Soviet and American journalist delegations took place over the next six years. Sims notes it is doubtful that the last four exchanges would have taken place at all had it not been for Mikhail Gorbachev's policy of openness—glasnost—"which led to laws guaranteeing newspapers the right to publish and permitting journalists greater freedom to travel and report news."[26]

The exchanges produced windows into other countries and showed the challenges that Soviet journalists faced in Russia and the states it controlled. It also gave journalists from both sides of the Iron Curtain a chance to discuss their contrasting styles. Sims notes the following instance, for example:

> During a 1987 meeting, Viktor Afanasyev, editor in chief of Pravda and chairman of the Union of Soviet Journalists, boasted that a telephone on his desk led directly to President Gorbachev. Boris Yeltsin, then Moscow city boss, had criticized the party's leadership, and Jim Gannon, editor of The Des Moines Register, had a suggestion: "Pick up the phone and ask Gorbachev what he's going to do with Yeltsin."

Although that would have been the action of an American journalist, it would have not fit the more restrictive parameters that Afanasyev and his Russian colleagues were operating under.

At times, visiting Soviet journalists would even remark in their own newspapers about differing conditions in the United States and even wistfully ask why Russia had to be so restrictive. Risky business, but it did happen. For example, Nadezjda Garifullina wrote the following in her Kazakhstan paper in 1988:

> *An attentive, respectful attitude toward the client, worrying about whether he is comfortable, whether he is satisfied—this is in the blood of the American service industry. We were not asked for documents in a single hotel, which is done so unceremoniously in our own country. I hope readers will not accuse me of lack of patriotism, but why can they and why can't we? Why is it that in any American store you can examine goods and no one demands to look into your purse when you walk out? Why are such things possible over there and not here?*[27]

"We once did not write about such things as crime or earthquakes," *Pravda* editor Afanasyev told an ASNE delegation in 1987, "but now we have no taboos." In Leningrad, an ASNE delegation found *Pravda* campaigning against the sale of stale bread in city bakeries and failure of the city's streetcars to operate on schedule. In Samarkand, a delegation found the newspaper *Lenin's Path* under fire for publishing an article on suicide among young Muslim women. Boris Shegolikhin, the newspaper's editor, said complaints came not only from the city council, but also from displeased readers. "Editors sit at different tables, but they eat the same bread," said Shegolikhin. "An editor's bread is tough to eat."

After the collapse of the USSR into smaller, individual states, the problem of publishing news worsened. Russia's newspapers were relatively free to publish, but where was no revenue stream coming from advertising or anywhere else to replace what the government used to provide via subsidies to the media under Communism. Thousands of newspapers were launched, only to fail for lack of support. In 1995, Vsevolod Bogdanov, chairman of the Union of Russian Journalists, which succeeded the Union of Soviet Journalists, reported that Russian journalists earned only $30 to $40 per month. "The economy is poor, and most journalists know their papers can close at any time," said Bogdanov. "When they work, it is under very dangerous conditions, with too many being attacked and murdered. Many journalists say they cannot live without subsidies." He noted that much of the media's support came from individuals, political parties, or criminal elements seeking to manipulate public opinion.[28]

NOTES

1. James P. Cannon, "The Voice of the Communist Movement." Retrieved from http://www.marxists.org/archive/cannon/works/1928/voicemvt.htm on October 14, 2011.

2. John C. Merrill (Ed.), *Global Journalism: Survey of International Communication* (3rd ed.). White Plains, NY: Longman, 1995, xiv.

3. Ibid.

4. Merrill, p. 5.

5. Ibid.

6. Merrill, p. 173.

7. Bruce I. Konviser, "A Journalist behind the Iron Curtain," *Global Post*, November 17, 2009. Retrieved from http://www.globalpost.com/dispatch/czech-republic/091117/journalist-behind-the-iron-curtain on October 11, 2011.

8. Ibid.

9. Ibid.

10. Ibid.

11. Ibid.

12. Hope Katz Gibbs, "Truly Amazing Women Who Are Changing the World." Retrieved from http://trulyamazingwomen.com/the-women/journalist-kati-marton on October 12, 2011.

13. Ibid.

14. Ibid.

15. Ibid.

16. Ibid.

17. Jonathan Yardley, "Behind the Iron Curtain," *Washington Post*, October 18, 2009. Retrieved from http://www.washingtonpost.com/wp-dyn/content/article/2009/10/16/AR2009101601236.html on October 12, 2011.

18. Gibbs.

19. Yardley.

20. Ibid.

21. Watson Sims, "Journalists Built a Bridge of Understanding between East and West," Nieman Reports, Spring 2003. Retrieved from http://www.nieman.harvard.edu/reportsitem.aspx?id=101263 on October 13, 2011.

22. Ibid.

23. Ibid.

24. Ibid.

25. Ibid.

26. Ibid.

27. Ibid.

28. Ibid.

9

THE FINAL YEARS OF EUROPEAN COMMUNISM

Like a singer who labors for years in obscurity and then lands the break making her an "overnight success," the menace of the wall vanished on the night of Nov. 9, 1989, in the blink of an eye that took almost three decades to shut.[1]

The fall of the Berlin Wall and the collapse of Communism in Europe did not happen overnight. And yet from the first moment in August 1961, when the East German government decided to put its people in a concrete-and-steel cage, the seeds of that collapse began to take root. The soil was rocky, to be sure, so the plants grew slowly. It would be three decades before the 16 million East Germans and the millions in other Soviet-controlled territories were to begin feeling significant relief.

Ironically, that relief would come from the leader of the Soviet Union itself. His name was Mikhail Gorbachev. For its part, the leadership of East Germany was unwilling to move as quickly as Russia did in granting greater freedoms to its people. But those same GDR leaders knew they could not rebel for long against the mother ship of the Soviet empire. Because Russia controlled the Soviet Union, and because Gorbachev led Russia, it is worth spending time looking at the ripple of reforms in Russia that became rivers that produced a tsunami of changes in Eastern European countries and the world at large.

THE REFORMS OF GORBACHEV

Certainly the collapse of Communism in Eastern Europe resulted from several stimuli. But Mikhail Gorbachev was one of the leading reasons that reform would come. This man who would redraw the face of Europe and reset the political climate of the world, came from humble beginnings. Gorbachev was born on March 2, 1931, in rural Russia to a peasant family in a small agricultural village. His father worked as a mechanic on a collective farm. In 1945, Gorbachev himself started out in farming as an assistant to a combine harvest operator. By the age of 18, he had shown his dedication and leadership skills, and was awarded the Order of Red Banner of Labour. The next year, he was accepted into the School of Law at Moscow University, and it was obvious Mikhail Gorbachev would not be spending his adult years on a farm.

A loyal Communist, Gorbachev had been a member of the Communist Youth Organization known as Komsomoi and then joined the Communist Party of the Soviet Union (CPSU). In 1955, he received his law degree at the age of 24. Over the next five years, he would rise in leadership positions in the local and regional Communist parties. He earned a second degree at Stavropol Agricultural Institute, becoming an expert in farm issues, and in 1970 was appointed First Secretary for the Stavropol territory, supervising an area of 2.4 million people. He was appointed to the CPSU Central Committee in 1971, moved to Moscow, and became Secretary of Agriculture in the Central Committee. In 1980, he became the youngest full member of the Politburo, and in 1985 was elected General Secretary of the CPSU.[2]

After assuming party leadership in 1985, Gorbachev ("Gorbi" as the East German protestors affectionately called him in their demonstrations) launched policies that set the collapse of Communism in motion. Soon after taking office, he drew up social and economic reforms for the Soviet Union. It would be wrong to say Gorbachev was abandoning Communist principles, however. He remained a staunch Communist, but he also was smart enough to see that the system was full of corruption and inefficiency.

He knew these twin problems were pulling the Soviet Union down, so several of his reforms were really meant to breathe new life into a failing system. He believed, for example, that the sagging economy might be revived by less government control. He also felt that Russians were responding to the pessimism they felt by drinking way too much and that widespread alcoholism endangered the mental and physical health of Soviet citizens. It also made them lazier in the workplace, which wasn't helping the economy either. Creativity and talent were being washed away not just by alcohol, but by the inefficient ways the government was using its people. Something had to be done if the Soviet Union had any chance of surviving and being a player on the world stage.

That "something" was *perestroika*, the Russian word for restructuring, but that also meant competition in business. Along with perestroika, Gorbachev launched a policy of *glasnost*, or greater openness and freedoms for the people of the Soviet Union. But restructuring would cost money. A lot of it. Since the biggest drain on Soviet resources was its military, Gorbachev took the unprecedented step of cutting military spending and transferring that money to his restructuring programs. This was a huge shift for a country that had been vying with the United States for leadership in the international arms race. The move was as controversial in Russia, as it always is in the United States whenever the government cuts the military budget. But Gorbachev knew that 25 percent of Soviet spending went to the military, and he decided to shift it to programs he thought would bear more fruit for the future.

PROBLEMS INCREASE

Russia's problems at home had been exacerbated when, in 1979, the Soviet Union invaded Afghanistan in an ill-fated attempt to stabilize the Communist government there, which was under assault from Muslim mujaheddin forces. Not only was this to be an expensive war with no end in sight—indeed many have referred to it as Russia's Vietnam—it also caused an even wider rift with the United States. Shortly after Ronald Reagan took office, he began publicly calling the Soviet Union "the evil empire," and the world seemed to become more polarized than before. To many, this military incursion by Russia across the borders of Afghanistan made the country and its Soviet bloc allies a band of outlaw nations in the world. The United States even went so far as to boycott the 1980 Olympics, which were held in Moscow.

In fact, Russia could not afford the nuclear arms race. Trying to keep up the pace—some would say *set* the pace—against the United States was costing the Soviet Union a lot of money, talent,

Red Square gives an impression of beauty to this part of the Soviet capital with St. Basil's Cathedral and its 10 domes in the foreground. In the background (right) is the historic museum and the medieval wall of the Kremlin with one of the Kremlin towers (left), July 1980. Moscow hosted the 1980 Summer Olympic Games. (AP Photo)

and energy. During Ronald Reagan's presidency, which began in 1980, the United States was pumping great amounts of money into arms spending, reequipping and expanding American military capabilities, particularly those of most concern to the Soviet Union.

So, by the mid-1980s when Gorbachev came to power, the Soviet Union was in serious trouble. One of the first things he ordered was a complete withdrawal from Afghanistan, refusing to throw more good money after bad and to put troops in harm's way without the promise of victory. Realizing the Soviet Union could no longer afford the nuclear arms race, Gorbachev began the Strategic Arms Reduction Talks (START) with America and then signed the Intermediate-Range Nuclear Forces Treaty in 1987.

Looking toward the USSR's economy, Gorbachev realized it was moving in reverse. Manufacturing plants had become outdated, and the goods produced lacked quality. These outdated factories were sending harmful pollutants into the air every day, and safety measures were lax at facilities, which could be dangerous to the population were accidents to occur there. One such major accident occurred at the nuclear power plant at Chernobyl, where an explosion occurred in 1986, killing many and rendering the surrounding countryside and water sources toxic. Instead of dealing with the Chernobyl incident outright, the Soviet government did what it always did: spent too much energy on trying to cover the problem up. It would be a long time before the world knew the full extent of this disaster.

These problems, and more, led to even worse economic conditions, and the Soviet Union contained some of the poorest populations in the world, without enough food and goods to go around. Public unrest was increasing because of the economic situation, but also because of continued state censorship and oppression by the KGB and local police.

Gorbachev's plan to reduce the government's role in the economy and its interference in people's lives smacked of democracy to many, and people all over Eastern Europe watched with hope and guarded optimism. Could their lives be about to change for the better? Could more freedoms finally be at hand? How could this one man pull it off?

INSPIRATION SPREADS TO POLAND

The inspiration that Gorbachev's reforms provided was widespread and immediate. In Poland, for example, changes were coming fast. The Communist government that had crushed the labor movement of Solidarity back in 1980 began allowing it to reorganize and even take part in free elections. Public support was important to the ruling Polish government and—as the GDR leadership was also seeing—it would be impossible to rule without public support. So, following Poland's first free elections since World War II, Solidarity not only survived as a political power, but became the party that launched the first non-Communist government in Eastern Europe. And the leader of that movement, Lech Walesa, became its first president.

SHOCK WAVES IN THE GDR

What happened in Poland produced shock waves in neighboring countries, and the Communist dominoes began to fall across Eastern Europe. Before long, the Communist regimes in Czechoslovakia, Hungary, Romania, and even East Germany became victims of the masses they had oppressed for so many years. And in the latter country—East Germany—the end came when GDR Chancellor

Erich Honecker declared the Berlin Wall open in 1989. That declaration was redundant, of course, because the East German people had already opened it for themselves on the night of November 9, 1989, when tens of thousands of them pushed through the border crossings, and past confused guards who let them pass into West Berlin. The next year, East and West Germany were reunited into a single country. Another peaceful revolution occurred in Czechoslovakia, while blood was shed in Romania as its Communist leader, Nicolae Ceausescu, was executed.

Mikhail Gorbachev did not have revolutions and the fall of European Communism in mind when he initiated perestroika. But like a wildfire ignited by a spark and fanned by high winds over a drought-ravaged countryside, there was no stopping the people's movements in Eastern Europe. Gorbachev himself, as the head of the most powerful country in the Soviet Union, couldn't even do it. He would have had to call up the might of the Red Army to do it, and the cost would have been destruction of the reforms he had launched and more international tensions with the West. It was too high a price to pay, so Soviet tanks stayed home while Gorbachev witnessed the crumbling of Communism. In doing so, he abandoned the Brezhnev Doctrine of deploying military force to preserve Communist rule in Eastern Europe. Instead, Gorbachev called upon the Communist leaders of Soviet bloc countries to find new ways of gaining popular support for their policies. That would prove impossible by any means short of leaving office and holding free elections.

In both Poland and Hungary, that meant sanctioning previously outlawed political parties and allowing free and competitive elections to take place. Whether rulers of the GDR liked it or not, these reforms were headed toward their country's borders.

ALL EYES ON THE WALL

All eyes were focused on the breaching of the Berlin Wall on November 9, 1989. That event was the high-water mark of all demonstrations and revolutions occurring in Eastern Europe, all of which were targeted at Communist leaderships. In one 24-hour period, the fall of the Wall became the most visible and focused symbol of the changes sweeping through these Communist countries. In country after country of the Soviet bloc of nations, demonstrators and reformists were taking to the streets and ripping power from the hands of the dictators who had oppressed and suppressed them for the four decades since the end of World War II.

The reform movements may have begun in Poland with Solidarity in 1980, but they coalesced at the border crossings of the Berlin Wall that night.[3] The revolutionaries in Hungary, Czechoslovakia, Romania, and other Soviet states were united in spirit with the joyous East Germans who sat boldly atop the wall with pick axes and hammers, chipping away at that barrier.

The televising of that celebration spurred on Czechs and Slovaks, who moved into the streets of their own cities to demand more freedoms. In Prague, the dissident playwright Vaclav Havel led the charge. For countries such as Czechoslovakia and East Germany, who had lived with the threat of government-imposed violence and bloodshed for so long, it is ironic that the people's revolutions in both of these countries took place without a shot being fired. In Prague, the Communist Party peacefully and quietly transferred its rule to Havel and his reformers in what was poetically called the Velvet Revolution. Before long, the Communist parties in both Albania and Bulgaria turned power over to reformers in those countries.

These were the demonstrations, protests, and revolutions—all occurring in 1989—that spelled the end of Communism in Eastern Europe. The revolutions spread into Russia itself as Communist regimes were overthrown in country after country. And the man who had inadvertently done so much to inspire them—Mikhail Gorbachev—was not spared the consequences, as he had to cede power in Russia to Boris Yeltsin. It would be Yeltsin who would oversee the final dissolution of the Soviet Union.

JOINING HANDS WITH ARTISTS

In the 1980s, after conditions had thawed between East Germany and the United States to allow the opening of a U.S. Embassy in East Berlin, the State Department had positioned cultural arts representatives like Peter Claussen to work with East German artists, musicians, and dramatists. Claussen, himself a former director and actor and not the most stereotypical State Department employee because of his opposition to the war in Vietnam, would prove helpful in making connections to the very people who were most often leading demonstrations in East Germany. These people were creative artists who, among other things, wanted to be able to express themselves more freely through their arts. It was the job of Claussen and other diplomats like him to make connections with these East Germans, develop joint creative projects, and bring the resources of America to help the arts grow in East Germany.[4]

The reality was that as the arts flourished there, so did the demonstrations for freedom. And it was these demonstrations that produced the fall of the Berlin Wall.

REAGAN AND GORBACHEV

These and other State Department efforts that helped lead to the end of the Cold War came, of course, under the American presidency of Ronald Reagan, the man who many sources credit with "winning the Cold War." Take, for example, the following assessment from historian Fred Kaplan, writing for *Slate* magazine:

> *So, did Ronald Reagan bring on the end of the Cold War? Well, yes. Recently declassified documents leave no doubt about the matter. But how did he accomplish it? Through hostile rhetoric and a massive arms buildup, which the Soviets knew they couldn't match, as Reagan's conservative champions contend? Or through a second-term conversion to detente and disarmament, as some liberal historians, including* Slate's *David Greenberg, argue?*
>
> *This is an uncomfortable position for an opinion columnist (and occasional Cold War historian) to take, but it turns out that both views have their merits; neither position by itself gets at the truth. Reagan the well-known superhawk and* Reagan the lesser-known nuclear abolitionist *are both responsible for the end of that era—along with his vital collaborator Mikhail Gorbachev.*[5]

Although it was not known at the time, both Gorbachev and Reagan shared a common fear and opposition to the buildup of nuclear weapons. Indeed, it was hard for many Americans and Russians to come to that realization since the two superpowers were seemingly engaged in an arms race at levels previously unknown. But here is how (after analyzing previously classified documents of the era) Samuel Wells, a Cold War historian at the Woodrow Wilson Center, described Reagan's view of nuclear arms: "His [Reagan's] staff, for all of the first term and most of the second, kept this out of the press. But Reagan was terribly, deeply opposed to nuclear weapons. He thought they were immoral."[6] Reagan believed his vision of a shield in outer space that would render nuclear weapons obsolete was the right way to go, even though many scientists thought the reality of that Strategic Defense Initiative (SDI) Program was impossible. Still, if it were to work, it might scare the Russians into talking seriously about mutual nuclear arms reductions.

A key moment in the thawing of the Cold War came in a face-to-face meeting between Gorbachev and Reagan in Reykjavik,

President Ronald Reagan and General Secretary Mikhail Gorbachev at the Pair's first summit in Geneva, Switzerland, on November 19, 1985. (Time & Life Pictures/Getty Images)

Iceland, in October 1986. As Fred Kaplan notes, "Reagan went far beyond Gorbachev's proposal of a 50 percent strategic-arms cut. To the alarm of some aides . . . he suggested that the two sides get rid of nuclear weapons altogether and *jointly* build an SDI system to guard against a nuclear revival."[7] Gorbachev, reacting with skepticism, initially dismissed the proposal. Later, however, he came to believe Reagan was genuine in his offer. Still, only limited progress was made in those 1986 talks. Gorbachev did say he would accept the "zero-nukes plan," but only if President Reagan agreed not to test nuclear weapons in outer space, which was a critical part of the SDI, or "Star Wars," plan. The American president countered he could not accept that condition.[8]

But Gorbachev returned to Russia convinced that his previous image of Reagan as a cowboy primed for a shootout was not accurate. He believed Reagan when he said America would not strike first in a nuclear war, and that was an important assurance for Gorbachev, who used it to convince the Politburo that Russian resources could safely be transferred from military to domestic spending without damaging Soviet security.

Kaplan concludes his assessment of the importance of the Reagan/Gorbachev relationship by writing:

> *In the last couple years of the Reagan administration, Reagan would propose extravagant measures in arms reductions. His hawkish aides would go along with them, thinking the Soviets would reject them (and the United States would win a propaganda victory). Then, to the surprise of everyone (except perhaps Reagan, who meant the proposals without cynicism), Gorbachev would accept them.*
>
> *In the end, Reagan and Gorbachev needed each other. Gorbachev needed to move swiftly if his reforms were to take hold. Reagan exerted the pressure that forced him to move swiftly and offered the rewards that made his foes and skeptics in the Politburo think the cutbacks might be worth it.*[9]

CIA ASSESSMENTS

It is interesting to look inside reports from America's Central Intelligence Agency (CIA) that were declassified years following the collapse of Communism, to see how intelligence experts depicted the then-coming changes in Europe in the last year or two of the Soviet Union. These CIA reports have been published in a book called *At Cold War's End: U.S. Intelligence on the Soviet Union and Eastern Europe, 1989–1991* (2000).

Some experts believe the most prophetic analysis of the late Gorbachev era was an informal CIA assessment prepared at the request of the National Security Council. This was Document 5 in the overall report and was titled "The Soviet Cauldron."[10] It was finished on April 25, 1991, and among other things predicted that "anti-Communist forces are breaking down the Soviet empire and system of governance." The prediction continued that there would be an attempted coup by Communist hardliners against Gorbachev, and that it would fail. This is exactly what did happen, actually. The intelligence experts said Boris Yeltsin would rise to become the first popularly elected leader in Russia's history. Further, the report predicted Yeltsin would set a new course for Russia, away from the old Communist guard. The analysis also accurately predicted that the surge toward independence by the Georgian, Baltic, Belorussian, and Ukranian republics would offer the most serious threat to the survival of the Soviet Union. While it didn't see the Soviet economic crisis as the most determining factor in the changes sweeping Russia, the Document 5 report did note that the country's entire economic system had fallen apart and was in the process of being replaced by Gorbachev's perestroika.

The new system was a mix of "republic and local barter arrangements, adding to already strong centrifugal forces."

After this April report came out, the administration of President George Herbert Walker Bush spent the summer watching the events in Russia and the Soviet Union with great interest and anticipation. Document 6 of the CIA analysis stated in part, "The USSR is in the midst of a revolution that probably will sweep the Communist Party from power and reshape the country within the five-year time frame of this estimate."[11] Of course it didn't take nearly that long. Six months would find the Communists gone from power in Russia and the Soviet Union. Not only were new governments put in place, but the Communist Party would be outlawed in the Soviet Union, which would itself break up into several different, independent republics. In place of the Union of Soviet Socialist Republics (USSR) would emerge the Commonwealth of Independent States (CIS). Further, Gorbachev would resign and Yeltsin would become his successor. As some experts said, the hard part was not predicting what would happen; just when.

A CONCERN ABOUT A BREAKUP

The United States was concerned, however, that the breakup of the Soviet Union into several independent states might make it harder to come to an international agreement on nuclear disarmament with these former Soviet states. Instead of dealing with one superpower, the United States would have to deal with several countries. There would be no "center" to maintain control over nuclear weapons production, research and development facilities, and test sites. What would happen to prevent a kind of "Dr. Strangelove" doomsday scenario where a mad general or nationalistic leader of one of the new independent states decided to push the button, sending his country's missiles toward Western targets? At least the current leadership of the Soviet Union was a known entity and somewhat predictable.

To forestall such possibilities, President Bush decided in September 1991 to remove or destroy all tactical nuclear weapons deployed in Europe and Asia, and on U.S. warships. He also canceled plans to deploy the mobile MX and certain other missiles. U.S. bombers and missiles that were scheduled for destruction under START were taken off 24-hour alert status. Bush then called upon Gorbachev to adopt additional arms control measures, including elimination of all land-based intercontinental ballistic missile systems (ICBMs) with multiple warheads. In response, Gorbachev—living out his last days as leader of the Soviet Union—announced his decision to dismantle all tactical nuclear weapons. He described this as "racing downhill" with America in arms control.[12] Both Bush and Gorbachev knew it was a race against time, however, and that it would be best to get it done before the USSR imploded and multiple leaders of individual republic states rose out of the ashes. No one in leadership on either side wanted renegade military officers to seize control of tactical nuclear weapons to use in localized conflicts or looming civil wars in the breakaway republics. The idea on both sides was to draft and sign binding disarmament agreements while the leadership in the Kremlin still had the power to complete this task.

In the end, American diplomats used CIA intelligence estimates to identify and seize an opportunity to bring the Cold War and the arms race to a close, and end the threat of mutual nuclear annihilation between the United States and the Soviet Union. Following up on work begun by Ronald Reagan and Mikhail Gorbachev, Presidents Bush and Gorbachev met five times at summits and maintained regular contact by phone and correspondence in between those meetings. This was in addition to the meetings between Secretary of State James Baker and Foreign Minister Eduard Shevardnadze. All of these meetings led to several formal and informal agreements that together led to the end of the Cold War era between the United States and the USSR. Many experts believe that even more than luck or deteriorating conditions in the Soviet Union in the 1980s, the end of the Cold War came because of the hard work of diplomats from both the United States and Soviet Union. According to this thinking, it proved ironic that it was diplomacy and détente—rather than confrontation and military might—that led to the collapse of the Soviet Union, Communism in Eastern Europe, and the nuclear arms race between Russia and the United States.

THE COLD WAR ERA ENDS

Along with the collapse of Communism in Eastern Europe came the end of the four-decades-old Cold War between the Communist world, headed by Russia, and the free democratic world, headed by the United States and countries of Western Europe. The end of that animosity, which had brought the world to the brink of nuclear war during the Cuban missile crisis of 1961, changed the political map of the world and allowed both sides to take a deep breath after holding it for so long. It allowed resources to be transferred from the full-scale nuclear arms race and let the U.S. government focus on something other than containing the expansion of Soviet power in Europe.

Not to be forgotten or minimized in any discussion of the end of the Cold War were the roles that U.S. diplomacy and American information policy (spearheaded by Radio Free Europe and Radio Liberty) played in the collapse of Communism in Europe. These efforts were responsible for providing a steady stream of information about democracy and freedom into the oppressed Communist regions. So many citizens of these countries were receptive to this information, and it helped inflame their zeal for democratic reforms. One senior embassy officer in Berlin, George Glass, said he would never want to diminish the role that the people of East Germany played in the fall of the Berlin Wall, but he would also not want to diminish the role that leaders like Ronald Reagan played either. Glass called the fall of the Wall, and the resulting end of the Cold War, "one of the great diplomatic success stories in history."[13]

The facts certainly appear to back that assessment up. Under Reagan's administration, the State Department was working behind the scenes to make the events of November 9, 1989, a reality. Without knowing how or when the breach of the Wall would take place, the Reagan administration knew it would happen because of the reports they had been getting from their embassy in Berlin.

NOTES

1. Jim Willis, "Fall of the Wall Saluted," *Oklahoman*, November 10, 1999, p. 1A.

2. "The Nobel Peace Prize 1990: Mikhail Gorbachev, Biography," Nobelprize.org. Retrieved from http://www.nobelprize.org/nobel_prizes/peace/laureates/1990/gorbachev-bio.html on January 2, 2012.

3. Interview with George Glass at the United States Embassy in Berlin on November 5, 2009, p. 175.

4. Interview with Peter Claussen at the United States Embassy in Berlin on November 6, 2011.

5. Fred Kaplan, "Ron and Mikhail's Excellent Adventure: How Reagan won the Cold War," *Slate*, June 9, 2004. Retrieved from http://www.slate.com/articles/news_and_politics/war_stories/2004/06/ron_and_mikhails_excellent_adventure.2.html on January 2, 2012.

6. Ibid.

7. Ibid.

8. Ibid.

9. Ibid.

10. Central Intelligence Agency (CIA), "At Cold War's End." Retrieved from https://www.cia.gov/library/center-for-the-study-of-intelligence/csi-publications/books-and-monographs/at-cold-wars-end-us-intelligence-on-the-soviet-union-and-eastern-europe-1989-1991/art-1.html on December 6, 2011.

11. Ibid.

12. Ibid.

13. George Glass interview.

10

NOVEMBER 9, 1989: THE NIGHT OF THE *MAUERFALL*

Jamila al-Yousef was born in a country that is no longer on the map. And her entry into the world came on the very night that changed the course of history in Europe; not only for her country but for the rest of the world.

The daughter of an East German mother and a Palestinian father, Jamila was born in East Germany on the night of November 9, 1989. That was the night that the Berlin Wall began to physically tumble under the axes and hammers of East Germans who had had enough and, in one massive stroke, breached that Wall.

Among the things that Jamila would not experience in her life were the following:

- The concrete and steel barrier that separated her country from freedom
- The heartbreaking news that some more of her countrymen—maybe even some relatives or friends—had been killed or imprisoned trying to get across the infamous "death strip" to scale the Wall itself
- The constant surveillance of the largest per capita secret police force in the world, commonly known as the Stasi

- The paranoia that came from knowing there is probably a Stasi informant embedded in your circle of friends; maybe even your family
- The threat of prison that awaited anyone who expressed too much of a desire to see the West or who applied more than once or twice to emigrate from East Berlin
- Living a schizoid life of appearing to believe what the East German Communist government leaders were telling you, all the while knowing you were probably being deceived
- The heavy restrictions placed on your travel to West Berlin to see friends and loved ones who were cut off from you or your family back in 1961 when the Wall went up and was named the "anti-Fascist protective rampart" by the East German government

Jamila's life would be different because the night of her birth signaled the death of not only the Berlin Wall, but also of European Communism. As the Christian Science Monitor *notes, "Ms. Yousef has known only freedom in her life, traveling through Europe, attending university in London, connecting with friends around the globe on Facebook, and talking on the cellphone. Whatever she knows about the Berlin Wall and the old East Germany has come from history books and family stories. Like millions of others in her generation, she has grown to maturity in a world where the wall no longer casts a shadow, a world where Germany is reunified."*[1]

"The fall of the Berlin Wall made my hometown disappear and gave birth to another Berlin," said Kira von Moers, an employment consultant. A native of West Berlin, Ms. von Moers says that in the years after the fall of the Wall, everything changed, from bus numbers to street names. "I like to live here, but it doesn't touch my heart anymore," she says. "Sometimes, I feel like a tourist."[2]

Beyond the city of Berlin, beyond the country of Germany itself, the everyday landscape of living would change dramatically from that night forward. With the Wall gone and East German Communism with it, at least as a ruling power, European Communism would wither and die over the next 14 months. As the *Monitor* notes, "From Bulgaria in the south to Poland in the north, the old order gave way to the new, change sweeping through Europe and later sweeping the Soviet Union into history. The cold war would eventually end. The United States and its allies won. The Soviet Union lost. Europe's eastern half was liberated. Germany was reunited."[3]

A LOOK AT THAT DAY

The morning of November 9, 1989, began like any other East Berlin morning. People were waking up to meet the day and go about their regular chores of getting ready for work or getting the kids ready for school. University students were headed to school, too, although this day seemed to provide a little anticipation for those who had been following—if not participating in—the student demonstrations that had grown louder and bolder in recent months. Students were pushing the government for reforms, and each day seemed to bring the question of how long the East German government could deny its own people some of the same newly given rights that Russian leaders were allowing their citizens. Everyone knew that the East German government could not hold out for long in the face of the Soviet Union's policies of perestroika and glasnost. But when would the day come that things would really change in East Germany? Could this be the day?

In the halls of power in East Berlin, government officials were mulling over how to respond to the latest round of pressure they were feeling. That pressure was being applied both from trying to fit in with relaxed Soviet policies as well from the streets outside where protest movements had been gaining steam and numbers. Still, no major announcements were being planned, which was why the early evening press conference of Guenter Schabowski, spokesman for the GDR government and its ruling SED Party, was so surprising. There was no reason to suspect that it would be anything but the dull briefing it always was, but that was not to be. A question from an Italian journalist changed the evening from routine to one of the most memorable times in European history.

Schabowski was asked by the reporter when a new law allowing East German citizens more freedom of travel would take effect. The reporter was referring to a statement that Schabowski had just made: "We decided today to make a regulation that will enable each citizen of the GDR to travel abroad over border crossings of the GDR."

Schabowski's famous response to the reporter's question—not sure of the correct answer but plunging ahead anyway—was, "As far as I know, that goes into effect now. Immediately." Since his press conference was being covered live on television, people watching the event across East Germany were stunned. Many headed toward the Berlin Wall to see if it was finally true, that they could finally travel more easily into West Berlin. When they arrived, they found tens of thousands of other East

During a news conference in East Berlin, November 9, 1989, East German politburo member Guenter Schabowski announces that those who want to visit other countries and then return still need a visa, but that visa requests will be handled without delay. (AP Photo/Lutz Schmidt)

Germans who were converging on the checkpoints in search of the same answer. As it would turn out, these everyday East Germans, emboldened by their numbers and feeling the tide had turned in their favor after 28 years of isolation from the West, would make their own answer that night by breaching the Wall.

DEMONSTRATIONS PAVE THE WAY

The night the Wall came down certainly did not happen without a prelude of demonstrations by GDR citizens that unfolded over several months prior to Schabowski's press conference on November 9. The demonstrators had been demanding political reform of its Communist leaders that included more individual freedoms, including the freedom to travel to the West. The demonstrations reached their zenith in the eastern city of Leipzig, where the Monday Demonstrators—whose numbers reached into the tens of thousands on a given night—were heard loud and clear across the GDR. Shouting, "We are the people!" and "Gorbi! Gorbi!," these demonstrators' voices reached the highest portals of power in East Berlin.

The latter chant was especially effective, referring as it did to Mikhail Gorbachev, the General Secretary of the Communist Party in the Soviet Union who had been initiating reforms in Russia since 1985. By praising Gorbachev, the demonstrators knew the GDR leadership would feel in a bind because of the influence that the Soviet Union still yielded over them. They couldn't very well arrest and jail demonstrators who were praising the leader of the Soviet Union. So, on October 9, one month to the day before the breach of the Berlin Wall in 1989, some 70,000 protestors took to the streets of Leipzig shouting their chants and pressing for reforms. Still, the hardline GDR government of Erich Honecker was not interested in implementing reforms. Refusal to back away from that position cost him his job just nine days after the Leipzig protest of October 9. He was replaced by Egon Krenz as head of the GDR, but the change was too little, too late. Most East Germans seemed to realize the end for the East German Communist regime was in sight.

THE NOVEMBER 4 DEMONSTRATION

Four weeks after the Leipzig demonstration, at least a half-million East Germans gathered on the morning of November 4 for a massive demonstration in Alexanderplatz. They had marched right past the East German parliament and the Privy Council Building. There would be no one in the GDR government that day who could evade knowing that the masses were rising up. Their chants demanding reforms in the GDR could be clearly heard across the Wall and the death strip separating the two Germanies. The massive demonstration and the rally that concluded it became a landmark in the democracy movement in East Germany. The idea and organization for the event was hatched by the New Forum, which was an alliance of those opposed to GDR policies, formed just two months earlier. At the core of the New Forum were Berlin's creative artists, who had voiced the loudest opposition against GDR leadership over the months preceding the rally.

The organizers registered the event officially beforehand, making it legal and challenging the government to actually deliver on the basic rights to freedom of assembly and of expression that were already in the GDR constitution. But those rights had never actually been granted nor implemented by the state, so the registration of this demonstration acted as a gauntlet thrown down for GDR leaders to pick up. Even the East German police seemed reluctant to intervene, as protest leaders promised there would be no violence. Actors with green and yellow sashes that bore the phrase No Violence *supervised the demonstrators. When the morning's demonstration unfolded, few police officers could be seen in Alexanderplatz.*

"Never before had Berlin experienced so much shared determination, spontaneous imagination and, despite all radicalism, circumspection," wrote German authors Hannes Bahrmann and Christopher Links.[4] Highly visible at the demonstration were many banners, voicing griev- ances and making demands, but doing both in clever ways and in witty articulations. Numerous speeches punctuated the morning. One speaker intoned, "The structures of this society must be changed if we are to become democratic and socialist. Let us create a democratic society, on a legal foundation, which is accountable!"[5]

Not all speakers were protestors, however. A few of them were actually GDR leaders like Guenter Schabowski himself, who drew choruses of criti- cism from many in the crowd. Bahrmann and Links wrote of the logic of allowing different kinds of speakers: "Even beforehand, there were solid arguments and discrepancies as to who one ... should let speak. [Organizer Henning Schaller said] My opinion was that the spectrum of speakers should be as broad as that which the whole collapsing GDR had to offer ... But then again and again we had to demand the crowd, who flared up at the hard-liners to let them talk and to listen carefully, because often enough of these speakers exposed themselves."[6]

For so many East Germans, the mere fact that this kind of massive dem- onstration against GDR leadership was allowed to take place at all was beyond belief. It certainly showed that, even in a tightly controlled society, the will of the masses of people must be heard by those in power. Otherwise, revolution is not far off. Equally amazing, for the first time in the history of the GDR, a demonstration for the democracy movement was broadcast live by GDR television. One of the news commentators noted in his coverage, "The people have overcome their speechlessness." And, on this same day, other large protest rallies were taking place in many other cities across East Germany. The moment of historic change was at hand.

CONFUSION AT THE HIGHEST LEVEL

This demonstration was the impetus behind Schabowski's state- ment the night of November 9 that the government would be allowing more freedom of travel. Whether this was actually a prom- ise the government had intended to keep or just another empty attempt at quelling the demonstrators, history will never know. When Schabowski added his unscripted response (that freedom to travel would start immediately), the floodgates opened, and a sea of East German citizens poured through the gates of the Berlin Wall.

The evening has been described by some as a comedy of errors and, by others, as one of the great accidents of history that resulted in one of the great victories for democracy. Mostly, though, it was an evening of confusion that turned into chaos for East German government leaders. As the *Christian Science Monitor* reported, "There was total confusion about precisely what it was that was supposed to happen 'immediately.' It had been expected that the leadership would ease travel abroad to try and stanch the flood of young East Germans who were escaping to the West every day via Hungary and Czechoslovakia, never to return. But it was clear that the party intended to maintain control by requiring official exit visas for travel and by preserving the presence of Soviet forces in East Germany."[7]

SCHABOWSKI RECALLS THAT NIGHT

Twenty years later, Schabowski talked candidly about his press conference that night in 1989. He became a sought-after interview for the world's media as they thronged to Berlin to cover the twentieth anniversary celebration. Speaking to the German English-language newspaper the *Local*, Schabowski deflected the descriptor of "hero" given to him by some East Germans. The following paragraph presents the gist of the interview he gave and the way the *Local* reported it.[8]

"I wouldn't say I was a hero who opened the border—truth be told, I acted to try to save the GDR [German Democratic Republic, as communist East Germany was officially known]," said Schabowski, 80 at the time of the interview. He said it had not been his intention that the Wall be breached that night or that this be the end of the barrier between East and West Germany. "On November 9, I was still a committed communist. The opening of the Wall wasn't a humanitarian, but a tactical decision taken because of popular pressure," he said.

Amplifying on that important statement on the effect public opinion had, even in a tightly controlled country, Schabowski said he felt there was no other choice than to open the Wall.

"The very existence of the GDR was at stake. Some 300 to 500 people were fleeing abroad each day (by way of Czechoslovakia and Hungary). We were bleeding. We had to do something to regain popularity," he said.

The decision to open the Wall for temporary travel followed the decision by the Politburo on October 17 to oust the regime's aging leader Erich Honecker, Schabowski recalled. "Normally in a communist party, you don't topple the secretary general—a secretary general leaves office or dies, but he isn't toppled," he said.

But again, because of pressure created by mass public demonstrations, "The Politburo then asked the government to prepare a law allowing for freedom to travel." Within weeks, the bill was ready and news of it was announced on November 6. But one sentence was badly phrased and suggested that a new body would be set up to deliver the visas, prompting new outcries, Schabowski said. "We couldn't believe it. We'd taken the most incredible of decisions to open the border and it was greeted by mass demonstrations! It was pure Kafka," he said. The government had to fix that straight away with a "governmental decree." The text of the decree was agreed upon by the council of ministers on the morning of November 9. Schabowski grabbed the text and put it in his pocket.

The aim was to "announce that as late as possible during the press conference to avoid questions," he said. But there was no holding back the tide once the news broke.

When East Berliners heard Schabowski's comments about the new law going into effect "immediately," they didn't wait to test the ambiguity of the statement. Instead they flooded en masse to the Wall and, by 10:30 P.M., the throng of people had reached gargantuan size at Bornholmerstrasse Crossing. Confusion reigned with the border guards at it did in the halls of the GDR government. They had no clear orders either to let the people through or to prevent them from passing. By this time, however, the guards were vastly outnumbered and let the first few people through the crossing. A few thousand others followed without waiting for permission. The same thing was happening at other crossings, like the one facing Checkpoint Charlie on Friederichstrasse. Before the night came to an end, tens of thousands were streaming across to freedom.

History has never witnessed another night like that of November 9, 1989.

THE GUARD WHO RAISED THE BARRIER

Although the historic events of that night took place in the larger context described in this and previous chapters, ultimately there was one border guard on that one night of November 9 who gave the order to raise the barrier and let the first East Berliners pass through the Wall to West Berlin. That man was Harald Jäger, then a lieutenant colonel in the East German army who was in charge of the border crossing at Bornholmerstrasse. He must have felt the weight of the world on his shoulders that night as he realized the decision was his and his alone at that moment: He could let the mass of East Germans mobbed at his crossing through, or he could try to stop them (although he had only a handful of guards to the 20,000 or so demonstrators standing in front of him). He could order his men to fire into the crowd, but only if they felt the guards' lives were in danger. His attempts to phone superiors to get clear-cut instructions had not been successful. Now it was his call. Not only his career, but the fate of Europe, lay in his hands. Jaeger talked about that moment in an interview with the German newspaper *Spiegel Online*, which appeared on November 9, 2009, twenty years to the day after that fateful night. That interview, reported by Cordt Schnibben, follows:[9]

SPIEGEL: When you saw the news conference in which the opening of the East German border was announced at 18:54 on Nov. 9, what went through your mind?

Jäger: I thought, "What's he going on about?" He's (Schabowski) reading something off and doesn't have any idea what the impact's going to be. He himself seemed very surprised at what he was saying, like someone who was reading it for the first time.

SPIEGEL: Was it clear to you what was going to happen in the following hours?

Jäger: No, not to that extent, but it was clear to me that people wanting to leave would appear at our border crossing. That didn't trigger any panic or fear in me. All I thought was: Now you've got to find out whether they're allowed to travel immediately or not. It wasn't government departments but the passport control offices at the checkpoints that had to deal with the situation. I immediately telephoned my superior in the operating command center in Berlin-Treptow. He had also seen the news conference and was just as surprised as all of us. His order was to turn the people away.

SPIEGEL: When did the first people start appearing at your checkpoint?

Jäger: The first ones came very quickly. But they stood at a distance, they were uncertain.

SPIEGEL: The border guards used to refer to anyone trying to cross the border without the right documents as 'wild boar.'

Jäger: Yes that's right, we would use that term for people who would turn up at night, often drunk, at our checkpoint and wanted to get across. But it was different that night. These were people who wanted to get across because they were referring to a statement by a member of the Politburo. I didn't regard them as wild boar.

SPIEGEL: At what point did things become tense?

Jäger: A police car turned up and announced through a loudspeaker to the waiting GDR citizens that they could report to a registry office where they would be issued with travel documents to let them leave. The GDR citizens started going to police stations. The next police station wasn't far from us, so it was five minutes there, five minutes back at most. The GDR citizens, not all but some of them, went there and came back very angry after 10 or 12 minutes. The police stations were closed. The GDR citizens felt they had been made fools of and said so loudly. "You're taking the piss! We demand to be let out." Schabowski had made the announcement on television, and they wanted us to implement it.

SPIEGEL: Did you try to explain the situation to your superior?

Jäger: I described the situation to Colonel Ziegenhorn in the command center and he said: "You know the order, there's nothing new." I said: "I just want to make you aware of the fact that hundreds of citizens are standing here and that the order has become a bit more problematic following the police announcement." He said: "Send them away." I said: "I can't send anyone away, I can only block off the border." That night one had to be braced for the possibility that GDR citizens might storm the border. One had to be braced for it.

SPIEGEL: Did these conversations keep taking place throughout that evening?

Jäger: Yes, over and over again. I told him: "A solution must be found." And at some point he said to me: "Listen,

I'll ring the ministry, you can listen in. We'll talk to the minister or one of his deputies." At that point he wanted to show me the chaos and that there wouldn't be any orders from the top. He wanted to show me that—I knew Colonel Ziegenhorn well enough, that's why he wanted me to listen in on the phone call. So I heard how someone in the ministry asked whether Comrade Jäger was in a position to assess the situation properly or whether he was acting out of fear. When I heard that, I'd had enough. I shouted down the phone: "If you don't believe me, then just listen." I took the receiver and held it out of the window.

SPIEGEL: Did you discuss the situation with your colleagues at the other checkpoints?

Jäger: I spoke repeatedly to all officers in charge that evening. On the street, but also in my office. They demanded: "Harald, you've got to do something!" I said: "What am I supposed to do?" I wanted to hear what they thought. They stood together in my office and I wanted them to tell me what I should do. "It's up to you, you're the boss," they said. I said: "Should I let the GDR citizens leave? Or should I give the order to open fire?" "For God's sake!" they said. I only mentioned opening fire as a provocation, I wanted to know if they would support me if I allowed the GDR citizens to cross over. It was clear that it would be my responsibility but I wanted to be sure I would have their support. But that wasn't forthcoming. That's how the meeting ended.

SPIEGEL: Would it have been possible to give the order to open fire?

Jäger: No, we had the order not to open fire even if the border was breached, unless our own lives were in danger.

SPIEGEL: So shooting at people in front of the barriers was not an option at any point on November 9?

Jäger: No, but people could have been injured or killed even without shots being fired. In scuffles, or if there had been panic among the thousands gathered at the border crossing. That's why I gave my people the order: Open the barrier!

ON THE OTHER SIDE OF THE WALL

On the other side of the Wall in West Berlin, there had been an expectation five days earlier that something was in the air. The November 4 demonstration by East Germans in Alexanderplatz was a straw in the wind to people like Christhard Lapple, then a 31-year-old reporter for German Television ZDF. Could something big be about to happen? Was it really possible after all these years?

Lapple, now in his 50s, sits in his ZDF office near the Brandenburg Gate. He is holding a fist-size chunk of the Berlin Wall that he had removed from the "monster" back in 1989.

"Something was in the air," he says about that November 4 demonstration. "But none of us knew that the Wall would fall just five days later. It was a total surprise."

Lapple echoed what many others have said about the momentous event on November 9, 1989, when the then 28-year-old symbol of the Iron Curtain was breached by everyday East Germans who carried no guns.

"It was a people's day," Lapple said. "The fall of the wall is a story about the power of the people," Lapple said in a private interview at his office a few days before the twentieth anniversary celebration of the fall of the Wall.

In another interview, George Glass—then the minister-counselor for political affairs at the U.S. Embassy in Berlin—agreed, at least in part. He said a lot of high-level government negotiations had been underway to help set the stage for that moment in history.

"The unification of Germany was one of a few really great historic diplomatic successes," Glass said. "In the first instance, it was a success brought about by the German people themselves. But in the second instance, it was the diplomats. They showed great restraint, and that helped greatly. In the end, reason and diplomacy prevailed. Today, Germany is a model country and contributes to a great Europe."

Still, the career diplomat had to admit, "I cannot say I saw the end of the wall coming. But for me, the images of that night live on."

Reflecting on the mob of East German citizens at Bornholmerstrasse Crossing on the night of November 9, 1989, Lapple said, "They just made a test with their bodies and started to move through the gate and past the guards. Twenty thousand East Berliners were starting to move against 50 to 60 East German guards, who had machine guns. The guards decided not to shoot."

Stores in West Berlin stayed open late and banks gave out 100 Deutsch marks in "welcome money," then worth $50, to each East

German visitor. The party lasted four days and by November 12, more than 3 million of East Germany's 16.6 million people had visited, nearly a third of them to West Berlin, the rest through gates, opening up along the rest of the fenced, mined frontier that cut their country in half. Sections of the nearly 100 miles of Wall were pulled own and knocked over. Tourists chiseled off chunks to keep as souvenirs. Tearful families reunited. Bars gave out free drinks. Strangers kissed and toasted each other.

TWO DAYS LATER: A PERSONAL ACCOUNT

The night of the *Mauerfall*, as Germans say it, was a great night to be a journalist in Berlin. The story of the century was unfolding on this night and on the next day of November 10, and the news programs and newspapers were full of the stories surrounding the historic fall of the Wall. This was a worldwide story, and many families in countries close to Germany wanted to see for themselves what was going on and if the news reports were really true. One such man, who was living in Denmark and heard the news that East Germany was collapsing, was Andreas Ramos. He asked his Danish wife Karen and two Danish friends to drive the eight hours with him to Berlin to join in the festivities. Ramos is an author and web consultant who was born in Colombia, grew up in the United States, and went to Europe to study. His ensuing account is detailed, but it is that detail that offers the best sense of what the average person was feeling during this unprecedented time that East Germany had dreamed about for 28 years. Here are quoted excerpts of Ramos's own account of that trip:[10]

We talked about what one should take to a revolution: it was a very cold, dry November day. We settled on a dozen boiled eggs, a thermos pot of coffee, extra warm clothes, sleeping bags, and a battery-powered radio. The four of us packed into my 25-year-old Volkswagen bug and we drove off.

It's normally an eight-hour drive from Aarhus, Denmark, to Berlin. We took the Autobahn down to Hamburg and then across one of the transit routes to Berlin. Berlin is in the center of East Germany. There are only three highways which allow access from West Germany. At the border city of Braunschweig (Brunswick), on the German side, we began to see the first Trabants. These are small East German cars. They don't just look like toy cars, they look like Donald Duck's car.

. . . After a pizza in Braunschweig, we drove towards the German/ German border. It was about 11 P.M. at night now. The traffic began to slow down. Soon there was very heavy traffic. In the distance there was a

tremendous cloud of light. No one knew what was going on. On the radio, reports followed one another, contradicting each other. Soon, we began to pass cars that were parked along both sides of the Autobahn. People were walking along, all heading towards the border.

We finally reached the border just after midnight. The East German border was always a serious place. Armed guards kept you in your car, watching for attempts at escapes. Tonight was a different country. Over 20,000 East and West Germans were gathered there in a huge party: as each Trabi came through, people cheered and clapped. East Germans drove through the applause, grinning, dazed, as thousands of flashbulbs went off. The traffic jam was spectacular. The cloud of light turned out to be the headlights of tens of thousands of cars in a huge cloud of Trabi exhaust fumes.

We got out of the car and began walking. Between lanes of cars, streams of people were walking, talking together. Under one light, a group of musicians were playing violins and accordions and men and women were dancing in circles. Despite the brilliantly cold night, car windows were open and everyone talked to each other.

We met people from Belgium, France, Sweden, Spain, England: they had all left their homes and come to see the wall be torn down. Germans were drunk with joy. Everyone spoke in all sorts of languages and half languages. French spoke German and Spaniards spoke French and everyone spoke a bit of German. We walked for a while with a French family from Belgium: the mother had packed her two young daughters into the car and came to see the German revolution.

Along with everyone else headed towards Berlin were thousands of East Germans; they had been in West Europe for a blitz tour with the kids and grandmother in the back, to look around and drive back again. Without passports, they had simply driven through the borders. Amused West European border guards let them pass. They smiled and waved to everyone.

At the checkpoint, which is a 25-lane place, people milled around. It was nearly 3 A.M. by now. It had taken us three hours to go through the traffic jam of cheering and applause. West Germans are environmentally conscious and if they're stuck in traffic, they turn off the engine and push their cars. East Germans, on the other hand, sat in their Trabis, putting out clouds of exhaust. Everyone had their radios on and everywhere was music. People had climbed up into trees, signs, buildings, everything, to wave and shout. Television teams stood around filming everything. People set up folding tables and were handing out cups of coffee. A Polish engineer and his wife had run out of gas; someone gave us some rope, so we tied the rope to his car and pulled them along.

We walked through the border. On both sides the guard towers were empty and the barbed wire was shoved aside in great piles. Large signs told us that we needed sets of car documents. The East German guard asked if we had documents. I handed him my Danish cat's vaccination documents, in Danish. He waved us through.

We were finally inside East Germany on the transit highway to Berlin. We could see headlights stretching into the distance, a river of light winding through hills and valleys as far as one could see. We counted our odometer and saw that in the opposite direction both lanes were filled and stopped for 35 kilometers. We counted people and cars for a kilometer and guessed that perhaps another one hundred thousand people were headed westward towards West Germany.

. . . We arrived in Berlin at 4:30 A.M., five hours longer than usual. We drove first to Brandenburgerplatz, where the statute of Winged Victory stands atop a 50-meter column, which celebrates a military victory in the 1890s over Denmark. Cars were abandoned everywhere, wherever there was space. Over 5,000 people were there. I began talking to people. We left the car and began to walk through a village of television trucks, giant satellite dishes, emergency generators, and coils of cables, and tents. Cameramen slept under satellite dishes.

At the wall, West German police and military [were] lined up to prevent chaos. West German military trucks were lined up against the wall, to protect it from the West Germans. Hundreds of West German police stood in rows with their tall shields. On top of the wall, lined up at parade rest, stood East German soldiers with their rifles. Groups of West Germans stood around fires that they had built. No one knew what was going on.

After a while, we walked to Potsdammer Platz. This used to be the center of Berlin. All traffic once passed through the Potsdammer Platz. Now it was a large empty field, bisected by the wall. Nearby was the mound that was the remains of Hitler's bunker, from which he commanded Germany into total defeat. We talked to Germans and many said that the next break in the wall would be here. It was still very dark and cold at 5 A.M. Perhaps 7,000 people were pressed together, shouting, cheering, clapping.

We pushed through the crowd. From the East German side we could hear the sound of heavy machines. With a giant drill, they were punching holes in the wall. Every time a drill poked through, everyone cheered. The banks of klieg lights would come on. People shot off fireworks and emergency flares and rescue rockets. Many were using hammers to chip away at the wall. There were countless holes. At one place, a crowd of East German soldiers looked through a narrow hole. We reached through and shook hands. They couldn't see the crowd so they asked us what was going on and we described the scene for them. Someone lent me a hammer and I knocked chunks of rubble from the wall, dropping several handfuls into my pocket. The wall was made of cheap, brittle concrete: the Russians had used too much sand and water.

Everything was open: restaurants, bars, discos, everything. Yesterday over two million East Germans had entered Berlin. The radio reported that over 100,000 were entering every hour. With Berlin's population of three million, there were over five million people milling around in delirious joy celebrating the reunion of the city after 28 years (Aug. 12, 196 to Nov. 9,

1989). A newspaper wrote banner headlines: Germany is reunited in the streets!

The East German government was collapsing. East German money was worthless. West Germany gave every East German 100 Deutschmark, which amounted to several months' wages. The radio announced that banks and post offices would open at 9 A.M. so that the people could pick up their cash with a stamp in their identification papers. Thousands stood in line.

We left our car in front of the Gedankniskirchen, the Church of Remembrance, a bombed out ruins of a church, left as a memorial to the victims of the war.

We walked into a bar. Nearly everything was sold out. A huge crowd was talking and laughing all at once. We found a table. An old woman came up and asked if we were Germans. We said no, Danish, and invited her and her family to our table. We shared chairs and beer. They were East Germans, mother, father, and daughter. She worked in a factory, her husband was a plumber, and the daughter worked in a shop. They came from a small village several hundred kilometers to the south. The old woman said that she had last seen Berlin 21 years ago and couldn't recognize it. They told us about the chaos of the last few weeks. I asked them what they had bought in Berlin. They all pulled out their squirt guns. They thought it was so funny to fill up the squirt guns with beer and shoot at everybody.

. . . Everything was out of control. Police on horses watched. There was nothing they could do. The crowd had swollen. People were blowing long alpine horns which made a huge noise. There were fireworks, kites, flags and flags and flags, dogs, children.

The wall was finally breaking. The cranes lifted slabs aside. East and West German police had traded caps. To get a better view, hundreds of people were climbing onto a shop on the West German side. We scampered up a nine-foot wall. People helped each other; some lifted, others pulled. All along the building, people poured up the wall. At the Berlin Wall itself, which is 3 meters high, people had climbed up and were sitting astride. The final slab was moved away. A stream of East Germans began to pour through.

People applauded and slapped their backs. A woman handed me a giant bottle of wine, which I opened and she and I began to pour cups of wine and hand them to the East Germans. Journalists and TV reporters struggled to hold their cameras. A foreign news agency's van with TV cameras on top was in a crowd of people; it rocked and the cameramen pleaded with the crowd. Packed in with thousands, I stood at the break in the wall. Above me, a German stood atop the wall, at the end, balanced, waving his arms and shouting reports to the crowd. With all of the East Germans coming into West Berlin, we thought it was only fair that we should go to East Berlin.

A counterflow started. Looking around, I saw an indescribable joy in people's faces. It was the end of the government telling people what not to do, it was the end of the Wall, the war, the East, the West. If East Germans were going west, then we should go east, so we poured into East Berlin.

East Berlin citizens climb up the Berlin Wall near the
Brandenburger Tor on November 10, 1989, to reach the
western part of the divided city. (AP Photo/Jockel Finck)

*Around me, people spoke German, French, Polish, Russian, every language.
A woman handed her camera to someone who was standing atop rubble so
that he could take her picture. I passed a group of American reporters; they
didn't speak anything and couldn't understand what was going on, pushing
their microphones into people's faces, asking, "Do you speak English?" Near
me, a knot of people cheered as the mayors of East Berlin and West Berlin
met and shook hands.*

*I stood with several East German guards, their rifles slung over their
shoulders. I asked them if they had bullets in those things. They grinned
and said no. From some houses, someone had set up loudspeakers and played
Beethoven's ninth symphony: Alle Menschen werden Bruder. All people*

Passersby crosses a memorial strip where the Berlin
Wall once stood, near the Brandenburg Gate in
Berlin. (AP Photo/Markus Schreiber)

*become brothers. On top of every building were thousands of people. Berlin
was out of control. There was no more government, neither in East nor in
West. The police and the army were helpless. The soldiers themselves were
overwhelmed by the event. They were part of the crowd. Their uniforms
meant nothing.*

The Wall was down.

NOTES

1. Bill Glauber, "When the Berlin Wall Came Down," *Christian Science
Monitor*, November 9, 1989. Retrieved from http://www.csmonitor.com/
World/2009/1108/p25s01-wogn.html on December 13, 2011.

2. Ibid.

3. Ibid.

4. Hannes Bahrmann and Christopher Links, *Cronik der Wende*, Christoph Links Berlin: Verlag, 1994, 79. Retrieved from http://uinic.de/alex/en/proj/4nov.html on December 14, 2011.

5. Ibid.

6. Hannes Bahrmann and Christoph Links (Eds.), Bilderchronik der Wende, Berlin 1999, 36. Retrieved from http://uinic.de/alex/en/proj/4nov.html on December 14, 2011.

7. Elizabeth Pond, "The Comedy of Errors That Caused the Wall to Fall," *Christian Science Monitor*, November 8, 2009. Retrieved from http://www.csmonitor.com/World/2009/1108/p25s02-wogn.html on December 14, 2011.

8. "Meet the Man Who Brought Down the Berlin Wall," Local, September 20, 2009. Retrieved from http://www.thelocal.de/national/20090920-22033.html on December 16, 2011.

9. Cordt Schnibben, "I Gave My People the Order: Raise the Barrier," *Spiegel Online*. Retrieved from http://www.spiegel.de/international/germany/0,1518,660128,00.html on December 16, 2011.

10. Andreas Ramos, "The Fall of the Wall: A Personal Account." Retrieved from http://andreas.com/berlin.html on December 16, 2011. Reprinted with permission.

11

RUSSIA AND GERMANY AFTER THE WALL

My life in Moscow was pretty much what it would be in America. I drove to work every morning. I drank beer with friends on the weekends. I shopped in grocery stores and ate out a lot. But it's different being a reporter in Russia—interviewing was never direct. There were different levels of truth. You always had to sort through what you thought was an outright lie and what was partly true. One general rule of thumb was this: come to a conclusion about what's really going on in a government or business quarrel. Then step back. Think about it ten times more cynically, and that will be the closest to the truth.

—Sabrina Tavernise[1]

A NEW RUSSIA UNFOLDS

What does the former world of European Communism look like, now that the Iron Curtain has disappeared and a new stage has been set for coming generations? To look at this question, it makes sense to look at the country that led Eastern Europe into Communism in the first place and that controlled some 15 Communist states during the era when Lenin, Stalin, and their successors held sway in a huge region of the world. Keep in mind that Russia is the largest country in the world and is 1.75 times the size of the United States. In the years since the fall of Communism and the splintering of the Soviet Union into separate states, much has been written about the changes that have taken place in Russia. This chapter will look at some of these findings.

In their book *Russia after Communism*, Anders Aslund and Martha Brill Olcott noted that in the decade following the collapse of the Berlin Wall and European Communism, Moscow went from being one of the world's most colorless cities to being one of the more colorful. "Bare-shelves state-owned stores have been replaced by glittering malls and boutiques filled with merchandize from all over the world. Placards and political slogans have all come down from billboards and other public spaces, their places taken by brightly-colored advertisements."[2]

That's the good news for Russia. The bad news is that these conditions that allowed many to prosper are also forcing others to the poverty end of the economic food chain. Whereas before there was something resembling a safety net for the poverty-stricken, that net is virtually gone now for the many homeless persons who have become more prevalent on city streets. Some of these homeless come from the ranks of hundreds of thousands of refugees from Chechnya and other former Soviet states. Many of these refugees are escaping violence and wars in their countries, choosing to take their chances in Russia instead. The city was not prepared for the huge numbers of refugees over the past two decades.[3]

In this chaotic and quickly changing climate, government leaders have had to find ways to adapt. The process has not been easy because so much has changed in Russia. Communism as an overarching institution is gone; in its place is a quasidemocracy that in some ways is in a "wild west" era with more than a little degree of lawlessness and corruption. Leaders are trying to find out what will work and what won't. As the American experience showed, 20 years is too little time to expect a new system like democracy to flourish. That is certainly true in Russia. While Russian voters do troop to the polls to elect their leaders, the support for these offices and the institution of democratic government is on a soft foundation. People seem unsure about embracing the new forms, wondering if they will really last.

The economy is in the same untested boat. Capitalism and a market economy are replacing Communism, but what final form will they take, and how successful will they be in a country where the economy is so poor and there are such huge gaps between rich and poor? Russia needs a middle class to help stabilize things and, as yet, it doesn't have a large one. There is much disagreement about the direction Russia should take in the future as well as what kind of country it should become and how. Russians realize their power in the world has shrunk dramatically because there is no longer a Soviet empire; just 15 different states, many of which are struggling hard to make it as independent countries.

RUSSIA AND CAPITALISM

Sabrina Tavernise, a reporter for the *New York Times* who lived and worked in Russia for six years and has written extensively on it, describes life in Russia after the fall of Communism and the splintering of the USSR into several independent nations. It is a Russia seemingly on the road to capitalism but finding it to be a long and winding road with plenty of rough places. Two of them are deception and corruption, and it's obvious from the reporter's comments here that she has found plenty of both. Nevertheless, by her own account, it has been a life-changing experience to have spent time in the old Russia and to see it evolve into the new Russia.

> *It was an amazing time in the country's history. Everyone's world had turned upside down, and people became immigrants in their own country. They had to scramble to survive. They're still scrambling. For the vast majority of Russians, life is worse than it was in Soviet times. But I don't think most people would choose to go back, though they remember the past with great fondness. They miss feeling like a great superpower, and they've had to swallow this bitter pill of being weak. But the young folks who didn't grow up with Soviet ideology are more pliable.*[4]

It may be surprising to some that—despite the differences she found in Russia—this *New York Times* reporter also finds similarities between life in America and in Russia. For example, she explains that the gap between rich and poor Russians—like the similar gap in America—has grown into a chasm. But while America has a safety net to catch many of its poor, Russia does not. The poor in Russia are very poor and often out of luck. Tavernise notes that if one is poor in Russia and lives in a rural area, it could be days before he or she ever gets transported to a hospital when he or she needs to go. Buses don't keep regular schedules, and owning a phone is not a given in Russian society. "Life is exhausting, and even the simplest of tasks can be very difficult," she says.[5]

Asked in 2004 about some of the biggest changes she has seen in Russia since the fall of Communism, she noted several. Most notably, Tavernise said life was settling into more of a predictable pattern where everyday Russians are going about their day-to-day jobs in the business world. This comes after several years right after the earth shifted in Russia and everything was "up for grabs and people grabbed it."[6] After that, she said, Russians had to learn how to manage what they'd grabbed and hang onto it. They're getting better at it.

And her idea about the country's biggest challenges?

Russia is not a law-based society. Simply, if you're big and strong and have money everything is for sale, even justice. The American idea of what was going to happen once the Soviet Union was gone was impossibly romantic. The Americans thought, here's this country that wants to be just like us, now at last they get to be free—all that needs to happen is we have to write some laws.

Well, it may have worked sort of like that in Poland and the Czech Republic, but Russia was too big and sprawling Russia is still an Eastern place. People don't say exactly what they mean. The government is this incredibly complex web of officials who get bribed and the businessmen who bribe them.

Russia's hope is definitely its young people. They are really different than their parents. Those who were born after the fall of the Soviet Union never saw lines—the wealthy ones have never ridden on the subway. There is more chance for them to travel, to speak foreign languages, and to be part of the rest of the world, than their parents ever had.[7]

Tavernise, who holds a bachelor's degree in Russian studies from Barnard College, did a report for the PBS show *Frontline* in which she reported on what it's like to be "Rich in Russia." She noted the following about how the economic climate has changed in Russia since the opening days of capitalism:

In the ten years since Russia chose capitalism, Moscow has been transformed into a party for the young and the rich. The nouveau riche are famous for their indulgent excesses, with high fashion, luxury automobiles and a night-life that rivals that of Paris or London. But beyond the bright lights of Moscow, the average salary in the country is just $4,000 a year. Moscow is an enclave where fortunes are being made.[8]

Russians are quick to observe that there is a vast difference between economic lifestyles in the big cities like Moscow and the lifestyles of the rest of Russia, which is a mostly rural country. It is as if there are actually two Russians contained within the country's border. For these everyday Russians outside the cities, shopping at the expensive boutiques in Moscow and having an opportunity to become rich are beyond the realm of possibility. In fact, most Russians found themselves in a worse economic position after the fall of Communism and the Soviet Union. Hardest hit are the retired and older adults whose meager pensions fall far short of covering their living expenses in many cases. The government continues to work on this problem, but the situation is still not good. In some cases, physicians have to supplement their income with night jobs in stores or driving taxis. The sea change that occurred in Russia after the breakup of the Soviet Union and the fall of Communism left many citizens in a daze about what to do next and how to do it. Tavernise says, "It is as if they are immigrants in their own country."[9]

RUSSIA NOW COURTING THE WORLD

A Russian journalist writing for *Pravda* wrote in 2011 that Moscow is taking yet another cue from the pages of Western capitalism in trying to boost its flagging economy. Journalist Svetlana Smetanina says the government is looking to tourism, but that it faces high hurdles in luring visitors to Russian cities. She writes that Moscow is building new 25-floor hotels that will be classified at the three-star level and which will be much less expensive than current hotels in the city. The goal is to double the tourist trade in Moscow in a few short years. Will these new hotels accomplish the tourism goal? She responds:

> For the time being, Moscow does not seem to be a very attractive city for foreign tourists. Sadly enough, the Russian capital does not attract many Russians either . . . A friend of mine, an Italian woman, asked me once what places of interest I would recommend her to visit in Moscow. I have to say that her question left me perplexed a bit. I didn't want to recommend Lenin's Tomb, although it could probably be of interest for foreign tourists—to take a look at the mummy of the world's greatest revolutionary.
>
> The friend arrived in Moscow in summer, so we took a pleasure boat ride on the Moskva River. However, in this situation a foreigner will only have the pleasure to enjoy the views. There are no boat excursions in foreign languages: the required technical means are not provided for it.
>
> Nikolai Koziorov, the director of ArtistSpace, a Moscow travel agency, also thinks that Moscow is not very friendly towards foreign tourists.

"All signs are only in Russian. There are no tourist buses with excursions in foreign languages. Such excursions would be great for those tourists who travel alone. The biggest problem is the absence of cheap hotels that would charge 100–120 euros a night," the specialist said.[10]

To be sure, a big problem for visitors to Moscow has been the price of hotel rooms, which in survey after survey have been judged to be the most expensive hotels in the entire world. A hotel room in Moscow has been averaging about $415 per night.[11] Smetanina continues:

Moscow will have to think a lot to compete. "Moscow loses the competition with many European capitals because there are not many places to visit in the city. Nothing new has emerged during the recent years either," Anna Trapkova of the Institute of Regional Politics said.

It seems that the Moscow government is aware of the problem. It has been recently reported that Moscow may build a Russian Disneyland on the place of the Tushino airdrome. If this idea becomes real, the number of foreign tourists visiting Moscow will increase considerably.

Moscow remains the only large capital that does not have its own theme parks. According to Forbes *magazine, four Disneylands—in Paris, Tokyo, Florida and California—are the most visited places in the world.*[12]

CELEBRATING THE FALL OF THE WALL

On November 9, 1999, and then again 10 years later, I covered the tenth and twentieth anniversaries of the fall of the Berlin Wall. Both celebrations were tributes to those who had resisted the Wall and those who helped to bring it down. In 1999, memories among all Germans were fresher about conditions that existed in the Cold War; 10 years later the memories were less vivid, and many of the children born after the Wall came down in 1989 saw the event as an abstract history lesson. The interesting thing to me was the number of former East Germans who seemed to wax nostalgic for the old days of the GDR although, given the economic hardships many former GDR citizens faced in the competitive environment of capitalism, that started to make some sense. Nevertheless, having spent a day at the Checkpoint Charlie Museum and seeing so many stories of courage and resistance by so many East Germans, the thought struck me that we all have short memories and we tend to remember the good times and forget—or diminish—the bad.

I made the following observations for stories appearing on page 1 of the American newspaper the *Oklahoman* and its web edition, *Newsok.com*, after interviewing several Germans and after attending the tenth and twentieth anniversary celebrations held in Pariser Platz at the Brandenburg Gate. The first story is from the November 10, 1999 edition of the *Oklahoman*.

BERLIN (November 9, 1999)—*To the "Ossis" it was a monster standing menacingly between them and freedom. To the "Wessis" it was a constant reminder that a third of their homeland had been abducted, possibly forever.*

Fared and loathed for years by East Germans and West Germans alike, it was one of the defining symbols of communism, whose collapse 10 years ago stunned a nation and a world.

The monster was the Berlin Wall, a concrete barrier that had divided a nation but also served as a reminder of a barrier between worlds. Tuesday night, a crowd of 40,000, including 1,000 youths who were in town for a European Youth Festival, helped mark the anniversary of the collapse of the Berlin Wall as they gathered beneath the historic Brandenburg Gate.

"The process that brought together what belongs together cannot be stopped," German Chancellor Gerhard Schroeder said in the Reichstag earlier in the day. "The wall did not fall only because of Bonn, Moscow or Washington. It fell because the people made it happen."

Former President Bush, who was in office when the wall collapsed, agreed: "The sweetness and harmony that exists in this chamber today is something I'd like to bottle . . . and take home."

Like a singer who labors for years in obscurity and then lands the break making her an overnight success, the menace of the Berlin Wall vanished Nov. 9, 1989 in the blink of an eye that took almost three decades to shut. During the 28 years of its existence, the wall created a lot of heroes among Easterners who refused to stop seeking freedom . . . Such stories were part of the legacy that spirited Germans commemorated on Pariser Platz Tuesday night in drizzly, 40-degree weather. Despite mixed feelings of some Germans, those gathered on this cold night seemed glad the wall was gone.

. . . The big party Tuesday night included floodlights at the gate and red flares attached to lightposts illuminating the path of the wall from Checkpoint Charlie to Humboldthafen. Smoke from the flares shrouded the areas in a fog reminiscent of the scene at the wall 10 years ago.

Chancellor Shroeder addressed the crowd, which included Helmut Kohl, Bush, and Mikhail Gorbachev. Bush was made an honorary citizen of Berlin on Monday. Not so fortunate was Egon Krenz, the chancellor of the former German Democratic Republic when the wall came down. A German appeals court upheld his conviction on manslaughter for his role in ordering the shooting of people at the border who were trying to escape to the West. He faced 61/2 years in prison.

But Tuesday was a day of celebration, and the city that has once again become the nation's capital after the government's move from Bonn in September was in a party mood . . . Still, while Germans Tuesday celebrated the reunification, many are disturbed that reconciliation has been expensive, time-consuming and frustrating.

Many compare it to a marriage. Ten years ago two lovers came together to start a relationship. They knew, despite their differences, that they belonged together. After the euphoria of the wedding and honeymoon, problems arose faster than they could be solved. Much work was needed to keep together what belonged together. This week some ordinary Germans spoke about the relationship now, 10 years after the wedding.

"For me, nothing really changed," said Katharina Borgmann, an employee of the Deutsche Bundesbahn, who is originally from the eastern part of Germany. "To be honest, now I might be able to buy everything, but the price I pay for this luxury is the fear of losing my job. The unemployment rate here is just so high. The freedom to travel; that's all we actually needed," she said.

Thomas Behrends agreed. "Well," he said, "if you can buy everything, nothing is special any more. Back in the old days, everybody had to stand in line to get some oranges for Christmas. That didn't only make Christmas something special, it also made you belong to a community."

This is an interesting comment, especially when compared to U.S. press attaché Peter Claussen's feeling—expressed later in this chapter—about the closeness that some East Germans felt because of the common enemy of the GDR leadership that they faced.

Among Western Germans, feeling are also mixed.

"It was good that the wall came down", said Wolfgang Kaedeng, a native of West Berlin. "It really had to happen sooner or later." But he added, "Financially I did much better before the reunification. Now we have to pay so much money out of our own pocket to solve damages that we aren't even responsible for—I guess this sometimes causes a lot of frustration."

In the weeks leading to the anniversary, the European media have been looking at where Germany is now compared with 10 years ago. Many reports argue that freedom has yielded mixed results. The festivities have been marred by complaints about a lack of prominence for East Germans at what is, after all, an event marking their liberation.

TWENTIETH ANNIVERSARY EVEN GREATER

In November 2009, the twentieth anniversary took on an even more celebratory tone, and the crowd in Pariser Platz was 100,000 on the night of November 9, instead of the 40,000 who participated in the 1999 celebration. It was also a carefully and comprehensively staged event wherein the Wall was made a symbol for all "walls of oppression" that still exist around the world. It was much more of an international event than in 1999, and Germans seemed to more strongly favor the reunified country than they had 10 years before. What follows is an account of the twentieth anniversary that appeared in stories on November 9 and 10 and in an accompanying blog, "The Berlin Wall," in the same newspaper's online edition that week.

All this week, Berliners have been waiting in eager anticipation for tonight when they will officially celebrate the 20th anniversary of the fall of the Berlin Wall. Some 100,000 people are expected to converge on Pariser Platz, the site of one of the most historic symbols of Germany, the Brandenburg Gate. The gate was a key dividing line between East and West Germany.

If the 10th anniversary celebration in 1999 was any indication, this will be quite a party. That celebration drew some 40,000 Germans out into the cold night air. Floodlights swept across the face of the Brandenburg Gate and torches were lit along the path that the wall had taken around the city. While those torches provided the main visual imagery 10 years ago, tonight that image will be provided by dominoes. More than 1,000 brightly painted, large Styrofoam dominoes painted by young Germans, together with other young people around the world, will topple in quick succession starting at the Brandenburg Gate. The dominoes carry a wide range of images, all

The twentieth anniversary "dominoes" that fell across the city of Berlin. Residents and visitors in Berlin could walk among these dominoes in the days prior to the anniversary celebration in November 2009. (Photo by Jim Willis)

connoting freedom, and they will follow the path that the wall took between Potsdamer Platz and the Reichstag Building. The event will be televised live in Germany and round the world.

The falling of the dominoes is part of the Festival of Freedom, as the 20th anniversary is called. All of this is to celebrate the night when the first of the East Germans decided to test an announcement they had heard earlier in the day from a leading East German Politburo member, Geunter Schabowski: East Germans were now free to travel to the west. As it turned out, that announcement carried no official status—at least in terms of orders conveyed to the border guards. So when East Berliners began to assemble at the main East-West gate on Bornholmerstrasse, the guards did not know what to do. Should they prevent them from leaving or not? And, if some tried to leave, should they shoot?

A PARTY FOR THE WORLD

Having Jon Bon Jovi and U2 perform in the same week on ground that was once known as the life-threatening no man's land is amazing enough. Having the men who championed perestroika in Russia and Solidarity in Poland on the same stage alongside the chancellor of a unified Germany and the U.S. Secretary of State added to the wonder.

But the sight that really got your attention Monday night [November 9] on the cold and wet pavement near the Brandenburg Gate were the more than 100,000 Berliners, fellow countrymen, and well-wishers from around the world who came on this night to remember what was and to give thanks for what is no more. You've never been happier to be squeezed into a one-foot square of personal space in your life. The company was great.

Chief among those things past, of course, is the structure that Berliners used to call simply the Monster. That was, of course, the 97-mile Berlin Wall, 10 feet high in most places, that encircled this city that was divided between Russian, American, British, and French sectors after World War II.

Although "Wessis" (West Germans) could leave and reenter at will, the "Ossis," (East Germans) were trapped and barred from moving West, except with special permits usually good for only a day now and then. And it was no cinch getting even those.

Those who tried to leave on their own faced being shot or blown up by explosives implanted in the infamous "death strip," which separated the actual Berlin Wall from a "hinterland" wall or inner barrier.

The death strip is another casualty of events that took place 20 years ago on November 9, 1989, when the Wall was rendered moot, quite by accident. An East German Politburo member made a premature announcement he had no authority to make early in the evening; a border commander at

Bornholmerstrasse Crossing was confused about whether to order his 30 guards to shoot when East Berliners approached his gate; he ordered his guards to shoulder their Kalashnikovs, and the rest is history.

Estimates are that 25,000 East Berliners risked their lives that night to walk through the gate, while others simply scaled the wall itself.

The thing that was—that monster—had lost its teeth. It was no more.

Following are some parameters of that Wall and its environment:

- *Length of the Wall: 155 kilometers*
- *Height of the Wall: 3.6 meters*
- *Length of metallic fence: 66 meters*
- *Guard towers: 302*
- *Concrete guard bunkers: 20*
- *Guard dog runs: 259*
- *Self-actuating shrapnel firing units (land mines): 54,000*
- *Lives lost trying to escape over, under, or through the Wall: 225*
- *Lives lost trying to escape elsewhere on the East–West border in Germany: 760*

All these things once were but are now no more. Sadly the 985 East Germans, who sacrificed their lives for a chance at freedom, are among them.

Other things that were but are no more? How about stories of mothers who wanted their children to grow up in freedom but didn't want to give them up to someone else to be raised, perhaps never to see them again? One such woman was Anneliese Trauzettel, an East German woman who—because she had epilepsy—already had four of her five children taken from her by the state. There was no way she was going to give up Mike. She knew she could probably get a one-day shopping pass to West Berlin, but she also knew the East German Catch-22 that said you couldn't take your children with you.

So Anneliese solved that problem in May 1987 by getting her day pass, spraying four-year-old Mike with deodorant to throw off the scent of the guard dogs, giving him a sleeping pill to calm him, and stuffing him into a wheeled shopping cart. She knew there was a 50–50 chance the bag would be searched at the Checkpoint Charlie crossing, so she picked the heaviest-trafficked time of day to attempt escape. It worked—the guards didn't search her bag, and she and Mike were free.

A postscript to this story is that Mike Trauzettel celebrated his sixteenth birthday in a party thrown for him back at Checkpoint Charlie on April 8, 1999.

A remaining stretch of the Wall in today's Berlin. Some strips are left as a historical reminder of the formerly divided Germany. (Photo by Jim Willis)

But this time, the Wall was no more.

All this week, Berliners have been waiting in eager anticipation for to-night, when they will officially celebrate the twentieth anniversary of the fall of the Berlin Wall. Some 100,000 people are expected to converge on Pariser Platz, the site of one of the most historic symbols of Germany, the Brandenburg Gate. The gate was a key dividing line between East and West Germany.

Today, the wall is nearly all gone, although some parts of it still stand, at an outdoor art gallery and as part of an open-air museum. There are also narrow segments of it standing in various locations around the city. Its route through most of the city is now overlain with streets, shopping centers, and apartment houses. The only reminder of it in those places is a series of inlaid bricks that trace its path. Potsdamer Platz, the vibrant square that was destroyed during World War II and became a no man's land during the days of the Wall, is now full of upscale shops selling every-thing from iPods to grilled bratwursts.

RETURN TO NORMALCY

Two decades after the fall of the Berlin Wall, the magic of November 9 has inexorably faded. But eastern Germany has become a gloriously normal place in the meantime.

—Marc Young, the *Local*[13]

It would help to be a *Deutschlander* to understand what Berlin journalist Marc Young meant when he wrote that during the twentieth anniversary celebration week in a Berlin newspaper, the *Local*. I'm an American, but I've been coming to Germany since 1995 and I think I see what he's driving at. There are sound cultural reasons for Germans just wanting to be normal.

This is a nation of many laws, written and unwritten, regulating behavior. As a result, it is a nation of cities like Berlin itself where you can feel safe walking down the street at night. It is also the only place I've been in the world where a total stranger could come up to you and scold you for not crossing the street at the right time or in the right place. It is a nation that conserves energy and where clothing colors that many Americans might find drab are on the backs of most Germans you pass on the street.

Some of this is changing, but change comes slowly to a country that has been pummeled with too much of it in its history. Much of that change was unwanted and took the guise of invading armies, home-grown tyrants like Adolf Hitler who wrested control of Germany from everyday Germans, and distant tyrants like Joseph Stalin who did the same thing—at least for the East Germans.

When you grow up with a volatile history like that, *normal* is not a dirty word. Normal is nice. And normal is what Germany—especially East Germany—has become.

Having said all that, let me balance it with this: A couple of new generations of Germans have grown up without knowing war, so *their* Germany is different from that of their parents and grandparents. While still a part of the long train of Deutsch culture, these younger Germans have made some pretty big breaks with the past. They are opening up more emotionally; they are looking for more excitement and change; they are starting to show their colors more, and I mean that in a literal sense. The feeling of national pride—especially in the realm of international sports—is back. Actually, it never left. What left was the *showing* of that pride. Germany hosting the World Cup in 2006 and finishing third changed all that.

A friend in the U.S. Embassy in Berlin in told me that Germans can be as emotional as anyone else, and she doesn't agree with the perception that the typical German is detached from feelings. "But you have to get on with life in the face of tragedy," she said. "You can't let emotions stop you. Germans are good at surviving and moving on."

I would echo all that. It sounds trite to say something like this, but I'll do it anyway because it's true: Many Germans are some of the best friends I've ever had. Distance and time apart don't damage these friendships, either. You just pick up where you left off when you come back next year.

The fact that Germany and the United States have become such good international allies over the seven decades since World War II has made America safer in the world. It has also meant good things to Germany. Do we disagree on things? You bet. Just like the best of friends often do. That's why public diplomacy—the kind the State Department's Foreign Service practices so well—is vitally important to so many in today's world. America must listen to other countries' needs and do what we can to help them out, these advocates say, and we have to practice that over the long term instead of scrambling to make "firehouse friendships" in times of crisis when we need help ourselves.

Whatever your politics, there is an inspiring sight to see right there near the Brandenburg Gate that trumpets the respect Germany has for some American leaders. The site is the Kennedy Museum, a privately funded tribute to the entire Kennedy family and specifically to the love that President John F. Kennedy showed for Germany with his famous "Ich bin ein Berliner" speech in 1963 Berlin. Now *there* was a one-on-one relationship that produced positive results.

President John F. Kennedy delivers his famous speech "I am a Berliner" ("ich bin ein Berliner") in front of the city hall in West Berlin on June 26, 1963. (AP Photo)

Just as inspiring is the large poster of President Barack Obama in the display window of the museum and the exhibit inside inter-mingling notable campaign moments of Presidents Kennedy and Obama. Both displays have been special exhibitions at the museum, offering testimony to the international alliance of Germany and the United States.

"Kennedy really means a lot to Berliners," said Kathy Alberts, director of the Kennedy Museum. "Memory is triggered again by the pictures you see. We're trying to bring back that time and make it alive again, especially for the younger generation of Germans."

The director also noted the similarity that many Germans see between Kennedy and Obama, and that similarity is the hope that both men have inspired, even in President Obama's short time in office. The museum has featured a special exhibit for several months of President Obama, and his picture in the window was seen clear across Pariser Platz during the time surrounding the twentieth anniversary of the fall of the Wall in November 2009.

The twentieth anniversary of the fall of the Berlin Wall was a huge success as the Wall was used as a metaphor for all the walls oppression still standing around the world. It appeared that the legacy of this anniversary will remain. Through the individual stories of heroism and through the changes in Germany since East–West days, we can all learn a lot about the universal need of people to always dream of and chase freedom whereever and whenever they can.

On the night of November 9, 1989, approximately 25,000 caged East Germans flew to freedom through the infamous Berlin Wall. They were given an inch, saw liberty straight ahead, and they took a mile.

GERMAN REUNIFICATION

In spirit, at least in the euphoria of the moment on that historic night, Germany became reunified. But the official reunification would not occur for another 11 months and would involve formal government ratification. In light of the increasing support for reuni-fication, Western diplomats travelled to the GDR a few weeks after the wall's opening.

France and England in particular reacted with mistrust to the prospect of the large and economically powerful German state that reunification would create in the heart of Europe. If they could not stop reunification entirely, the two countries at least hoped to apply political sanctions on Germany. Helmut Kohl, then the chancellor of Germany, kept their position in mind as he delivered a speech in front of the ruins of Dresden's Frauenkirche cathedral that drew worldwide attention. Kohl declared that German unity would be possible only in the context of a more unified Europe. He said German and European unification were just two sides of the same coin. His speech garnered thunderous applause from the GDR citizens in attendance. Nevertheless, French President Francois Mitterrand travelled to the GDR two days later in an attempt to prevent West Germany from annexing the East.

By early 1990, the international community watched closely the process of German reunification to ensure that the interests of Germans as well as of the four conquering allied powers from World War II (England, France, the United States, and the Soviet Union) were respected. German negotiators worked out the conditions of a German reunification internally, while both West and East German officials consulted with the four powers about the international ramifications of the proposal. This "2 plus 4" process (representing the two German states and the four allied powers) concluded with a declaration of sovereignty for Germany on September 12, 1990. German negotiations had already resulted in an August 31, 1990, contract that specified all aspects of the new relationship between East and West Germany.

On October 3, 1990, the former East German states officially joined the Federal Republic of Germany. The date marked the end of the GDR and the beginning of a reunified federal republic.

IS GERMANY REALLY REUNITED?

A writer for Der Tagesspiegel, Helmut Schuemann wrote about Germany after the Wall in a November 2009 article headlined "What Is Germany in 2009?" He phrased his observations in a series of questions, starting with, "Are We Reunited?" Noting several advances—not the least of which is twice electing a woman chancellor, who comes from the East, no less—Schuemann points out the country has a ways to go in spreading the wealth and workload. He concludes this answer by noting, "The nostalgia for the East and the supposed desire for the past spring from the same melancholy that infects West Berlin."[14] Simply stated, we all tend to take refuge in the familiar past, remembering the decent times and forgetting the worst.

One informed perspective on Germany after the Wall comes from Peter Claussen, press attaché for the U.S. Embassy in Berlin. Claussen was stationed in East Berlin from 1987 to 1990, and was stationed in Germany again in 2006 and was still in Berlin in 2011. Interviewed at the embassy, next to the Brandenburg Gate, Claussen said the situation in Germany today is somewhat complex related to whether Germans consider themselves unified and the degree of nostalgia for the past.

Claussen said there was a clearer definition of cultural identity, especially for East Germans, when the Wall was in place. "I could walk down the west side of the Wall and everything would be colorful and diverse. People were laughing and talking and exchanging ideas. I could walk down the other side and everything was gray, black or white. Not so much laughing or talking. There is no doubt which side I preferred."[15] But he said that to East Germans, there was a familiarity with their lifestyle, and they had become accustomed to it. They knew what they were, what they could do, and what they couldn't do, and they worked within those parameters. They were very aware of the deceptions that their government was engaging in. They had their own thoughts about it, and everyone knew that the government rhetoric about utopia didn't match the practice of Communism, at least not the way the SED party leadership was practicing it.

"But for former East Germans today their sense of place, identification, and purpose are unclear," Claussen said. Now they are part of a larger Germany and they are still trying to find their way in that larger and more diverse world. Some seem to pine for the past but, he said, most don't. He cited one journalist, a friend of his who was about 60 years of age and a former "Ossis," or East German. "She tells me that people grumble, but we are all better off now."[16]

Complicating the picture is that three generations of Germans are involved in the reunified Germany, and each has a different perspective. First are those who lived behind the Wall as adults and saw the Wall come down in 1989. Second are those who were born behind the Wall and maybe lived there as children before it came down. Third are those who were born after the Wall came down and knew nothing—firsthand anyway—of life in the GDR. Says Claussen, "For the post-wall generation, the Wall is not in their hearts, although they are still in its shadow."[17] They hear narratives from their parents and others, but the reality of contact with Westerners is an everyday thing for them, while their parents had no such contact.

Claussen said he senses that some former East Germans may miss one thing, although it may seem ironic: they may miss the closeness of some relationships they had in the GDR. It is ironic because the GDR leadership was paranoid about people talking too much and knew that dissident conversations were more likely to take place among close friends. To be sure, given the degree that the Stasi's Department 20 infiltrated social groups and even marriages at times, East Germans were slow in coming to place trust in other individuals, even friends. But once an East German decided you were trustworthy and vice-versa, there was a tight bond to that relationship that was made even closer by the common threat of arrest and imprisonment represented by the Stasi. Take away that threat, and the relationship loses some closeness.

Reflecting on the former East Germany where he worked for three years, Claussen recalled a typical kind of irony that was reflected in the GDR leadership. The year was 1961, and the government decided to do two things that they hoped would show their distinctive nature and their fight against Fascism. In that year, East Germany turned the former Nazi concentration camp of Sachsenhuasen into a public memorial for those victims of the Holocaust. They also started to build the Berlin Wall. Commenting in a 1990 television documentary, Claussen said, "The purpose of both [the concentration camps and the Wall] was the same: to keep people in." He added, "Countries like this limit people because they are afraid of them; afraid of differences. I'd like to see the contact we do [the State Department] alleviate a little of that fear."[18]

He recalled that his job while a diplomat in East Berlin was to bring information about the United States and that it was a tricky job. "The most difficult thing was to avoid paranoia. You knew it was there and you were vulnerable, but you had to avoid it. Gut reaction is what they [the State Department] told you to go on."[19] Since the USIA (United States Information Service, which has since been subsumed by the State Department) was the eyes and ears of the State Department, Germans wound up transmitting a lot of information back and forth about East German needs and desires and how the United States might help out. In Claussen's case, since he is a former actor and director, he focused much of that effort on the arts and culture needs of East Germany.

Today, Claussen believes that contact with America is better in the west part of Germany than in the east. He said the State

Department is trying to encourage more Americans to travel to the east and would like to see more student exchange programs at universities there. As for Berlin itself, the city is still somewhat divided psychologically, although there are parts such as the *mitte*, or center, where easterners and westerners mix well on a regular basis. Still, he notes, "The geographical stasis of Berliners is partially true. Regional identities from the past—after all, there were some 50 towns represented in greater Berlin—are still strong." Many former East Berliners choose to stay there and live, and many former West Berliners choose to stay and live there. Certainly the lure of employment can uproot one or the other, because unemployment is high in Germany, more in the east than in the west. In another irony, however, Claussen noted that women in the former GDR seem to be doing better than men in finding employment because they appear to be more flexible and willing to move.

Claussen said that despite claims by former East Berliners that work was easier to get in the days of the GDR, there are some safety nets that today's German government has put in place to catch the unemployed. There is the German version of unemployment insurance that, he said, Americans might find too socialistic. Still, there are few homeless people in Berlin and other German cities.

As of 2012, the big stories in Germany were in the economic crisis that also gripped America, the war in Afghanistan (which the German constitution requires to be voted on annually if troops are to continue being stationed there), and immigration. So the big issues in Germany appear to be the same ones confronting America. About immigration, however, Germans have their own reasons for finding it troubling. Not only are jobs at stake but— maybe just as important—German identity is also a consideration. Claussen said Turkish and North African populations enter the country asking, "How do I become a German?" And, he said, a typical German might find that question "astonishing." Germany is not a country like America where virtually everyone is an immigrant. There is a longstanding identity that Germans have, and the answer to the question of becoming a German is that you are *born* a German. In the past, that has been about the only way to become a German citizen, unless a parent was born German. Today, that is changing, and it's not an easy thing for many Germans to fathom, Claussen explains. "Being German is in their DNA," he said. "It's easier for immigrants to get German citizenship today than before, but it's still not easy."[20]

GERMAN UNITY DAY

Although the Berlin Wall fell on the night of November 9, 1989, it was not until October 3, 1990, that the two Germanies were officially reunited. That date has become the nationally celebrated German Unity Day, although many in Germany feel it doesn't carry the clout of the Fourth of July celebration in the United States. Still, they would say Germany has a lot to celebrate about where it has come from since 1989. Journalist Marc Young of the newspaper the *Local* in Berlin, made the following observations in a 2010 article:[21]

> *Twenty years on, only a few nut jobs publicly pine for the country's Cold War division, but the waning east-west antagonism is still reflected in an utter lack of interest in German Unity Day. Unlike America's Independence Day or France's Bastille Day, Germany's national day on October 3 is not much of a celebration. The official party is unlovingly rotated among the country's 16 federal states (this year it's in Bremen) and privately Germans mark the day by doing absolutely nothing special.*
>
> *On November 9 last year, there were huge commemorations for the 20th anniversary of the fall of the Berlin Wall. But few people seem to be halfway as excited about remembering the day when their country became whole again. Still, as Unity Day approaches, it's important to point out how much has actually been achieved in the past 20 years.*
>
> *Germany . . . has come a long way from the grim upheaval of post-reunification. While (former GDR) cities such as Leipzig and Dresden are flourishing, the east's natural wonders from Thuringia's lush forests to the pristine Baltic Sea are once again attracting tourists in droves. And only a decade ago, the German economy, saddled with rebuilding the east, was dubbed the "sick man of Europe," poised to drag everyone else down with it.*
>
> *But these days it's touted as the continent's 'economic motor' that should be emulated rather than pitied. Joblessness has dipped to levels not seen since the early 1990s and is expected to dip further still in the coming months.*
>
> *And perhaps, just as important, Germany finally appears to be on the upswing culturally as well as economically.*
>
> *The country's neighbors have come to realize over the years that they have nothing to fear from a reunified Germany, making it easier for younger generations to put Second World War–era resentments firmly in the past.*

BERLIN TODAY

The city of Berlin has been through so many momentous and catastrophic eras during its long existence, with the last two coming at the hands of the Nazis and the government in the GDR that built a wall around the entire city to separate it from the free democratic world. In the process, families, loved ones, and friends were cut off from each other, some of them forever. Since 1989, although that Wall has come down and Communism has fallen in Europe, many still debate whether Berlin—indeed all of Germany— is really reunited. The reality is that Germans on both sides of the for- mer Iron Curtain work and live together, freely coming and going wherever they want. But as one taxi driver put it while taking a trav- eler from the upscale Kurfurstendahm district of the western part of the city to the still-greyish district along Frankfurterallee in the eastern half, "Berliners are reunified politically, but not in the brain. Those who lived in the east before the Wall came down, mostly still live there; those who lived in the west mostly still live here. Germans don't like to change that much." The taxi driver also noted what was obvious to the passenger in the back seat: You could tell when you passed from the west to the east in Berlin. The colors became more muted; the buildings along Karl Marx Allee still bespoke the greyness of the East under the days of Communism and the GDR.

But Germans have also had more than two decades to get reac- quainted with each other and, at significant events like the tenth

A man looks at photographs in the Window of Remembrance at the memorial for the Berlin Wall, in Berlin, Germany, on Thursday, May 20, 2010. (AP Photo/Sebastian Willnow)

and twentieth anniversaries of the fall of the Berlin Wall, they seemed to get along just great. The generation born after the fall of the Wall is living in an entirely new world, and the hope of the future—in terms of true German reunification—lies with them.

NOTES

1. "Frontline World: Interview with Sabrina Tavernise." Retrieved from http://www.pbs.org/frontlineworld/stories/moscow/tavernise.html on October 25, 2011.

2. Anders Aslund and Martha Brill Olcott, *Russia after Communism*. Washington, DC: Carnegie Endowment for International Peace, 1999, as presented on pp. 1–2 in a synopsis retrieved from www.carnegieen dowment.org/files/Russia_After_Communism_Intro.pdf

3. Ibid.

4. "Frontline World."

5. Ibid.

6. Ibid.

7. Ibid.

8. Ibid.

9. "Frontline World: Rich in Russia: The Story." Retrieved from http://www.pbs.org/frontlineworld/stories/moscow/thestory.html on October 26, 2011.

10. Svetlana Smetanina, "Moscow to Build Cheap Hotels and Disneyland to Attract Tourists." Retrieved from http://english.pravda .ru/society/stories/25-10-2011/119434-moscow_foreign_tourists-0/ on October 25, 2011.

11. Ibid.

12. Ibid.

13. Marc Young, "Return to Normal," *Local*, November 9, 2009, as quoted in "The Berlin Wall" blog by Jim Willis on November 11, 2009. Retrieved from http:blog.newsok.com/berlinwall/ on December 7, 2011.

14. Helmut Schuemann, "What Is Germany in 2009?" *Der Tagesspiegel*, November 10, 2009, as quoted in "The Berlin Wall" blog by Jim Willis on November 11, 2009. Retrieved from http://blog.newsok.com/berlinwall/ on January 3, 2012.

15. Interview with Peter Claussen at U.S. Embassy Berlin, November 9, 2011.

16. Ibid.

17. Ibid.

18. Ibid.

19. U.S. State Department documentary on diplomacy in East Berlin, "Peter Claussen als Diplomat in der DDR." Retrieved from http:// www.youtube.com/watch?v=MaYWhfMPkWc on November 9, 2011.

20. Claussen interview.

21. Marc Young, "Celebrating the Late Blossoms of German Reunification," *Local*, September 30, 2010. Retrieved from http://www .thelocal.de/opinion/20100930-30181.html on January 3, 2012.

SELECTED BIBLIOGRAPHY

Ash, Timothy Garton. *The Magic Lantern: The Revolution of '89 Witnessed in Warsaw, Budapest, Berlin, and Prague* (New York: Vintage Books, 1993).

Baldwin, Kate A. *Behind the Color Line and the Iron Curtain: Reading Encounters Between Black and Red, 1922–1963* (Durham, NC: Duke University Press, 2002)

Barta, Peter I. (Ed). *The Fall of the Iron Curtain and the Culture of Europe* (New York: Routledge, 2012).

Berlin, Isaiah (author), Henry Hardy (editor), and Strobe Talbott (Foreword). *The Soviet Mind: Russian Culture under Communism* (Washington, DC: Brookings Institution Press, 2011).

Boyn, Oliver. *The Divided Berlin: 1945–1990: The Historical Guidebook* (Berlin: Christopher Links Verlag, 2001).

Brager, Bruce and James I. Matray. *The Iron Curtain: The Cold War in Europe* (London: Chelsea House Publications, 2004).

Buckley, William F. Jr., and Henry Kissinger. *The Fall of the Berlin Wall* (20th anniversary ed.) (Hoboken, NJ: Wiley, 2009).

Bukovskiĭ, Vladimir and Semyon Gluzman. *A Manual on Psychiatry for Dissidents* (New York: Keuffel and Esser, 1976).

De Senarclens, Perre and Amanda Pingree. *From Yalta to the Iron Curtain: The Great Powers and the Origins of the Cold War* (London: Berg Publishers, 1995).

Edwards, Harold. *From Newbury with Love: Letters of Friendship across the Iron Curtain* (Brooklyn: Melville House, 2007).

Engel, Jeffrey A. *The Fall of the Berlin Wall: The Revolutionary Legacy of 1989* (Oxford: Oxford University Press, 2011).

Fundler, Anna. *Stasiland: Stories from Behind the Berlin Wall* (New York: Harper Perennial, 2011).

Geder, Laszlo. *Faith and Devotion: Escape from Behind the Iron Curtain* (Bloomington, IN: Author House, 2008).

Grant, Bruce. *In the Soviet House of Culture: A Century of Perestroikas,* (Princeton, NJ: Princeton University Press, 1995).

Gvosdev, Nikolas. *The Strange Death of Soviet Communism* (Piscataway, NJ: Transaction Publishers: 2008).

Haynes, John Earl and Harvey Kiehr. *In Denial: Historians, Communism and Espionage* (Jackson, TN: Encounter Books, 2005).

Helmchen, Hanfried and Norman Sartorius. *Ethics in Psychiatry: European Contributions* (Berlin: Springer, 2010).

Hill, T. H. E. *The Day before the Berlin Wall: Could We Have Stopped It?: An Alternate History of Cold War Espionage* (Charleston, SC: CreateSpace, 2010).

Holian, Anna. *Between Nationalism and Soviet Communism: Displaced Persons in Post-War Germany* (Ann Arbor: University of Michigan Press, 2011).

Hutton, John Bernard. *Struggle in the Dark: How Russian and Other Iron Curtain Spies Operate* (Toronto: Harrap, 1969).

Kelly, Jerry. *In the Grip of the Iron Curtain* (Bloomington, IN: Author House, 2006).

Kempe, Frederick. *Berlin: 1961* (New York: Putnam Adult, 2011.)

Kirby, David, *The Baltic World 1772–1993: Europe's Northern Periphery in an Age of Change* (London: Longman, 1995).

Kortsha, Gene X. *One Man's Journey to Freedom* (Rochester, MI: Joseph Karl Publishing, 2010).

Kotkin, Stephen. *Armageddon Averted: The Soviet Collapse: 1970–2000* (Oxford: Oxford University Press, 2008).

Marx, Karl. *Economic and Philosophical Manuscripts of 1844* (New York: Prometheus Books, 1988).

Marx, Karl. "Stasimuseum Berlin: Information and Explanations" (English version), distributed at the Stasimuseum, Ruschestrasse 103, Haus 22, Berlin, Germany.

Merill, John C. (Ed.), *Global Journalism: Survey of International Communication* (3rd ed.) (White Plains, NY: Longman, 1995).

Meyer, Michael. *The Year That Changed the World: The Untold Story behind the Fall of the Berlin Wall* (New York: Scribner, 2009).

O'Heffernan, Patrick. *Mass Media and American Foreign Policy: Insider Perspectives on Global Journalism and the Foreign Policy Process* (Westport, CT: Ablex Publishing, 1991).

Ostermann, Christian F. and Charles S. Maier. *Uprising in East Germany 1953: The Cold War, the German Question, and the First Major*

Upheaval Behind the Iron Curtain (Hemden, VA: Central European University Press, 2001).

Reed, John. *Ten Days That Shook the World*. (New York: Penguin Classics, 1990).

Richmond, Yale. *Cultural Exchange and The Cold War: Raising the Iron Curtain* (Happy Valley, PA: Penn State Press, 2000).

Rose, Brian and Anthony Bailey. *The Lost Border: The Landscape of the Iron Curtain* (Princeton, NJ: Princeton Architectural Press, 2004).

Rottman, Gordon and Chris Taylor. *The Berlin Wall: And the Inner German Border, 1961–1989* (Oxford, England: Osprey Publishing, 2008).

Sheffer, Edith. *Burned Bridge: How East and West Germans Made the Iron Curtain* (Oxford: Oxford University Press, 2011).

Siebert, Fred S., Theodore Peterson, and Wilbur Schramm. *Four Theories of the Press: the Authoritarian, Libertarian, Social Responsibility and Soviet Communist Concepts of What the Press Should Be and Do* (Urbana: University of Illinois Press, 1963).

Sis, Peter. *The Wall: Growing Up behind the Iron Curtain* (New York: Farrar, Strauss and Giroux, 2007).

Smyser, W. R. *Kennedy and the Berlin Wall* (New York: Rowan & Littlefield, 2010).

Stokes, Gale. *The Walls Came Tumbling Down: The Collapse of Communism in Eastern Europe* (New York: Oxford University Press, 1993).

Taylor, Frederick. *The Berlin Wall: A World Divided* (New York: Harper Perennial, 2008).

Van Ginneken, Jaap. *Understanding Global News: A Critical Introduction*. (London: Sage, 1998).

Villaume, Poul and Odd Arne Westad. *Perforating the Iron Curtain: European Detent, Transatlantic Relations, and the Cold War, 1965–1985*. (Copenhagen: Museum Tusculanum Press, 2010).

Ward, Janet. *Post-Wall Berlin: Borders, Space, and Identity* (New York: Palgrave/Macmillan, 2011).

Weaver, David H. *The Global Journalist: News People around the World* (Cresskill, NJ: Hampton Press, 1998).

White, Philip. *Our Supreme Task: How Winston Churchill's Iron Curtain Speech Defined the Cold War* (Jackson, TN: Public Affairs Books, 2012).

Wright, Patrick. *Iron Curtain: From Stage to Cold War* (Oxford: Oxford University Press, 2009).

Wurmbrand, Richard. *100 Prison Meditations: Crises of Truth from behind the Iron Curtain* (Bartlesville, OK: Voice of the Martyrs, 2004).

INDEX

Adamec, Ladislav, 105
Adenauer, Konrad, 35, 36, 38
Afanasyev, Viktor, 165
Afghanistan, Soviet war
   in, 171, 172
Agriculture: communal, 18–19;
   Russian, 4–6, 20, 170;
   Ukrainian, 13
Albania: Communism in, 35, 175;
   final years of Communism in,
   175; movie based in, 3; World
   War II in, 24
Alexander I, Emperor, 72
Allen, Woody, 147
al-Yousef, Jamila, 183–84
American Society of Newspaper
   Editors (ASNE), 163–66
Andropov, Yuri, 163
Appelius, Stefan, 125–26
Arkin, Alan, 147
Arms race, 143–46, 171–72, 176–78,
   179–81. *See also* Nuclear
   weapons

Austria: World War II in, 28
AVO (Hungarian Secret Police),
   159–62

Baker, James, 180
Baltic states (Latvia, Estonia,
   Lithuania): Baltic Way protest
   in, 11; Bolshevik support from,
   24; independence of, 10–11;
   resistance in, 10–11, 82, 94–95;
   Singing Revolution in, 11;
   Soviet Union relationship to,
   10–11, 24, 28, 94–95; World
   War II in, 10
Barbed Wire Sunday, 37–39
Bauer, Shane, 85
Becker, Erwin, 122–23
Becker, Wolfgang, 133
"Behind the Berlin Wall"
   (television special), 41–43
Behrends, Thomas, 210
Belgium: World War II in, 28
Benes, Eduard, 12

Berlin, Germany: Barbed Wire
   Sunday in, 37–39; Berlin
   Dynamo team in, 78;
   Brandenburg Gate in, 44, 84,
   194, 200, 209, 211, 212, 214, 216;
   capital of Germany in, 210;
   celebrations of fall of Wall in,
   104, 195–200, 208–14; current
   status of, 222–24; escape
   attempts from East to West in,
   36, 38, 39, 53, 58–61, 82, 83,
   109–28, 135–36, 141, 213; Four
   Power Agreement on, 48;
   Kennedy Museum in, 216–17;
   Mauerfall (Berlin Wall fall/
   opening) in, 2, 3, 20, 43–44, 68,
   76, 82, 90, 104, 132–33, 156,
   174–76, 181, 183–200, 208–14;
   movies depicting, 131–33,
   139–41, 142–43; partitioning
   of, 7, 29–30, 33–34, 36–39, 53
   (*see also* Berlin Wall); post-
   Communism changes and
   challenges, 183–84, 208–24;
   Potsdamer Platz in, 84, 212, 214;
   Ramos' personal account of trip
   to, 195–200; resistance in, 38–39,
   40, 43, 76, 82–85, 89–90, 127, 156,
   185, 186–88 (*see also escape
   attempts subentry*); return to
   normalcy in, 214–17; travel
   restrictions in, 42, 48–50, 89,
   184, 185–86, 188–93
Berlin Wall: Barbed Wire Sunday,
   37–39; celebrations of fall of,
   104, 195–200, 208–14; escape
   attempts beyond, 36, 38, 39, 53,
   58–61, 82, 83, 109–28, 135–36,
   141, 213; establishment of,
   29–30, 36–39, 53; fall/opening
   of, 2, 3, 20, 43–44, 68, 76, 82, 90,
   104, 132–33, 156, 174–76, 181,
   183–200, 208–14; family and
   friends divided by, 37–38, 48, 61,
   113, 119–20, 223; guard who

raised the barrier at, 190–93,
   212–13; media coverage of, 36,
   37, 38–39, 41–43, 184, 185–86,
   188, 189, 191–93, 194, 195, 197,
   198, 209–10, 211–14; memorial
   for, 200, 223; as metaphor, 31,
   217; as "The Monster," 29,
   39–41, 109, 194, 209, 212–13;
   parameters and dimensions of,
   213; post-Wall changes and
   challenges, 183–84, 208–24; protests against, 38–39, 40, 43, 76,
   84–85, 127; Ramos' personal
   account of trip to, 195–200;
   "shoot to kill" order at, 58–61,
   112, 126; travel restrictions
   beyond, 42, 48–50, 89, 184,
   185–86, 188–93
The Berlin Wall in the World
   (Kaminsky), 48
Bierman, Wolf, 93
Bikel, Theodore, 147
Birthler, Marianne, 60
Bloody Sunday (Russian), 21
Blue, Ben, 147
Boettger, Bernd, 120–21
Bogdanov, Vsevolod, 166
Bohley, Barbel (Brosius), 89–90, 91
Bolshevik Commission for
   Combating Counterrevolution
   and Sabotage (Cheka), 88
Bolsheviks/Communist Party of
   the Soviet Union, 4, 6, 22–24,
   137–38, 139
Bon Jovi, Jon, 212
Borgmann, Katharina, 210
Brandenburg Gate, anniversary
   celebrations at, 209, 211, 212,
   214; Berlin Wall memorial near,
   200; Kennedy Museum near,
   216; protests at, 84; Reagan's
   speech at, 44; ZDF office
   near, 194
Brandt, Willy, 40, 47
Brezhnev, Leonid, 13, 73–74

Brisbane, Albert, 19
Brook(s) Farm Community, 18–19
Bryant, Louise, 136–38
Brynner, Yul, 148
Buccholz, Horst, 142, 143
Buhler, Hans-Jorg, 121
Bukovsky, Vladimir, 99
Bulgaria: Communism in, 35, 175;
  East German escape attempts
  via, 125–26; final years of
  Communism in, 175; World
  War II in, 24
Burton, Richard, 139
Bush, George H. W., 179–80, 209

Cagney, James, 142
Call, Harry (movie character), 132
Ceausescu, Nicolae,
  15–16, 101, 174
Chaplin, Geraldine, 138
Checkpoint Charlie, 84, 110–12,
  190, 209, 213. *See also* Berlin Wall
Checkpoint Charlie Museum,
  escape attempts documented at,
  59–60, 110, 112, 114, 117, 123,
  133, 208; establishment of, 112
Cheka (Bolshevik Commission for
  Combating Counterrevolution
  and Sabotage), 88
Chernobyl nuclear disaster, 14,
  172–73
Christie, Julie, 138
Chukseev, Vitaly, 164
Churches. *See* Religion and
  religious organizations
Churchill, Winston, 8, 35
CIA (Central Intelligence
  Agency) assessments,
  178–79, 180
Clark, Zsuzsanna, 64–65, 67
Claussen, Peter, 63, 175, 210,
  219–21
Committee for State Security.
  See KGB (Committee for State
  Security)

Communism: American interest
  in, 18–19, 136–38; anti-
  Communist response to, 10–11,
  13, 38–39, 40, 43, 52, 63, 65–67,
  76, 77, 81–106, 112, 127, 148, 156,
  173, 174–76, 185, 186–88; daily
  life under, 40–43, 62–67, 77–78;
  Eastern Europe under, 1–16, 18,
  20, 22–24, 28–30, 32, 35–36, 43,
  47–78, 81–106, 109–28, 129–49,
  151–66, 169–81, 183–200 (*see also*
  specific countries); establishment
  of, 4–16; fascism *vs.*, 25, 26, 27,
  28–29, 53; final years/fall of
  European, 102, 169–81, 183–200;
  indoctrinating young in tenets
  of, 64, 67–69; interpretations of,
  19–20, 52–53; McCarthyism on,
  147; media under, 33, 67, 71, 103,
  122, 151–66, 188; movies depicting, 35, 50, 121, 129–49; post-
  Communism changes and challenges, 16, 66, 183–84, 203–24;
  religion and, 58, 67, 69–77,
  98–101, 103; resistance to, 10–11,
  13, 38–39, 40, 43, 52, 63, 76, 77,
  81–106, 112, 127, 148, 156, 173,
  174–76, 185, 186–88 (*see also*
  Escape attempts); rise of, 17–18,
  22–24, 28–30; rules under, 47–78;
  travel restrictions under, 35, 42,
  48–50, 63, 89, 104, 184, 185–86,
  188–93
The Conversation (movie), 132
Cuban missile crisis, 143, 180
Currency, East German, 49, 198
Czechoslovakia/Czech Republic:
  Communism in, 12–13, 82,
  104–6, 157–59, 173, 174, 175; East
  German escape attempts via,
  189; establishment of, 11–12;
  final years of Communism in,
  173, 174, 175; independence of,
  13; media in, 157–59; Prague
  Spring in, 158; resistance in, 82,

104–6, 175; Soviet Union
relationship to, 12–13, 157–59;
travel restrictions in, 104; Velvet
Revolution in, 105, 158, 175;
World War II in, 12, 28

Dana, Charles A., 19
Demonstrations. *See* Resistance
Denisovich, Ivan (movie
character), 141–42
Denmark: Ramos' trip to Berlin
from, 195–200; World
War II in, 28
Détente or *rapprochement:* East
German, 56, 85, 115–16; Soviet
(*see Glastnost; Perestroika*)
Drapalova, Iva, 157–59
Dreyman, Georg (movie
character), 131
Dr. Strangelove (movie), 133,
143–46
Dr. Zhivago (movie), 138–39
Dubcek, Alexander, 158
Dzerzhinsky, Felix E., 88

Eastern Europe: CIA assessments
of, 178–79, 180; Communism in,
1–16, 18, 20, 22–24, 28–30, 32,
35–36, 43, 47–78, 81–106, 109–28,
129–49, 151–66, 169–81, 183–200;
countries of, 2–3 (*see also specific
countries*); final years/fall of
Communism in, 102, 169–81,
183–200; media in, 33, 67, 71,
103, 122, 151–66, 188; movies
depicting, 3, 35, 50, 121, 129–49;
post-Communism changes and
challenges in, 16, 66, 183–84,
203–24; religion in, 58, 67, 69–77,
98–101, 102, 103; resistance in,
10–11, 13, 38–39, 40, 43, 52, 63,
76, 77, 81–106, 112, 127, 148, 156,
173, 174–76, 185, 186–88 (*see also
Escape attempts*); Velvet
Revolution in, 102, 105, 158, 175

East Germany/German
Democratic Republic: arts
movement in, 175–76; Berlin
and Berlin Wall in, 2, 3, 7, 20,
29–30, 31, 33–44, 48–50, 53,
58–63, 68, 76, 78, 82, 83–85,
89–90, 104, 109–28, 131–33,
135–36, 139–41, 142–43, 156,
174–76, 181, 183–200, 208–24;
Communism in, 3, 7–9, 32, 35,
43, 47–63, 67–69, 74–78, 81–94,
109–28, 130–33, 140–41, 142–43,
169–70, 173–76, 183–200;
currency in, 49, 198; daily life in,
40–43, 62–63, 77–78; *détente* or
rapprochement in, 56, 85, 115–16;
education in, 42, 43, 67–69;
escape attempts from, 36, 38–39,
50, 53, 58–61, 77, 82, 83, 87,
109–28, 135–36, 141, 189, 213;
establishment of, 3, 7–9, 32,
34–35; final years of
Communism in, 169–70, 173–76,
183–200; indoctrinating young
in Communist tenets in, 67–69;
international recognition of, 56,
85; movies depicting, 50, 130–33,
139–41, 142–43; post-
Communism changes and challenges, 183–84, 208–24; prisoner
negotiations and sale by, 56, 85,
88, 114; religion in, 58, 74–77;
resistance in, 38–39, 40, 43, 52,
76, 81–94, 127, 156, 174–76, 185,
186–88 (*see also escape attempts
subentry*); return to normalcy in,
214–17; reunification with West,
3, 132–33, 174, 194, 197–98, 210,
211, 217–22, 223–24; "shoot to
kill" order in, 58–61, 112, 126;
Socialist Unity Party in, 51,
52–55, 58, 67–68, 78, 84, 86, 88,
122, 126, 131; Soviet Union relationship to, 3, 7–9, 32, 33–34, 35,
38–39, 67, 84, 115–16, 123–24,

169–70, 185, 187; Stasi in, 5, 8–9, 40–41, 50–61, 78, 81–94, 109, 110, 112, 113, 115, 116–19, 121–28, 130–32, 135–36, 161, 183–84, 220; student descriptions of life in, 41–43; travel restrictions from, 35, 42, 48–50, 63, 89, 184, 185–86, 188–93; youth organizations in, 68–69, 78. *See also* Germany

Edith K. (student story), 41–42

Education: East German, 42, 43, 67–69; Hungarian, 64; indoctrinating young in Communist tenets via, 64, 67–69; Soviet, 65

Ellis Farm/Ellis Brook Farm, 18–19

Emerson, Ralph Waldo, 18–19

Enemies of the People: My Family's Journey to America (Marton), 159, 161–62

Engels, Friedrich, 53

England. *See* Great Britain

Escape attempts: aerial, 116, 124, 135–36; "barrier-breakers," 112–13, 114–15; cable-based, 109–10, 118–19; documents used in, 113, 119, 120; East German, 36, 38–39, 50, 53, 58–61, 77, 82, 83, 87, 109–28, 135–36, 141, 189, 213; escapee demographics, 113–14; failed/casualties from, 58–59, 61, 87, 112, 113, 115, 121, 122, 125–28, 135, 141, 213; movies depicting, 121, 135–36, 141; nautical or aquatic, 116–18, 120–21; "shoot to kill" order in response to, 58–61, 112, 126; simple, 123–24; southern route, 50, 125–26, 189; subterranean, 114, 121–23, 128; timing of, 114–16; train-based, 118; vehicular, 112–13, 116, 117, 120, 123–24, 126, 135

Estonia. *See* Baltic states (Latvia, Estonia, Lithuania)

European Union, 15, 33. *See also specific countries*

"Evil empire," 2, 171

Family and friends: East/West separation of, 37–38, 48, 61, 113, 119–20, 127–28, 184, 223; of escapees, 110, 113, 118, 119–20, 127–28; informants among, 51–52, 55–57, 82, 87, 88, 90–91, 92–94, 160–61, 184, 220

Famines and hunger: German, 32–33; Russian, 5, 6, 13, 20, 173, 204; Soviet, 13, 173

Farming. *See* Agriculture

Fascism: Communism vs., 25, 26, 27, 28–29, 53; Nazism or National Socialism as, 17, 24, 25, 26–28, 34, 134; resistance to, 24; rise of, 17, 24, 25–28

Fattal, Joshua, 85

Fechter, Peter, 58–59, 127

Federal Commission for the Stasi Records, 86–87

Fiedler, Daniel, 87

Fiedler, Edith, 87

Fiennes, Ralph, 134

Fischer, Erna, 90

Fischer, Werner, 90–91, 93

Ford, Paul, 147

Forest Brothers, 10

Forum for Education and Rehabilitation, 83

Fourier, Charles/Fourierism, 18–19

Four Power Agreement, 48

France: Berlin occupation by, 31, 33–34, 48; German reunification involvement of, 217–18; World War II involvement of, 12, 28

Free German Youth (FDJ), 68

The Front (movie), 147

Furrer, Reinhard, 121

Garifullina, Nadezjda, 165
Gaspon, George, 21
Germany: Berlin (*see* Berlin, Germany); famines and hunger in, 32–33; German Unity Day in, 222; immigration in, 221; Nazism/fascism in, 17, 24, 25, 26–28, 34, 134; partitioning of, 3, 7–9, 31–32, 34–35 (*see also* East Germany/German Democratic Republic; West Germany/Federal Republic of Germany); post-Communist changes and challenges in, 183–84, 208–24; return to normalcy in, 214–17; reunification of, 3, 132–33, 174, 194, 197–98, 210, 211, 217–22, 223–24; unemployment in, 32, 210, 221; World War II involving, 7–10, 12, 28 (*see also* Hitler, Adolf; World War II); World War I impacts on, 26
Gheorghiu-Dej, Gheorghe, 15–16
The Girl Who Spelled Freedom (movie), 136
Glass, George, 181, 194
Glasnost, 74, 90, 102, 104, 115–16, 155–56, 158, 163, 165, 171, 185, 187. *See also Perestroika*
Gluzman, Semyon, 99
Goodbye Lenin (movie), 132–33, 143
Good Night and Good Luck (movie), 147
Gorbachev, Mikhail: arms race reduction under, 171–72, 176–78, 179–80; background of, 170; Baltic states under, 11; Bush's relations with, 179–80; celebrations of Berlin Wall fall including, 209; economic policies of, 170–71, 172–73; *glasnost* and Communism decline under, 74, 90, 102, 104, 115–16, 155–56, 158, 163, 165, 171, 185, 187; military changes

under, 171, 172, 176–78, 179–80; *perestroika* under, 13, 158, 171, 174, 185, 187; Reagan's relations with, 43, 171–72, 176–78; reforms under, 169–73 (*see also Glastnost; Perestroika*); religion under, 74; removal from office/resignation of, 175, 179; Ukrainian relations under, 13
GPU (State Political Directorate), 88
Great Britain: Berlin occupation by, 31, 33–34, 48, 140–41; German reunification involvement of, 217–18; movies depicting, 139–41; World War II involvement of, 7, 8, 12
The Great Escape (movie), 121
Greeley, Horace, 19
Grimm, Heinz, 127
Guilty by Suspicion (movie), 147

Haack, Peter, 81
Habedank, Karola, 38
Havel, Vaclav, 82, 104–6, 175
Hawthorne, Nathaniel, 19
Hayden, Sterling, 144, 146
Hazeltine, Scarlett (movie character), 143
Hetze, Barbara (Hille), 125
Hetze, Olaf, 125
Hildebrandt, Rainer, 112
Hitler, Adolf: Czech invasion under, 12; *Mein Kampf* by, 26; Nazism under, 26, 27–28; Poland invasion under, 9–10. *See also* World War II
Hohlbein, Hubert, 121
Holbrooke, Richard, 159, 160, 162
Holzapfel, Carl-Wolfgang, 82, 84–85
Holzapfel, Heinz, 118–19
Honecker, Erich, 76, 77, 88, 116, 131, 174, 187, 190
Horovitz, Israel, 134

The Hungarian Revolution (Kovacs), 97
Hungary: Communism in, 14–15, 35, 50, 63–65, 82, 95–98, 101, 134, 148, 173, 174, 175; daily life in, 63–65; East German escape attempts via, 50, 189; education in, 64; final years of Communism in, 173, 174, 175; Hungarian Secret Police (AVO), 159–62; Hungarian Workers Party in, 96–97; independence of, 15; isolation of, 14–15; media in, 159–62; movies depicting, 134, 148; religion in, 101; resistance in, 82, 95–98, 101, 148, 175; Smallholders Party in, 96, 97; Soviet Union relationship to, 14–15, 35, 96–98, 161; travel restrictions in, 50; World War II in, 24

Intermediate-Range Nuclear Forces Treaty, 172
Iron Curtain: references to, 35, 40, 43. *See also* Communism
Italy: fascism in, 25–26

Jäger, Harald, 191–93
Jaruzelski, Wojciech, 103
Jennings, Peter, 159, 162
Jewish people: movies depicting, 134; Nazi Germany treatment of, 26, 28, 134
John Paul II (Pope), 102, 103
Journalism. *See* Media
The Journey (movie), 148

Kadar, Janaos, 64
Kaedeng, Wolfgang, 210
Kaminsky, Anna, *The Berlin Wall in the World*, 48
Keller, Lukas, 135
Kennedy, John F., 35–36, 216–17
Kennedy Museum, 216–17

Kerensky, Aleksandr F., 22, 23, 137
Kerner, Alex (movie character), 132–33
Kerner, Mrs. (movie character), 132–33
Kerr, Deborah, 148
Kersten, Holger, 61
KGB (Committee for State Security): AVO (Hungarian Secret Police) relationship to, 161; files, records and paperwork of, 94; genesis of, 5, 88, 94; Okhrana as forerunner of, 5; religious organization infiltration by, 72, 73–74; resistance suppression by, 94, 95; Stasi modeled after, 88
Khrushchev, Nikita, 13, 36, 73, 99, 100
Kisov, Dimitri (movie character), 146
Knabe, Hubertus, 60
Kockrow, Wolfgang, 121
Koehler, Kevin, 65
Kohl, Helmut, 209, 218
Kornilov, Lavr, 23
Kovacs, Bela, 96–97
Krenz, Egon, 60, 187, 209
Kroener, Hans, 42–43
Kubrick, Stanley, 144, 146
Kulbeik, Helmut, 127
Kuodyte, Dalia, 94–95

Lapple, Christhard, 194
Lara (movie character), 138–39
Lateran Treaty, 26
Latvia. *See* Baltic states (Latvia, Estonia, Lithuania)
Latvian National Partisans, 10
Lauks, Adam, 88
Leamas, Alec (movie character), 140–41
Lean, David, 138
Le Carré, John, 139–40

Lenin, Vladimir Ilyich, 19, 23, 29,
137, 151, 155
Lithuania. *See* Baltic states (Latvia,
Estonia, Lithuania)
Lithuanian Partisans, 10
The Lives of Others (movie), 50,
130–32
Liz (movie character), 140–41

MacNamara, C. R. "Mac" (movie
character), 142–43
Makeeva, Valerya, 100
Mandrake, Lionel (movie
character), 144
Mann, Delbert, 136
Manual on Psychiatry for Dissenters
(Bukovsky & Gluzman), 99
Marshall, George C., 33
Marshall Plan, 33
Marton, Endre, 159–62
Marton, Illona, 159–62
Marton, Kati, 159–62
Marx, Karl, 19, 29, 52, 69, 155
Mauerfall (Berlin Wall fall/
opening), 2, 3, 20, 43–44, 68, 76,
82, 90, 132–33, 156, 174–76, 181,
183–200, 208–14
McCarthy, Joseph, 147
Media: agitator role of, 152–54;
Berlin Wall coverage by, 36, 37,
38–39, 41–43, 184, 185–86, 188,
189, 191–93, 194, 195, 197, 198,
209–10, 211–14; Communist, 33,
67, 71, 103, 122, 151–66, 188;
Drapalova, Iva in, 157–59; end
of Communism coverage by,
184, 185–86, 188, 189, 191–93,
194, 195, 197, 198; end of
Communism influenced by, 181;
escape attempts covered by, 125,
127; freedom of the press for, 67,
71, 156–57, 164, 165, 166;
funding for, 166; *glastnost*
impacting, 155–56, 158, 163, 165;
Marton, Kati, Endre and Illona

in, 159–62; movie reviews by,
132, 133, 134, 137–38, 146;
national development and,
152–54; Nazi control of, 27; post-
Communist coverage by, 203,
205–8, 209–10, 211–15, 218–19,
222; press theories on, 154–56;
religious coverage by, 74, 75–76;
resistance coverage by, 81, 83,
85, 90, 91, 92–93, 94, 95, 97–98;
Stasi coverage by, 51–52, 60–61
Mein Kampf (Hitler), 26
Mielke, Erich, 53, 54, 83, 88, 109
Mikosha, Vladislav, 72
Ministry of State Security. *See* Stasi
(Ministry of State Security)
Mitterrand, François, 218
Morley, Robert, 148
Movies: availability of, in East
Germany, 42; Communism
depicted in, 35, 50, 121, 129–49;
The Conversation, 132; *Dr.
Strangelove*, 133, 143–46; *Dr.
Zhivago*, 138–39; Eastern Europe
depicted in, 3, 35, 50, 121,
129–49; escape attempts
depicted in, 121, 135–36, 141;
The Front, 147; *The Girl Who
Spelled Freedom*, 136; *Goodbye
Lenin*, 132–33, 143; *Good Night
and Good Luck*, 147; *The Great
Escape*, 121; *Guilty by Suspicion*,
147; *The Journey*, 148; lack of,
depicting Communism, 148–49;
The Lives of Others, 50, 130–32;
Night Crossing, 135–36; *One, Two,
Three*, 142–43; *One Day in the Life
of Ivan Denisovich*, 141–42; *Reds*,
136–38; *The Russians Are Coming,
the Russians Are Coming*, 143,
146–47; *The Spy Who Came in
from the Cold*, 139–41; *Sunshine*,
134; *Wag the Dog*, 3; *The Way We
Were*, 147
Muehe, Ulrich, 130

Muffey, Merkin (movie character), 146
Murrow, Edward R., 147
Mussolini, Benito, 25–26

NATO (North Atlantic Treaty Organization), 15, 36
Naumann, Frieda, 38
Nazism/National Socialism: Jewish treatment under, 26, 28, 134; Nuremberg Trials for leaders of, 34; rise of, 17, 24, 25, 26–28
Neumann, Joachim, 121
New Forum, 90
Newspapers. *See* Media
Nicholas, Tsar of Russia, 72
Nicholas II, Tsar of Russia, 5–6, 20–22, 137
Night Crossing (movie), 135–36
NKVD (People's Commissariat for Internal Affairs), 94, 95
Nobel Prizes: to Solzhenitsyn, 141; to Walesa, 103
Noffke, Siegfried, 127–28
Norway: World War II in, 28
Nuclear disaster, Chernobyl, 14, 172–73
Nuclear weapons, 89, 91, 144–46, 171–72, 176–78, 179–81
Nuremberg Trials, 34

Obama, Barack, 217
Okhrana (Department for Protecting Public Security and Order), 5
One, Two, Three (movie), 142–43
One Day in the Life of Ivan Denisovich (movie), 141–42

Pasternak, Boris, 138
Patriot Act, 63
People's Commissariat for Internal Affairs (NKVD), 94, 95

Perestroika, 13, 158, 171, 174, 185, 187. *See also Glastnost*
Petschauer, Attila, 134
Piffl, Otto Ludwig (movie character), 143
Pilsudski, Jozef, 9
Poland: Communism in, 1, 35, 74, 82, 101–4, 173, 174; final years of Communism in, 173, 174; religion in, 74, 102, 103; resistance in, 82, 101–4, 173, 175; Sanacja Movement in, 9; World War II in, 9–10, 28
Pollack, Sydney, 147
Poppe, Ulrike, 52
Potsdam Conference, 7, 33
Potsdamer Platz, 84, 212, 214
Prague Spring, 158
Protests. *See* Resistance
Psychiatric prisons, 98–100

Rajk, Laslo, 96
Rakosi, Matyas, 97–98, 161
Ramos, Andreas, 195–200
Rathenow, Lutz, 93
Reagan, Ronald: Soviet relations with, 2, 43–44, 171–72, 176–78, 181
Reds (movie), 136–38
Reed, John, 136–38
Reiner, Carl, 147
Religion and religious organizations: Catholic, 26, 70, 74–75, 102, 103; Communism and, 58, 67, 69–77, 98–101, 103; freedom of religion for, 67, 69, 70–71, 74, 99; Jewish, 26, 28, 134; KGB infiltration of, 72, 73–74; Mussolini agreement with, 26; Protestant, 74–75; religious dissidents, 98–101; Russian Orthodox, 69–70, 72, 73–74, 98, 100; Stasi infiltration of, 58
Resistance: anti-Communist, 10–11, 13, 38–39, 40, 43, 52, 63,

76, 77, 81–106, 112, 127, 148, 156, 173, 174–76, 185, 186–88 (*see also* Escape attempts); antifascist, 24; Baltic states, 10–11, 82, 94–95; by Bohley, Barbel, 89–90, 91; Czech, 82, 104–6, 175; East German, 38–39, 40, 43, 52, 76, 81–94, 127, 156, 174–76, 185, 186–88; end of Communism and, 174–75, 185, 186–88; by Fischer, Werner, 90–91, 93; by Havel, Vaclav, 82, 104–6, 175; by Holzapfel, Carl-Wolfgang, 82, 84–85; Hungarian, 82, 95–98, 101, 148, 175; Polish, 82, 101–4, 173, 175; religious, 98–101; Romanian, 100–101, 175; by Walesa, Lech, 82, 101–4, 173; by Welsch, Wolfgang, 81–82, 83; by Wollenberger, Vera, 91–94
Riemann, Erika, 8–9
Ripley, George, 18–19
Ripley, Sophia Dana, 18–19
Ripper, Jack D. (movie character), 144
Robards, Jason, Jr., 148
Robinson, E. G., 148
Romania: Communism in, 15–16, 35, 100–101, 173, 174, 175; final years of Communism in, 173, 174, 175; independence of, 15; religion in, 100–101; resistance in, 100–101, 175; Revolution in, 15–16; World War I in, 15; World War II in, 15, 24
Roosevelt, Franklin D., 8
Rosenthal, A. M., 164
Rusk, Dean, 38
Russia: agriculture in, 4–6, 20, 170; Bloody Sunday in, 21; Bolsheviks in, 4, 6, 22–24, 137–38, 139; Communism in, 4–7, 22–24, 137–39, 141–42, 143–47, 169–81; daily life in, 65; education in, 65; famine and hunger in, 5, 6, 13, 20, 173, 204;

Hungarian relationship to, 14; indoctrinating young in Communist tenets in, 67; media under policies of, 67, 71, 151–52, 154–66; movies depicting, 136–39, 141–42, 143–47; Okhrana in, 5; post-Communist changes and challenges in, 203–8; pre-1917, 4–6, 20–24, 138–39; religion in, 69–74, 98–100; Russian Revolution in, 4, 6–7, 20–24, 136–39; tourism in, 207–8; unemployment in, 22; World War I involvement of, 5–6, 21–22, 139. *See also* Soviet Union, former
The Russians Are Coming, the Russians Are Coming (movie), 143, 146–47

Sadesky, Alexi de (movie character), 146
Sanacja Movement, 9
Schabowski, Guenter, 185, 186, 188–90, 191, 192, 212
Schmidt, Helmut, 77
Schroeder, Gerhard, 209
Schultz, Egon, 122
Schulze, Frieda, 47
Scott, George C., 145, 146
Selle, Peter, 119–20
Sellers, Peter, 144, 145, 146
Sharif, Omar, 138
Shegolikhin, Boris, 166
Shevardnadze, Eduard, 180
"Shoot to kill" order, 58–61, 112, 126
Sieland, Christa-Maria (movie character), 131
Simanaitis, Edmundas, 95
Sims, Watson, 163–65
Singing Revolution, 11
Smallholders Party, 96, 97
Smetanina, Svetlana, 207–8
The Social Destiny (Brisbane), 19

Socialist Unity Party (SED), 51,
    52–55, 58, 67–68, 78, 84, 86, 88,
    122, 126, 131
Solzhenitsyn, Alexander, 99,
    141–42
Sors, Ivan (movie character), 134
Soviet Union, former: Afghanistan
    war of, 171, 172; Albanian
    relationship to, 35; arms race in,
    143–46, 171–72, 176–78, 179–81
    (*see also* Nuclear weapons);
    Baltic states relationship to,
    10–11, 24, 28, 94–95; Berlin
    occupation by, 31, 33–34, 35–36,
    48; Bulgarian relationship to, 35;
    Bush's relations with, 179–80;
    CIA assessments of, 178–79, 180;
    Communism in, 2, 7–15, 28, 29,
    32, 35–36, 65, 67, 69–74, 84,
    94–100, 141–42, 143–47, 151–52,
    169–81; countries comprising, 3
    (*see also specific countries*); Cuban
    missile crisis with, 143, 180;
    Czech relationship to, 12–13,
    157–59; daily life in, 65; demise
    and dissolution of, 2, 43, 178–79,
    179–80, 204; East German
    relationship to, 3, 7–9, 32, 33–34,
    35, 38–39, 67, 84, 115–16, 123–24,
    169–70, 185, 187; education in,
    65; establishment of, 2, 7, 24; as
    "evil empire," 2, 171; famine
    and hunger in, 13, 173; final
    years of Communism in, 169–81
    (*see also* Glastnost; *Perestroika*);
    German reunification
    involvement of, 218; *glastnost*
    and Communism decline in, 74,
    90, 102, 104, 115–16, 155–56, 158,
    163, 165, 171, 185, 187 (*see also*
    Perestroika); Hungarian
    relationship to, 14–15, 35, 96–98,
    161; indoctrinating young in
    Communist tenets in, 67; KGB
    in, 5, 72, 73–74, 88, 94, 95, 161;

media under policies of, 67, 71,
    151–52, 154–66; movies
    depicting, 136–39, 141–42,
    143–47; *perestroika* in, 13, 158,
    171, 174, 185, 187 (*see also*
    Glastnost); Polish relationship to,
    35; psychiatric prisons in,
    98–100; Reagan's relations with,
    2, 43–44, 171–72, 176–78, 181;
    reforms in, 169–73 (*see also*
    Glastnost; *Perestroika*); religion
    in, 69–74, 98–100; resistance
    suppression by, 84, 94, 95,
    98–100; Romanian relationship
    to, 15, 35; Russian Revolution
    leading to formation of, 4, 6–7,
    20–24, 136–39; Ukrainian
    relationship to, 13–14; World
    War II involvement of, 7, 8, 13,
    24, 28, 73; Yugoslavian relation-
    ship to, 35. *See also* Russia
The Spy Who Came in from the Cold
    (movie), 139–41
Stalin, Josef: Communism under,
    12–13, 29, 72, 96, 98, 141–42;
    Czech relations under, 12–13;
    death of, 84; Hungarian relations
    under, 96; religious suppression
    under, 72, 98; Ukrainian relations
    under, 13; Yalta Conference
    participation by, 8
Stasi (Ministry of State Security):
    American arrest by, 40–41; AVO
    (Hungarian Secret Police) based
    on, 161; Department 20 of, 58,
    220; escape attempt response of,
    58–61, 109, 110, 112, 113, 115,
    116–19, 121–28, 135–36;
    evolution of, 52–55; files,
    records and paperwork of,
    51–52, 86–87, 90, 92–93;
    informants of, 51–52, 55–57, 82,
    87, 88, 90–91, 92–93, 113, 161,
    184, 220; KGB as role model for,
    88; movies depicting, 50, 130–32;

Okhrana as forerunner of, 5; prisoner negotiations and sale by, 56, 85; punishment under, 8–9, 51–52, 55–56, 78, 87–88, 89–90, 91; resistance suppression by, 52, 81–94 (*see also escape attempts response subentry*); "shoot to kill" order by, 58–61, 112, 126; sports club founded by, 78; Stasi Museum, 51, 54, 56, 87, 126; surveillance by, 50–52, 53–58, 130–32, 183–84 (*see also informants subentry*)
State Political Directorate (GPU), 88
Sterenberg, Tatiana, 87–88
Steve (American in East Berlin), 40–41
Strangelove, Dr. (movie character), 144–45
Strategic Arms Reduction Talks (START), 172
Strategic Defense Initiative program, 176, 177
Strelzyk, Peter, 124, 135–36
Sunshine (movie), 134
Szabó, Istvan, 134

Taskforce Against Inhumanity, 112
Tavernise, Sabrina, 203, 205–7
10 Days That Shook the World (Reed), 136
Tiffin, Pamela, 142
Tokes, Lazlo, 101
Trauzettel, Anneliese, 213
Trauzettel, Mike, 213
Travel restrictions, Czech, 104; daily living conditions including, 63; East German, 35, 42, 48–50, 63, 89, 184, 185–86, 188–93; fall of Berlin Wall lifting, 185–86, 188–93; permission to travel under, 48–50; protests over, 42; resistance leader, 89, 104
Treaty of Versailles, 28

Trotsky, Leon, 137
Turgidson, Buck (movie character), 145
Tuskulenai genocide/Tuskulenai Memorial, 94–95

Ukraine: Chernobyl nuclear disaster in, 14, 172–73; Communism in, 13–14; independence of, 13, 14; resistance in, 13; World War II in, 13
Ulbricht, Walter, 76
Unemployment: German, 32, 210, 221; Russian, 22
Union of Soviet (Russian) Journalists, 162–63, 164, 166
Union of Soviet Socialist Republics (USSR). *See* Soviet Union, former
United Kingdom. *See* Great Britain
United Nations: Declaration on the Elimination of All Forms of Intolerance and of Discrimination Based on Religion or Belief, 71; International Covenant on Civil and Political Rights, 71; Universal Declaration of Human Rights, 70–71
United States: Americans in East Berlin, 40–41; arms race in, 143–46, 171–72, 176–78, 179–81 (*see also* Nuclear weapons); Berlin occupation by, 31, 33–34, 35–36, 48; Bush's Soviet relations, 179–80; CIA assessments for, 178–79, 180; Communist interests in, 18–19, 136–38; Cuban missile crisis in, 143, 180; German international relations with, 216–17, 220–21; German reunification involvement of, 218; government surveillance in, 63;

media under policies of, 154, 157–59, 159–62, 163–66; movies depicting Americans, 136–38, 142–47; prisoner negotiations with, 85; Reagan's Soviet relations, 2, 43–44, 171–72, 176–78, 181; sixties protest movements in, 74; World War II involvement of, 7, 8, 28

Vatican City, 26
Velvet Revolution, 102, 105, 158, 175
Victor Emmanuel III, King of Italy, 25
von Donnersmarck, Florian Henckel, 130–31
von Moers, Kira, 184

Wag the Dog (movie), 3
Walesa, Lech, 82, 101–4, 173
Wasserman, Charles, 41
The Way We Were (movie), 147
Weisler, Gerd (movie character), 130–32
Weisz, Rachel, 134
Welsch, Wolfgang, 81–82, 83
West Germany/Federal Republic of Germany: anti-Communist resistance and protesters from, 38, 40, 85, 112, 127; Berlin Wall fall impacting, 194–95, 197–200, 210; escape attempt helpers from, 112–13, 118, 119–20; establishment of, 3, 32, 34–35; prisoner negotiations and sale to, 56, 85, 88, 114; reunification with East, 3, 132–33, 174, 194, 197–98, 210, 211, 217–22, 223–24. *See also* Germany
Wetzel, Guenter, 124, 135–36
Wilder, Billy, 142, 143
Winkler, Irwin, 147
Winters, Jonathan, 147
Wollenberger, Knud, 91, 92
Wollenberger, Vera, 91–94
Wollweber, Ernst, 54

Women for Peace, 52, 89
Wordel, Kurt, 112–13
World War I: Czechoslovakia establishment after, 11–12; German postwar status, 26; Romania in, 15; Russian involvement in, 5–6, 21–22, 139; Treaty of Versailles ending, 28
World War II: Albania in, 24; Austria in, 28; Baltic states in, 10; Belgium in, 28; Bulgaria in, 24; Czechoslovakia in, 12, 28; Denmark in, 28; France in, 12, 28; Great Britain in, 7, 8, 12; Hungary in, 24; Marshall plan after, 33; Norway in, 28; Poland in, 9–10, 28; postwar German partitioning, 3, 7–9, 31–32, 34–35; Potsdam Conference, 7, 33; Romania in, 15, 24; Soviet Union in, 7, 8, 13, 24, 28, 73; Ukraine in, 13; United States in, 7, 8, 28; Yalta Conference, 7, 8, 33; Yugoslavia in, 24
Wowereit, Klaus, 60
Wurmbrand, Richard, 100–101
Wurmbrand, Sabina, 100

Yalta Conference, 7, 8, 33
Yandushev-Rumiantsev, Alexey, 69–70
Yeltsin, Boris, 165, 175, 178, 179
Young Pioneers (JP), 64, 68–69
Yugoslavia: Communism in, 35; World War II in, 24

Zaisser, Wilhelm, 53, 54
Zhivago, Tonya (movie character), 138–39
Zhivago, Yevgraf (movie character), 138–39
Zhivago, Yuri (movie character), 138–39
Ziegenhorn, Colonel, 192–93
Zobel, Christian, 121

About the Author

JIM WILLIS is an author and college professor living in southern California. He holds the PhD in Journalism from the University of Missouri and has spent much of his life working as a journalist. He has covered both the tenth and twentieth anniversaries of the fall of the Berlin Wall for Oklahoma City's metro daily, the *Oklahoman*. He has also conducted numerous lecture tours in Germany about the American media, several of them sponsored by the U.S. State Department's Foreign Service. He has been instrumental in developing media and educational partnerships between Germany and the United States. *Daily Life behind the Iron Curtain* is Willis's thirteenth book, and his second focusing on Germany. He is Professor of Journalism at California's Azusa Pacific University, is married to Anne Willis, and has two sons and three stepdaughters.